THE AMERICAN ORTHODOX CHURCH
A HISTORY OF ITS BEGINNINGS

By
George C. Michalopulos
&
Herb Ham

ISBN 1-928653-14-6

Regina Orthodox Press
PO Box 5288
Salisbury MA 01952

800 636 2470
Non-USA 978 463 0730
FAX 978 462 5079

www.reginaorthodoxpress.com

This book is dedicated to Don G. Metevelis,
mentor, friend, veteran of D-Day
and all-around great guy,
but most of all, a fellow-laborer
in the Vineyard of our Lord.

May your labors not have been in vain.

Contents

Acknowledgements viii

The Ruling Bishops of the Russian-American Greek Catholic
    Church of America xi

Prologue...…... xiii

Part I
The Church United:
The Archdiocese of the Aleutians and North America
1794-1918

Chapter 1: From Sitka to San Francisco 1

Chapter 2: The American Crucible 16

Chapter 3: The Calm Before the Storm: 1898-1918 39

Chapter 4: The Bolshevik Revolution 54

Part II
The Church as Ghetto:
The Creation of the Exarchates
1918-1960

Chapter 5: Moscow and the Church Abroad 73

Chapter 6: The Greek Archdiocese 86

Chapter 7: The Antiochian Archdiocese 109

Chapter 8: The Other Jurisdictions 122

Part III
The First Steps Towards Unity:
SCOBA, Ligonier and the Emerging Orthodox
Consciousness
1960-1994

Chapter 9: The Post-War, Cold War and SCOBA 141

Chapter 10: The Secularist Challenge 159

Chapter 11: Ligonier and the Challenge to the Old World 179

Chapter 12: Towards an American Orthodox Church 195

Epilogue 211

Notes 215

About the Authors

George Michalopulos was born in Tulsa, Oklahoma, where he has been active in church affairs throughout his adult life. He is a registered pharmacist engaged in private practice in his hometown where he lives with his wife, Margaret, and his two sons, Denny and Mikey.

Herb Ham is an Adjunct Professor of History at the University of Central Oklahoma. He embraced the Orthodox Faith in 1990. He was ordained a Subdeacon in 1999 and serves as the Administrator of St. Elijah Orthodox Church in Oklahoma City.

Acknowledgements

In addition to several primary, secondary and even tertiary sources, some of which are no longer in print, oral sources have also been used. Those oral sources that have allowed the use their names for references have been so noted. Others have asked to be quoted only "on background" or only in paraphrase, as they are otherwise unwilling to lend their names for attribution. They are referenced only as "a priest in the Diocese," or "a highly placed source in the Archdiocese," or "a layman on the diocesan council" and so forth.

Many people assisted in the undertaking of this book. Taras Tikhomerov provided Russian documentary sources as well as valuable explanations of the intricacies of the Church of Russia *vis a vis* the Church Abroad and quite a few other matters. Father Bill Christ gave much theological insight into the canons of the Church as well as historical sources. John Sames explained the hymnography of the Church and provided access to several patristic sources. Chapter 10 could not have been written without his help. Photius (Shannon) Ware provided invaluable assistance in researching materials. Special thanks also goes to Amanda Hamm, who has served as typist, copy-editor and cheerleader. By virtue of the fact that Amanda was a catechumen when this project started, she provided me with much insight into American Christianity to which I was not privy as well as a deeper appreciation of my own faith. For this I am extremely grateful.

This book is as much the product of Herb Ham as it is mine. As co-author, he rewrote the initial drafts and crafted the research into its final form. The final product is an example of a collaborative process that joined research methodology with historical writing skills. Herb is not merely a collaborator and mentor, but an all-around great guy as well.

Special thanks must go to the publisher, Frank Schaeffer, whose belief in this book never wavered and whose encouragement ensured this project became a reality.

Paramount thanks must go to my wife, Margaret, who has patiently borne my burdens, and my two sons, Denny and Mikey, who thought for a time that their dad was plugged into a computer. Without their support, this book could not have been started, much less completed. It is because of my wife and sons that I can envision an American Orthodox Church, and it is on their behalf (and on behalf of all the children of the fourth and fifth generation) that I pray for such an outcome.

George Michalopulos
Pascha 2003

THE RULING BISHOPS
OF THE
RUSSIAN-AMERICAN GREEK CATHOLIC
CHURCH OF AMERICA

(As known by their official titles)

The Leader of the Kodiak Mission[1]
    Joasaph Bolotov............1794-1799, Bishop of Kodiak

The Bishops of Novoarkhangelsk[2]
    Innocent Venamianov..... 1840-1858
    Peter Ekaterinovsky....... 1859-1866
    Paul Popov.................. 1866-1870

The Bishops of the Aleutians and North America[3]
    John Mitropolsky.......... 1870-1877
    Nestor Zakkis.............. 1878-1885
    Vladimir Sokolovsky...... 1887-1891
    Nicholas Adoratsky........ 1891
    Nicholas Ziorov............ 1891-1898
    Tikhon Bellavin............ 1898-1907[4]
    Platon Rozhdestvensky... 1907-1914
    Evdokim Meschersky......1914-1918
    Alexander Nemolovsky... 1918-1922

---

[1] Auxiliary of the Diocese of Irkutsk.
[2] Auxiliaries of the Diocese of Kamchatka.
[3] Diocese relocates to San Francisco in 1868.
[4] Diocese relocates to New York City; Tikhon elevated to archbishop.

The Metropolitans of All America and Canada[5]
    Platon Rozhdestvensky... 1922-1934
    Theophilus Pashkovsky... 1934-1950
    Leonty Turkevich..........1950-1965
    Ireney Bekish............... 1965-1977[6]
    Sylvester Haruns........... 1974-1977 (*locum tenens*)
    Theodosius Lazor..........1997-2002
    Herman Swaiko............2002-present

---

[5] Archbishop Platon, St Tikhon's successor, had become Metropolitan of Odessa, so he kept his title during his second pastorate in North America. Henceforth, the Russian-American archdiocesan district would be known as the "Metropolia" and enjoy *de facto* autonomy from Moscow.

[6] In 1970, the Patriarchate of Moscow granted autocephaly to the Metropolia, now known as the Orthodox Church in America.

PROLOGUE

THE ROOTS OF THE ORTHODOX CHURCH IN NORTH AMERICA

According to Alexander Bogolepov, in his book *Towards an American Orthodox Church*:

> The Orthodox Church traces its origin from the Mission of the Russian Orthodox Church that arrived in Alaska in 1794. The Mission was made a diocese and eventually became the Russian Archdiocese of the Aleutian Islands and North America. Subsequently, this Archdiocese became the Russian Orthodox Greek Catholic Church of America...[f]rom its very inception [it] was designed as a "permanent church of the settled Orthodox population" and not merely a church to take temporary pastoral care of Russian émigrés until their return to their homeland.[1]

How, then, did we get to the present uncanonical state in which we find ourselves today, where almost a dozen competing jurisdictions are, in effect, dependencies of the Old World? For the answer to this question, we must examine several different facets of Orthodoxy in America, including immigration patterns, tribalism, run-of-the-mill episcopal squabbling and the massive Islamic and atheistic oppression of the last 500 years. Almost all of these issues can be ascribed to the Ottoman conquest of the Near East and the Balkans; quite simply, the various Orthodox patriarchates of the Old World ossified into Christian ghettos as the sultans forced all of the patriarchates under their control from functioning as living, breathing churches of Christ.

Gone was evangelism, the establishment of monasteries, infirmaries and theological schools. No more were monks being sent out to translate the scriptures and liturgies into foreign languages. No more were new alphabets being created for the purpose of educating illiterate tribes. Orthodox bishops had to go hat-in-hand to Constantinople to receive their offices, having to pay exorbitant sums to the sultanic bureaucracy, a stricture which led to simony, an ecclesiastical crime condemned by the Church since Apostolic times. All of the worst excesses of the Renaissance Church in the West that we have long condemned were in fact practiced under other names in the East. Instead of indulgences, *psychokhartia* ("forgiveness documents") were sold, verifying that the bearer had indeed obtained the proper ecclesiastical remittance of his sins. In order to build churches, priests were pressured to charge for the sacraments they performed for the people. Under the Ottoman occupation, the Church survived, but we cannot say that it thrived.

The question arises, how have individual Orthodox Christians, parishes and even bishops from competing dioceses managed to put aside their differences and agitate for unification? Both aspects, the positive as well as the negative, need to be addressed. The ultimate answer, however, must tell us how we are going to resolve these differences and when, not if, an American Orthodox Church will arise from the ashes of the past.

The Russian Mission: From Sitka to Ft. Ross[2]

As far as missions go, the seeds of Orthodoxy were planted in the new world not with monastics or missionaries, but in the waning days of the Age of Discovery by explorers and adventurers. According to Timothy Ware in his seminal book, *The Orthodox Church,*[3] the first documented Orthodox presence in the North America occurred when the Russian explorers Vitus Bering and Alekseii Chirikov sighted the coast of Alaska on July 15, 1741. Five days later, on the feast of the Prophet Elijah, the first Orthodox liturgy was celebrated on the *St. Peter,* a Russian ship anchored at Sitka Bay.[2] This was, in fact, the first *official* Russian presence in

North America. In reality, Russian fur-trappers had already beaten Bering and Chirikov to the punch by almost a century.

These men, known in Russian as *promishlenikii* (traders), plied their trade on an itinerant basis and, being on the whole bachelors, married many of the native women. In reality, it would be a stretch to consider these men European Slavs, as they themselves were descended from previous Russian explorers who had married Siberian women in the preceding centuries. They were, therefore, of Russian descent. Their Orthodox identity was intact, however, and by a slow process of intermarriage had acclimated the natives of the Aleutian Islands to Slavic Orthodoxy, incorporating the natives' pre-Christian practices into a truly native expression of Orthodox Christianity.

This was the manner in which Orthodoxy had spread across the vast Siberian expanse since the inception of the Church in Russia. In itself, it was normative and, in any other circumstance, would have resulted in the creation of a dominant Orthodox culture in Alaska and possibly North America. As to why it did not, however, we can point to several factors, among them: (1) the Russians were the last of the explorers in the New World, (2) the dominant cultures in North America were already Christian and relatively advanced, (3) immigration patterns in the "lower 48" would overwhelm the native Church and (4) Old World Orthodoxy would be convulsed in due time by pressures that very nearly destroyed many of the ancient patriarchates.

This book is the story of these events and how they have led us to the present situation.

PART I

THE CHURCH UNITED:

THE ARCHDIOCESE OF THE ALEUTIANS AND NORTH AMERICA

1794-1918

CHAPTER 1

FROM SITKA TO SAN FRANCISCO

The first official Orthodox presence in North America occurred when the Russian explorers Vitus Bering and Aleksei Chririkov sighted the coast of Alaska on July 15,1741. Five days later, on the Feast of the Prophet Elijah, the first Orthodox liturgy was celebrated on the *St. Peter*, a Russian ship anchored on Sitka Bay.[1] In reality, an unofficial Orthodox presence had been established by Russian fur-trappers almost a century earlier. The Russian explorer Simeon Dezhnev founded a trading post on Anadyr on the Bering Strait, directly opposite Alaska in 1648.[2]

For several years thereafter, Siberian *promishlenikii* (traders) would embark from Anadyr to trap sea otters and trade with the Eskimo and Aleut peoples of North America on an annual and semiannual basis. They intermarried with the local women and produced a significant population of mixed Slav-Alaskans called *mestizos*.

According to the folklore of the descendants of these original *mestizos*, many of the Russo-Siberian men brought priests over to legitimize their marriages and baptize their wives and children.[3] Chapels of a rudimentary sort were built as well, usually converting the typical native spirit-house by placing a Russian three-bar cross on the top. Regardless of the fact that this period produced no permanent Russian settlements, an Orthodox presence had been established among the *mestizos*. Within 150 years, the cross-assimilation of Orthodox Russians and natives was virtually complete. When the famous British explorer Sir James Cook visited the Aleutian islands in 1793, he could not distinguish the Slavs from the natives.[4]

Economically, the fur trade proved so lucrative that, by the time Bering and Chirikov arrived in 1741, it became evident that a

1

permanent settlement was necessary. In 1780, Gregory Shelikov petitioned the imperial authorities in St. Petersburg for permission to set up an official trading colony. Shelikov's settlement of Kodiak Island was greeted with significant armed resistance, and he was only able to subdue the natives with extreme violence.[5]

After founding the "Russian-American Trading Colony" on Kodiak Island, Shelikov returned to Russia basking in his newfound glory as the "Russian Columbus." He left behind a subordinate named Alexander Baranov as supervisor. By all accounts, Baranov was a most unfortunate choice, as he treated the natives, the *mestizos* and even his Russian subordinates with contempt. He ruled the Russian-American Trading Company with an iron fist for 27 years.

The base of operations for the Trading Company was located on Sitka Bay in the town of Novoarkhangelsk (New Archangel). From Sitka, the Russian presence extended to most of sub-Arctic Alaska; the Pacific coast of the Yukon Territory; and all the way south to California, where just north of San Francisco (immediately north of the boundaries of Spanish America) the Russians established Ft. Ross. The boundaries of the Russian province were ratified by the United States, Spain and Great Britain by the turn of the 19th century.[6]

Meanwhile, Shelikov, having established an economic presence in North America, set out to establish an ecclesiastical presence in Russian America. He personally traveled across Russia to the venerable monastic center of Valaam, located near the Finnish border, to recruit monks to set up a formal mission in Alaska. He found a receptive audience. "One archimandrite, three priest-monks, one deacon-monk, one lay monk, together with several staff members, left St. Petersburg on December 21, 1793. They arrived in Kodiak on September 24, 1794, having traveled 7,300 miles in 293 days."[7]

When the group of missionaries arrived in Kodiak, they were horrified at what they encountered. According to their own recollection, "it was not the poor living conditions, inhospitable weather, nor the strange customs and foods of the native peoples that so upset [them], but the violent and exploitative behavior of their own Russian countrymen."[8]

Believing Shelikov would intervene, the leader of the mission sent vivid reports of abuse back to Shelikov. Receiving no reply, Frs. Joasaph, Macarius and Stephen returned to Russia in 1798 to report firsthand the outrages that Baranov had perpetrated in Alaska. In order to augment Joasaph's authority, the Holy Synod of Russia consecrated him as an auxiliary bishop of the Diocese of Irkutsk. With this new title, it was hoped that he would be able to institute reforms. On his return trip to Alaska, he sailed on *The Phoenix*. The ship sank before reaching its destination and all aboard, including Bishop Joasaph, perished.

While these events were taking place, the remaining five monks had undertaken in the interim an evangelistic mission. Baranov had prohibited the baptism of Aleut natives, since baptism conferred upon them automatic Russian citizenship. The monks, being aware that baptism would result in imperial protection, secretly baptized hundreds of Aleuts, very often immersing entire villages in the harbors and writing baptismal certificates on whatever type of parchment they could find. Such clandestine activity forced Baranov to acts of desperation, some of which included sending henchmen led by brutes such as Ivan Khuskutov, who pressed the natives into slavery.[9]

Outraged by the meddling of the missionaries and temporarily free from immediate episcopal oversight, Baranov placed the five remaining monks under house arrest and forbade them from having any further contact with the natives.

The First American Saints

(1) St. Herman

Father Herman, one of the monks of the Russian mission, escaped from Kodiak sometime after 1808 and set up a hermitage on Spruce Island, three miles to the north. He named his sanctuary "New Valaam" in honor of the monastic center from which he and his brethren had come. He lived as an ascetic, caring for Aleut orphans, the sick and dying. He built a hut for himself that also served as a chapel for the Reader's Services that he conducted for the natives. He tended a garden in which he pioneered the new agricultural techniques of using seaweed as a fertilizer. Due to his experimentation, he was able to increase agricultural yields, thereby improving the diets of the natives.

According to the accounts of pilgrims who visited him at the hermitage, his existence was spartan to the extreme: his only coat was a smock made of deerskin; his blanket, a wooden board; bricks comprised his pillow.[10] Despite his meager accommodations, his company was sought by people from all stations of life. One such man, Constantine Larianov, a pilgrim of mixed descent, commented that, "during my stay in the cell of Father Herman, I, a sinner, sat on his 'blanket' - and I consider this the acme of my fortune."[11] The successor of Baranov was so impressed by Fr. Herman's piety and concern for the natives that he eventually gave up his worldly possessions and entered the monastic life.[12]

Like the other monks of the original mission, Fr. Herman was well-loved by the natives, not only because he did everything he could to protect them from harassment, but because he strived to understand them on their own terms. Soon stories of miracles associated with Herman circulated and, given his ascetic and kindly temperament, gained currency. By the time of his death in 1837, most of the natives he had come in contact with had embraced Orthodoxy.

Father Herman's solitary approach, though brought on by Baranov's harassment, was in fact the traditional Russian form of monasticism. In Russia, holy men traditionally went into the wilderness to live as ascetics. Eventually others would find them and become their disciples. The solitary hermitage then became a skete and would often evolve into a full-fledged monastery.

Father Herman was the last surviving member of the original mission. He served the cause of Christ for over 40 years in Alaska. Almost immediately after his death, the local faithful of Alaska considered Fr. Herman to be a saint. His name spread across Russia, Finland and North America. On August 9, 1970, clergy and laity from the Orthodox world gathered in Kodiak to canonize St. Herman as the Wonderworker of America. He is the first saint glorified on this continent.[13]

(2) St. Juvenal

One of Herman's brothers, the priest-monk Fr. Juvenal (another refugee from the mission), undertook a whirlwind evangelistic mission that began in 1795 and lasted until his death two years later. Father Juvenal pioneered the practice of mass-baptism of entire villages and was a tireless preacher, stopping at the most remote areas to spread the Gospel. At Nunchek, on the coast of Alaska, he baptized more than 700 Chugach Sugpiaq Indians.

Father Juvenal became the first martyr for the faith in North America. According to his Tanaina Indian guide, who escaped by swimming away, Juvenal was murdered by a native hunting party led by a shaman in the Kuskokwim Bay. As Fr. Juvenal stood to speak to them, the shaman, frightened by the outsiders, ordered that the strangers be killed. As the spears and arrows flew at him, Fr. Juvenal made the sign of the Cross, which looked to the natives like he was "swatting flies." Upon his death, the shaman tried to remove the large brass pectoral cross that he wore but was unable to lift it. According to oral accounts passed down within that tribe, the shaman fell into a trance and regretted his actions. He warned the natives not to harm any man who came to them wearing that symbol. Ironically, subsequent Protestant missionaries were very well-received by the members of that tribe.[14] St. Juvenal was glorified and proclaimed a martyr by the Diocese of Alaska in 1977.[15]

(3) St. Innocent

As dedicated as Ss. Herman and Juvenal were, in order to survive in North America, the Church needed someone with tremendous organizational skills, tenacity and broad-based knowledge to oversee the work in North America. Into this fray stepped one of the most interesting saints of the Orthodox Church, Fr. John Popov-Veniaminov, the future St. Innocent.

Father John was, by all accounts, a man for all seasons: linguist, author, scientist, craftsman, architect, adventurer and diplomat. In due course he would not only solidify the Alaskan church but would return to Russia and be ordained first as Bishop (1840); then as Archbishop of Kamchatka (1850); and finally as Metropolitan of Moscow (1868), the senior hierarch in the Russian Orthodox Church.[16]

There was nothing in Veniaminov's origins that would lead one to believe that he would rise to the pinnacle of the Russian church. Born to poverty in 1797, he was orphaned while still a child and raised by an uncle. At nine years of age, he was sent to the monastery of the Ascension, the site of the relics of St. Innocent of Irkutsk (d 1731), one of the great missionaries of the Russian church.[17] While there, he received an excellent education. He excelled academically, especially in Greek and Latin.

Upon graduation, the future St. Innocent married and was ordained to the priesthood. In 1824, six years after the death of Baranov, he arrived in Alaska with his wife, children and mother-in-law. Because of his facility with languages, he set about learning the Unangan Aleut language and, together with a *mestizo* named Ivan Pan'kov, set about translating the Gospel of Matthew and a catechism into that language.

In 1828, both men opened a parish school, the first educational institution in Alaska. Innocent also built an infirmary and orphanage and even introduced the practice of vaccination. He strived to contain drunkenness and polygamy, which were rampant among the natives. Innocent "took a close and sympathetic interest in the native customs and beliefs, and his writings in this field remain a primary source for modern ethnography."[18] His writings on the flora and fauna of the Aleutians were published in a series of volumes entitled *Notes on the Unalaska District*, a work which earned him honorary membership in the Russian Geographical Society and the Moscow Royal University.

Besides his erudition, he was know for his tremendous physical strength and, like St. Juvenal before him, undertook hazardous missionary journeys to remote villages. Many of these voyages would last over several months, and his only mode of transportation was nothing more than a kayak. Despite his great stamina, this extreme privation resulted in his suffering from crippling and almost constant pain in his legs during his later years. Innocent would also travel to less harsh climes: in 1836 he boarded a Russian ship headed for Ft. Ross, where he made lasting friendships with the local Spanish clergy, conversing with them in Latin. While there, he built two pipe organs for them. (According to some oral accounts, one of the organs was a player-piano type that played Russian folk tunes.)

In 1839, Innocent and his family were recalled to Russia, and his wife died during the journey home. Upon the advice of

Metropolitan Philaret of Moscow, he reluctantly accepted monastic tonsure, receiving the name Innocent after his boyhood hero. In 1840, the Holy Synod, which had heard glowing reports of his work in Alaska, created the new "Diocese of Kamchatka, the Kuriles and the Aleutian Islands," and consecrated him as its first bishop.

Upon his return to Sitka, he founded the "All-Colonial School for the training of native and creole clergy, seamen, navigators, physicians, accountants, cartographers and artisans." He set about learning the Tlingit language and designed the cathedral of St. Michael, building with his own hands the clock which adorned the tower. Because his diocese covered both sides of the Bering Strait, he spent the next 11 years traveling back and forth between Alaska and Siberia, setting up missions and learning some of the Siberian languages as well.

In April 1865, the now Archbishop Innocent of Kamchatka was elevated to the office of Metropolitan of Moscow. Keenly aware of his own lack of formal seminary training, in a speech noted for its humility, Innocent begged the assembled hierarchs for their forgiveness in assuming such a lofty post over men "eminently more qualified" than himself.[19] His singular achievement as metropolitan was the establishment of the Orthodox Missionary Society, which guided and nurtured the Alaskan church for several years thereafter. Upon the sale of Alaska to the United States, Innocent recommended that the diocesan seat be relocated from Sitka to San Francisco and emphasized the need for English-speaking priests who could celebrate the services of the Church in that language.[20]

No better epitaph for the career of St Innocent can be written than the one given by the present-day Patriarch of Russia, Alekseii II:

> The apostolic preaching of Metropolitan Innocent spread to a vast territory including Alaska and Chukotka, the Aleutians, Kuriles and Commander Islands, eastern Siberia, the Amur region, Kamchatka and the Far East. [He] brought the light

of Christian faith to the Aleutians, Koloshes, Kuriles, Eskimo, Kenai, Chugaches, Kamchadals, Oliutores, Negidales, Mongols, Amogires, [etc]...He never missed an opportunity to preach and talk to people and tirelessly instructed his clergy to do the same.[21]

In 1977, the Holy Synod of the Church of Russia proclaimed him "St. Innocent of Moscow, Enlightener of the Aleuts and Apostle to America."[22]

(4) Ss. Peter the Aleut and Jacob Netsvetov

According to Orthodox ecclesiology, a church has not taken root in a new land until four things have transpired: (1) the translation of the Bible and the liturgies into the native tongue, (2) the establishment of a native clergy, (3) the establishment of a monastic presence and (4) the canonization of native saints. Thanks to the Kodiak mission and the evangelistic program of Ss. Herman, Juvenal and Innocent, three of the four had been achieved.

Born on Kodiak Island, Cungagnag took the name Peter when baptized by monks of St. Herman's missionary party. In 1815, Peter participated with other Aleuts and Russians in a trading mission to the Russian-American Trading Post located 50 miles north of San Francisco at Ft. Ross.[23] Spain still owned California at the time, and they took a dim view of Russian incursions into their territory, fearing the possibility of the loss of California. As Peter and the others approached Ft. Ross, Spanish sailors captured them and took them to San Francisco for a mock trial reminiscent of the Spanish Inquisition.

Roman Catholic priests in California put pressure on the Aleuts to embrace Catholicism. The prisoners responded by telling the priests they were already Christians. They showed their baptismal crosses as evidence they had been baptized. The Catholic clergy, perhaps unaware of the Russian mission, told them that if they did not convert they would be tortured.

A second time, Peter and his fellow Aleuts refused to renounce their Orthodox faith. The authorities cut off a toe from each of Peter's feet. Peter continued to repeat, "I am a Christian. I will not betray my faith." The Spanish priests then ordered some their native Californian Indian henchmen to cut off each finger of Peter's hand, one knuckle at a time. They eventually cut off his hands as well. Still, Peter refused to betray his faith. The Indians were then order to disembowel Peter. Peter died as a result of these tortures.

Upon receiving word of Peter's death, St. Herman went to his home altar, crossed himself and prayed out loud, "Holy new-martyr Peter, pray to God for us!"[24] In 1980, Peter the Aleut was formally glorified a saint as the "Martyr of San Francisco."[25]

Saint Jacob Netsvetov is another example of a profound native Christian witness. The son of a Russian father and an Eskimo mother, Jacob developed an affinity for the priestly life. He was the first known *mestizo* to receive a seminary education. While in seminary in Siberia he met his future wife, a Russian woman. Like Innocent before him, Jacob engaged in missionary journeys that separated him from her for months at a time.

In 1828, he was sent to assist newly consecrated Bishop Innocent as Innocent sought to stabilize the frontiers of Orthodoxy in the Aleutians. He developed local schools and worked with St. Innocent in developing a written form of one of the local languages, into which Jacob then translated the Scriptures and liturgical texts. Beginning in 1844, Jacob served the Yukon river area and worked primarily with the Yup'ik Indians for the next 20 years.[26]

Jacob kept meticulous journals of his activities that give valuable insights into the work of these Christian missionaries in Alaska. His diaries reveal horrendous privation. At one point, things got so bad for him and a small mission he had established that it looked like starvation would finally overcome them. A subdeacon named Constantine, sent out by Jacob to find game, had been gone for several days. His last-minute capture of some caribou averted the mass starvation they faced. (A certain Bishop Peter, who had access to Jacob's diaries, later marked in the margins, "What!? Meat during Lent?")

One of Jacob's successes was his intervention between the Yup'iks and the Athabascans. His intervention prevented a full-fledged intertribal massacre. The climax of Jacob's ministry was the mass-baptism of several hundred Athabascans in the Innoko River in 1852. In recognition for his years of service, he was knighted by Emperor Nicholas I of Russia, the first *mestizo* to receive such an honor.[27]

Shortly after, Jacob's wife died and he conducted her funeral service. He then returned to his missionary activities. Upon his own death, he was unable to be buried next to her, as all the available space was already taken. His gravesite to this day is unknown. Despite the fact that no one has access to his relics, he was proclaimed a saint as "Enlightener of the Peoples of Alaska" in 1994.[28]

The Success of the Russian Church in Alaska

The Russian Orthodox mission to Kodiak and Alaska succeeded in every sense of the word. When Russia sold Alaska in 1867, the Russian mission in Alaska had grown from eight monks to include 12,000 native Christians, nine parishes, 35 chapels, 17 schools (including the All-Colonial School) and three orphanages. Alaska was a mission in the truest sense of the word and not a diaspora. The Russian presence in Alaska itself was never great in proportion to the native population,[29] therefore the Russian mission was not a ministry among and for native Russians who had immigrated to Alaska.

The Aleuts and native Alaskans were clearly identified as being worthy of receiving the Orthodox faith. And they were worthy to receive the Gospel in their native language. The natives were not required to learn Russian, nor were they forced to attend services in languages they could not understand. To the credit of the eight Russian monks, they recognized that the natives had a deep pre-Christian spirituality and were to be brought into the faith with their own customs, languages and traditions intact.

The mission to America clearly demonstrated the Orthodox Church's understanding of the Day of Pentecost, when each one heard the Gospel in his own language.[30] For the Orthodox Church, Pentecost not only confirmed the universality of the Gospel as established by Christ in the Great Commission,[31] but the Day of Pentecost also indicated the manner in which the gospel was to be taken to all nations: in the native language of each people. Indeed, one of the differences historically between the missionary work of the Roman Catholic Church and the Orthodox Church was the issue of language. The Orthodox Church always adopted the native language of the people; whereas until recently, the Roman Catholic Church always used Latin in its services. It should be noted that one of the results of using the language of the people was the creation of ethnic churches, for example, the Greek Orthodox, the Russian Orthodox, the Macedonian Orthodox and so forth. They each express the same Orthodox Faith, but each in their own language. This is indeed a manifestation of the spirit of Pentecost, which marks the evangelistic nature of the Orthodox Church.

Alaska Becomes Part of the United States—1867

With the sale of the former Russian colony to the United States, the future of Alaska was sealed: if Orthodoxy was to survive, then the original missionary thrust exhibited by the Russian presence would have to be transferred to the contiguous United States. Despite the success of the Kodiak mission and the establishment of the native church in Alaska, the future of Orthodoxy in America could not be maintained from Sitka.

As part of the agreement transferring sovereignty of Alaska from Imperial Russia to the United States, all Russian nationals were allowed to accept American citizenship or migrate back to Russia. The overwhelming majority of European Russians, admittedly a small number overall, chose to repatriate. The immediate effect upon the Alaskan church was that this repatriation created a dearth of clergymen. Nevertheless, despite the absence of trained clergy, the Orthodox Church did not wither. In fact, it "continued to grow, largely through the efforts of indigenous leaders. Despite the fact that the mission never had more than 15 priests, scores of new parishes and chapels, as well as schools and orphanages were built. Lay leaders continued to conduct services, preach and even teach in the absence of clergy."[32]

The success of the native church was due in large measure because "from its very beginning, it was envisioned in the best tradition of Orthodox missionary spirituality, as an indigenous church, not as a 'diaspora'."[33] The process of Orthodox acculturation was so profound that photographs from the mid-to-late-19th century Aleuts reveal natives who were indistinguishable from white Americans of the "lower 48." What is striking was that they embraced these manners because of the Russian example rather than having it forced upon them. The effects of Orthodox Christianity were profound: intertribal slavery, massacres, drunkenness, polygamy and the exposure of the aged were eliminated. This was all done without forced conversions or the removal of tribes from ancestral homelands, as happened during the expulsion of the Five Civilized Tribes that occurred elsewhere on the North American continent in the same century. The contrast could not be more striking.

To be sure, the abandonment of Alaska by many Russian clergymen was not a high moment, nor was the tyrannical rule of Baranov. But the kindliness of the average Russian monk and the hundreds of laymen who intermarried with the native women, in the final analysis, planted the Orthodox Faith deep into the often frozen soil of Alaska. The tenacity with which the natives of Alaska still cling to the Orthodox faith in the present day is a testament to the success of the mission. Indeed, the fact that Alaska has more Orthodox parishes per capita than any other state in the union is a proud testament to the enduring legacy of the Russian Orthodox mission to Alaska.

The "Missionary Diocese" of San Francisco

With the incorporation of the territory of Alaska into the United States in 1867, Metropolitan Innocent recommended the relocation of the diocesan seat from Sitka to San Francisco. In addition, Innocent suggested several other reforms that he felt could expedite the growth of Orthodoxy in America: (1) the translation of the services and liturgical books into English, (2) the rapid ordination of American-born men to the priesthood, (3) the immediate installation of an English-speaking bishop and (4) the erection of a cathedral. Furthermore, Innocent asked that the Sitka mission not be closed but turned into a diocese of its own.[34]

A confluence of events made the relocation inevitable. For one thing, the tiny Russian émigré community of Ft. Ross had asked for a priest. Secondly, the harbor at San Francisco had already served as a debarkation point for the long ocean voyage to St. Petersburg, which was quicker than the overland route across the vast Siberian expanse. And finally, the climate of Alaska mitigated against any further European migration. By the mid-19th century, it was obvious to most people around the world that the continental United States would serve as a beacon for immigrants for the

14

foreseeable future. In 1868, Bishop John Mitropolsky (who spoke English), erected a diocesan office and mission school on the grounds of the newly erected cathedral of St. Aleksandr Nevsky in the "Russian Hill" section of San Francisco.[35]

Saint Innocent's vision was realized with a rapidity that is remarkable in the annals of Orthodoxy. His vision of evangelism for the entire United States created the subdivision of the new diocese into vicariates that were headed by priests who reported directly to San Francisco. Saint Innocent's commitment to the use of the vernacular resulted in the publication of the first Orthodox Church periodical in America. *The Russian-American Messenger* was published entirely in English until demographic pressures in the early 20th century forced it to put out a multilingual edition.

From San Francisco efforts to take the Orthodox Faith to North America in the languages of North America continued. Alaska was not forgotten; indeed, it remained part and parcel of the overall missionary fervor. Bishop John Mitropolsky's successor, Bishop Nestor Zakkis (1879-82), for example, attempted to translate the Gospels into Eskimo but died before he could finish the task. Nestor's successor, Vladimir Sokolovsky (1888-91), translated many of the Church Slavonic chants into English. He appointed the first American-born Orthodox priest, Fr. Sebastian Dabovich (the son of Serbian immigrants), as the "English Preacher" of the cathedral.[36] Because of this momentum, a new cathedral was required, and, in 1888, the Cathedral of St. Nicholas was erected in San Francisco.

As the 1800's drew to a close, Orthodox Christianity had planted itself in the New World in largely the same method it had implanted elsewhere: by monks, itinerant preachers, native conversion and émigré colonists. However, tumultuous events were to overtake this normal, organic process. As the 19th century ended, international political realities and massive waves of immigration to the United States would alter the American landscape forever.

CHAPTER 2

THE AMERICAN CRUCIBLE

Historical Influences

The history of Christianity began dividing into East and West with the sack of the city of Rome by Alaric, king of the Visigoths in A.D. 410. The western half of the Roman Empire entered a period of decline now known as the Middle Ages. The Medieval Period lasted approximately 1,000 years, from the fall of the city of Rome in A.D. 476 to the Italian Renaissance in the 15th century. Forces that created and shaped Western Christianity and Western culture included St. Augustine's *The City of God,* Charlemagne's influence on the Patriarchate of Rome, the creation of the Holy Roman Empire and the Germanizing of the Roman papacy under Pope Nicholas I. The final break between East and West occurred with the Great Schism of 1054, the end-result of ecclesiological and theological fissures that had been simmering for decades. With Rome's separating herself from the rest of Christianity, two churches existed instead of one: the Roman Catholic Church in the West and the Orthodox Church in the East.

Unlike the West, the East did not have a dark age. Blocked by Islam to the south and east, the Eastern church sent missionaries northward through the Balkans. Photius, the Patriarch of Constantinople, selected two brothers from Thessalonica, Cyril and Methodius, to begin taking the Orthodox Faith to the Slavs of Moravia, Bulgaria, Serbia and Russia. In 863, the two brothers began the massive work of creating an alphabet for the Slavonic language in order to translate the Scriptures and liturgical services into the language of the Slavs. The Moravians (modern day Czech Republic and Republic of Slovakia) were the only people of Western Europe, at this time, who heard the Gospel and liturgical services in their own language, unlike the Germanic peoples who had been evangelized by Rome.

The missionaries to Bulgaria, "lacking the vision of Cyril and Methodius, at first used Greek in Church services, a language as unintelligible as Latin to the ordinary Bulgar."[1] Soon, however, Slavonic replaced Greek and "the Christian culture of Byzantium was presented to the Bulgars in a Slavonic form which they could assimilate."[2] The conversion of Bulgaria spread, and in 926, an independent Bulgarian patriarchate was established, the first "daughter" patriarchate. Beginning also in the 860's, and following the pattern of Cyril and Methodius, missionaries took Christianity to Serbia. The Patriarchate of Serbia was created in 1346. With the institution of autocephalous churches, both Serbia and Bulgaria were brought even more into alignment with Byzantine culture. The conversion of Romania, largely Latin in its national identity, followed suit. In 988, Prince Vladimir of Kievan Rus' converted to Christianity, and the conversion of Russia began in earnest. It was the Russian Orthodox Church that, in turn, would send the first Orthodox missionaries to North America.[3]

Unlike Russia, where Orthodox Christianity was practiced freely, the rest of the Orthodox world soon lived under the bondage of Islam. The traditional date for the beginning of Islam is A.D. 622, and within 100 years Islam had conquered half of the Eastern Roman Empire. Antioch fell in 711 as Muslims conquered Syria and Palestine and "pillaged Jerusalem, looting and burning churches, killing thousands of Christians."[4] The Crusades waged by the Christian West (1100-1300), ostensibly to rescue Jerusalem from the "infidels," revealed their true purpose in the Fourth Crusade. Begun under the pretext of attacking the Islamic navy wintering at Alexandria, the Western fleet of the Fourth Crusade changed course midway and sailed toward Constantinople where, in 1204, the Christian West attacked the Christian East and raped and pillaged Constantinople for three days. The Western fleet returned to Venice loaded with the stolen treasures of books, art, gold and silver that gave birth to the Italian Renaissance. Severely weakened, Constantinople never fully recovered. Turkish Islam achieved what Arab Islam and Persian Islam had failed to do when in 1453, with the fall of Constantinople and the end of the Roman Empire, the Ottoman Turks created their empire.

Under Islam, Christianity suffered severe restrictions.[5] In order to survive, Orthodox Christianity accommodated itself to these restrictions. By the 1850's, after 1100 years of Islamic domination and 400 years of Turkish rule, Christianity's accommodation to Islam had taken its toll. Evangelism was gone, an educated clergy was almost non-existent and an autocratic or aristocratic management of the parish and its finances was deeply entrenched—all in the name of self-preservation. To their credit, Orthodox Christians maintained the liturgical practice of their faith. They may not have understood what they were doing, but they understood it was important to do it. In this sense, Orthodox Christians under Islam were like the sensible steward Christ commended in his parable, "blessed is that slave whom his Master finds doing what he was supposed to do when he comes."[6] This is to say, the outward forms were maintained and consistently practiced with very little change through the centuries. Orthodox Christians continued attending the liturgical services of the church, but through the centuries the faithful stopped receiving the Eucharist regularly and stopped participating in the singing and liturgical responses. The non-communicant status of the laity unfortunately became the norm for Orthodoxy.[7]

After 400 years of power, the Ottoman Turkish Empire began to weaken. In 1830, the Egyptian army attempted to take Lebanon and Syria away from the Ottomans. In 1840, the Ottomans, along with Great Britain, Russia, Austria and Prussia, signed the Convention of London, which demanded that the Egyptians withdraw their troops. After a show of force the Egyptians were driven out of the region. However, peace never returned.

The Ottomans, fearful of a growing Arab nationalism within their Empire, sought to divide Arab unity by creating sectarian strife between the Christian Arabs and the Muslim Arabs. With Turkish orchestration, conflicts between Christians and Arab Muslims, which began in 1861, reached a climax in the massacre of 11,000 Christians in 1860. One hundred and fifty Christian villages were burned.[8] Across the Ottoman Turkish Empire unrest grew. By the 1890's, a flood of Arab emigrants from Eastern Europe and the Middle East began making their way westward to the United States, Canada, Chile, Brazil and Argentina.

America and the Immigrant Experience

Following the American Civil War, the United States went from being the fourth largest industrial power in the world to being number one by 1900, by then producing more than England and Germany combined. Industrialization required workers. From around the globe workers flooded into the Untied States. So many came that the United States replaced the old term *emigrant*, which described one who left a place, with the newly invented American term *immigrant* to describe someone who came to a place.

Before 1880, over 85% of the immigrants to the United States had come from Western Europe: England, Germany, Ireland and Scandinavia. After 1880, 80% of all new arrivals came from Southern and Eastern European countries: Italians, Greeks, Turks,[9] Hungarians, Eastern European Jews, Armenians, Poles, Russians and Slavs. The numbers were staggering. Between 1870 and 1910, more than 20 million immigrants came to the United States. In 1888, more than half a million Europeans arrived in the United States. By 1907, more than one million came into the United States via Ellis Island in New York City. Unlike immigrants from Western Europe who were mainly Protestants, these new immigrants from Southern and Eastern Europe were primarily Catholics, Jews and Orthodox Christians.

American society, created out of Protestantism and democratic political theory, confronted the new immigrants with ways of life to which they were unaccustomed, be they Catholic, Jewish or Orthodox. Europe and its customs appeared retrograde in comparison, and this produced a profound culture shock in many of the immigrants. Many could not cope and returned to their homelands. Most of the others who remained occupied the bottom wrung of the socio-economic ladder, taking jobs that nobody else wanted.

Many of those who came, particularly if they were Orthodox, were single males. Their goal was to make their fortune and return to their homeland, where they would marry and live out their lives. They came, in other words, for temporary employment, planning on an eventual return to their homelands. The Romanian immigrants of this era had a common expression: *mia su drumul* (A thousand [dollars] and home).[10] The only purpose of the typical Orthodox migrant was to make enough money to endower his sisters or otherwise alleviate the grinding poverty of his immediate family.

The massive flood of immigrants into the United States created a negative backlash among the old-stock Americans, especially those living in the cities of the Midwest and Northeast. To them the immigrants were invading armies that threatened to dilute their cherished American values and identities.[11] By 1890, one-fourth of Philadelphia's population, one-third of the populations of Boston and Chicago and four out of five New Yorkers were foreign born. By 1893, Chicago was the largest Bohemian city in the world and, by 1920, had become the third largest Polish city in the world. New York had twice as many Irish as Dublin and as many Germans as Hamburg.

The attendant societal strains which mass immigration placed on 19th century America were manifested not only in open hostility (for example signs, that said "No Irish Need Apply") and violence, but in profound intellectual changes as well. It was during this time, for example, that Charles Darwin had published his theories of evolution, which were amplified into racist genetic doctrines by several of his followers such as Josiah Strong, Charles Spencer and Stewart Houston Chamberlain. The effects on governmental policy both in the United States and northern Europe were profound and would ultimately have devastating consequences. In the United States, for example, old-stock Americans used the theories of "natural selection" and "survival of the fittest" to justify White, Anglo-Saxon, Protestant superiority, thus creating the WASP yardstick against which to measure and judge all non-WASPs. Southern and Eastern European immigrants likewise were labeled as "morons" and "imbeciles," and great efforts were made to segregate their children in the public schools from the children of the more established Northwest Europeans.[12]

In addition, Orthodox immigrants were often used to undercut the wages of earlier Irish, German and Scandinavian immigrants. Their success in this regard often resulted in the Orthodox domination of the coal-mining industry and the railroads. An unfortunate by-product of this, however, was violence against them by the nascent labor movement, which considered them to be "scabs."[13] Nativist organizations such as the Ku Klux Klan also contributed to the violence against them. On rare occasions, entire communities of Orthodox immigrants could be wiped out, as happened in 1912 in Omaha, Nebraska, when a young Greek ne'er-do-well shot and killed a policeman in cold blood. In the ensuing rampage, the entire Greek immigrant community of some 1,200 persons had their homes and businesses destroyed by an angry mob.[14]

The stresses of immigration were profound for all immigrant groups. For the Orthodox, however, there were other factors that made the immigrant experience all the more difficult. Catholic and

Jewish immigrants often immigrated in entire family units. Catholic hierarchies were established immediately, as were parishes, then parish schools in due course, then universities and hospitals. This pattern often held true for the established Orthodox presence, as was noted in chapter one. With the newer Orthodox immigration, however, chaos reigned. Sometimes whole Orthodox villages migrated to the United States and settled as neighbors in the new world. More often than not, immigrants settled where they could, and if numbers justified, sought to establish fraternal organizations based on common ethnicity. In time, these fraternities would establish parish churches, something that had never happened before within Orthodoxy.

The Orthodox way had been for the hierarchs to send missionaries into a region and to oversee the planting of new parishes. But the Orthodox immigrants did not come as missionaries. To their credit, they brought their faith with them. But there was no historical pattern for the oversight of an immigrant community. The only pattern was that oversight in a new country fell to the first Orthodox Church to send missionaries to that country. It therefore fell to the Russian Orthodox Church and the Russian bishops in San Francisco to oversee the throngs of Orthodox Christians pouring into the United States and Canada. The Russian bishops faced a monumental task. The erratic and scattered settlement across the continent of the new Orthodox immigrants, together with their inevitable tribalistic tendencies and ethno-nationalistic loyalties, as well as there being division within communities over whether to assimilate into American culture and acclimate themselves to their new country or to remain a diaspora in exile, were but a few of the problems. But others issues, including the use of the English language and submitting to the oversight of the Russian bishops, presented even greater problems if a unified American Orthodox Church were to be established.

The Missionary Diocese of San Francisco and the Challenges of the New Immigration

Although the diocesan seat of the Aleutians and North America had relocated to San Francisco in the hope of greater outreach to the American public and to minister to the growing number of Orthodox immigrants, the migration patterns of the various Orthodox ethnic groups, as well as their traditional xenophobia, made the mission of the Russian bishops in San Francisco all the more difficult.

Still, San Francisco was not without its successes. Parishes were established in all parts of the United States; often they were ethnocentric in nature, concentrated as they were in mining camps and in fishing villages along the Atlantic and Gulf coasts. Others were surprisingly "pan-Orthodox" in scope. According to the parish records of the church of St. Aleksandr Nevsky in Pittsburgh, Pennsylvania (1895), for example, there were "476 Uhro-Rusins [sic], 162 Galicians, 603 Serbians, 150 Syro-Arabs, 29 Greeks, 2 Montenegrins, 1 American, 1 Negro, 1 Moldavian, 4 Poles and 118 Russians."[15] The services in this polyglot parish were conducted in a mixture of Slavonic, Greek, Arabic and Serbian. Parish records from Holy Trinity Orthodox Church of New Orleans (the first Orthodox church built in the contiguous United States) reveal Greeks, Serbians and Arabs among the worshipers and services being conducted in a variety of languages, including English.[16] Indeed, parish council meetings had to be conducted wholly in English, because English was the only common language of the parish.

In due time, San Francisco was able not only to build parishes but to send young men of different backgrounds to Russia, some on full scholarship so that they could study for the priesthood. The Diocese of the Aleutians and North America (which was the 65th diocese of the Russian Orthodox Church) was subdivided into smaller units, each headed by a vicar who reported directly to San

Francisco. These vicars were priests of senior rank, not all of whom were Russian.

Although the North American diocese was situated entirely in a different country, it was part of the See of Moscow and was governed as such. It subsisted on a yearly stipend of roughly one-half million dollars, from which it paid the salaries of priests, parochial teachers and other diocesan functionaries.[17] From 1868 (when it relocated to San Francisco) until its effective demise in 1917, it experienced significant growth: 350 churches and chapels, one seminary, an orphanage, an unaccredited women's college, two monasteries and even a bank.[18] In comparison to the more massive Catholic immigration, which boasted several hundred dioceses, such an accomplishment is nothing short of astonishing.

Part of the reason for this growth was the insistence of the Russian Missionary Society that its North American diocese take its mission as an evangelistic church seriously. All of its bishops, beginning with Bishop John Mitropolsky, spoke fluent English. Outreach was made to all Orthodox immigrant groups as well, going to great lengths to set up ethnic parishes if the numbers warranted. Priests from Greece, Serbia, Syria and so forth were encouraged to emigrate to the United States in order to care for these parishes. In turn, the Old World patriarchates respected the prerogatives of the Russian bishops and refused to send ethnic bishops despite the loud clamor for such men from Greeks, Romanians and Albanians who feared "pan-Slavism."[19] Indeed, Patriarch Joachim III of Constantinople had written in 1903 a warm letter to Fr. Vladimir Alexandrov, a Russian priest in Seattle, thanking him for his pastoral care of Greek expatriates in that city.[20]

Among the men of non-Russian background who attained positions of authority during the period in question (1867-1917) were the aforementioned Fr. Sebastian Dabovich, who was also the first American-born Orthodox priest; Fr. Michael Andreades, a Greek who served as vicar of the western states; and Fr. Ambrosius Vlettas, another Greek who was also active in ministering to Greek immigrants. Converts to Orthodoxy were not unknown at this time. One of them, Nathaniel Irvine, actually was ordained as priest. The bishops in San Francisco and the Russian Orthodox Church in general, made a concerted effort to evangelize the non-Orthodox (at least to an extent) and to minister to Orthodox immigrants in their own parishes.

The Trustee Parish

Despite the best efforts of San Francisco to establish parishes and to endow them with vestments and other religious implements, the overwhelming majority of parishes in the late-to-early-20th century were independently established entities, usually along ethnic lines. Since laymen were responsible for raising the money necessary to build them in the first place, they became known as "trustee parishes." In short order trustee parishes were built all over the United States and Canada, most along ethnic lines.[21]

American laws mandated that churches be incorporated with boards of directors, or trustees, who would be responsible for them to the state. This was a new phenomenon in Orthodoxy; before this time, all churches were endowed by the state or some benefactor. The idea that a village or a community could come together to build a church and have responsibility for its upkeep was revolutionary. In America, however, this became, by necessity, the norm.

The reason for this is due to the fact that, despite the best efforts of San Francisco to establish parishes, there was only so much that could be accomplished on the amount of money received from Moscow. The annual stipend of 500 thousand dollars was half of what was actually needed.[21] Simply put, the pace of immigration exceeded the finances necessary to keep up the pace of building new churches. Immigration figures bear this out. According to the best estimates 40,000 Serbs, 25,000 Arabs, 25,000 Albanians, 250,000

Ukrainians and Carpatho-Russians and 300,000 Greeks permanently settled in the United States.[22] When these figures are added to perhaps twice that number who eventually returned to their points of origin,[23] then there were easily close to one million Orthodox immigrants living in North America within a space of 40 years. The strains on one diocese headed by one bishop therefore were too much to bear.

Furthermore, the fact that America was already a Christianized nation only added to the novelty of the situation *vis a vis* Orthodoxy. Up to this point in history, Orthodox Christianity had penetrated into lands that were previously pagan. Asia Minor, the Balkans, the Near East, the Eastern European plain and the vast Siberian expanse all succumbed in due time to Orthodox Christianity. The realization that the citizens of the United States were not only Christian but comprised a relatively more advanced culture complicated the picture immensely: it was no longer the case of civilized Byzantine monks going into the wilds of Moravia to Christianize uncivilized barbarians. This was readily apparent to every Orthodox immigrant, especially those from the Balkans and the Levant.

Because of this, xenophobia as well as the traditional Orthodox tribalism set in almost at once. That many immigrants viewed their stay as temporary played an even greater role as well. Why would the typical immigrant contribute his meager funds to build a pan-Orthodox parish when he was not going to remain in America for much longer anyway? When it became clear to more than a few that they were not going back, then the idea of an ethnocentric parish became the ideal.

Of course tribalism played a role in this mentality, but there were other economic reasons as well: an established Orthodox parish with a fixed address served as a point of contact by which a relationship with the homeland could be maintained. This went both ways: if the people back home only knew the name of a town and state in which an Orthodox church existed, then they could conceivably make their way to that town and be received by compatriots. This was vitally important in an era in which the priest was, more often than not, the only literate man in a typical Balkan or Levantine village, and the overwhelming majority of newer immigrants could not speak one word of English. They needed the parish priest to help them get settled and to help them translate their official documents for the immigration authorities.

The ethnocentric "trustee" parish, therefore, served not only as a way-station for the immigrant, but as an unofficial consulate and a clearing-house of information about the "old country." Although the typical village church had always served as a place of spiritual focus for the typical Orthodox peasant, the rich community life of the village provided emotional support as well. With immigration, however, the emotional and cultural ties were severed, and it was this emotional vacuum that the trustee parish filled. An immigrant parish became the cultural center of the immigrant group in a particular city or region as well as its spiritual center.

In order to accommodate the spiritual needs of the overwhelming number of Orthodox immigrants, the Russian hierarchy wisely decided to make a virtue out of necessity. Because the yearly remittances from Moscow were not enough to adequately staff priests for every parish, San Francisco allowed the trustee parishes to recruit priests from their villages back home. The only stipulation was that they should submit their credentials to the Russian bishop in San Francisco before they would be allowed to liturgize. It appears that, more often than not, this protocol was observed.

Russian bishops, whenever possible, traveled the length and breadth of the United States and Canada and consecrated these ethnic parishes, endowing them with gifts of religious implements and vestments, some of these being gifts from Czar Alexander III himself.[24] Although the expense of such gifts (as well as the necessary travel) made such endowments rare, almost every ethnic trustee parish "regularly" received the *antimensia* (the altar cloths) necessary for the celebration of the Divine Liturgy from the bishops in San Francisco.[25]

Eventually however, many of the non-Slavic trustee parishes chafed at Russian oversight: the Greeks especially, but also the Romanians. Even several of the Serbian parishes requested separation from the Russians, and in 1913, Fr. Sebastian Dabovich led 16 of the 19 Serbian parishes out of the Diocese of the Aleutians and North America, hoping to set up an exarchate under the Patriarchate of Belgrade.[26] The Serbian-Americans were rebuffed by Patriarch Dmitrij, and three years later a reconciliation was effected with the Russian hierarchy.[27]

It is hard to overestimate the feeling of empowerment that the new immigrants felt when they realized they had within their own power to endow a new church. Rather than being dependant on the czar or some other potentate to build a church, immigrants realized that, by banding together into a brotherhood or some such organization, they could each pool their meager resources, pledge future amounts of money and then go to a bank that could loan them the credit necessary.[28] Attendant with such independence was the responsibility for these parishes that the civil laws of the United States required. In other words, the benefactors had a stake in the church and were shareholders and thus trustees, responsible to the state and local governments for their church's conduct. Priests therefore came to be viewed as employees of the parish and could be hired and fired, often at will, in total disregard of normal Orthodox ecclesiology.

This new-found freedom, together with the traditional tribalistic pressures of the Orthodox immigrants, emboldened many parishes to ask not only for priests from their respective homelands but bishops as well. Surprisingly, Bishop Tikhon (1898-1907) welcomed the possibility of ethnic "auxiliary" bishops to administer the nascent ethnic sub-jurisdictions and worked hard to lobby the old patriarchates for qualified clergymen to lead them.

In this instance, however, both Bishop Tikhon and the ethnic parishes were consistently rebuffed by every one of the Old World patriarchates. The Greeks especially were cut adrift, not only by the autocephalous Church of Greece, but the ecumenical patriarchate as well. The reasons were many: the Greek monarchy did not want to anger the Romanov dynasty (with whom it was related), and the See of Constantinople had been ordered by the Ottoman government not to have anything to do with Greeks of the diaspora.[29]

Regardless of the growing ethnic tensions, the Russian diocese continued to grow and anticipate new challenges. Bishop Vladimir Sokolovsky (1888-1891) began the process of translating the liturgy into English and brought over seminarians and faculty from the Seminary of Kholm to help him standardize liturgical worship.[30] (It was Bishop Vladimir who had created the title of "English Preacher" for the cathedral in San Francisco, to which Fr. Sebastian Dabovich had been appointed.) It was under Bishop Vladimir's successor, Bishop Nicholas Ziorov (1891-1898), however, that the Church in America displayed a visionary outlook that resulted in its most productive evangelical outreach.

The Conversion of the Uniates: Bishop Nicholas and St. Alexis Toth

The slow but steady growth of Orthodoxy during this time received an explosive boost when tens of thousands of Eastern-Rite Catholics ("Uniates"), mostly from Ukraine, Galicia and Carpatho-Russia, entered the Church *en masse* between the years 1892-1917. The Uniate branch of Roman Catholicism traced its origin back to the Council of Ferrara-Florence, in which a union was effected between the Greek East and Latin West. The reasons for this union were complex, but the growing Ottoman threat to the ever-dwindling Byzantine Empire was clearly a motivating factor. Almost all of the

Eastern clergymen who attended the Council (save for Mark Eugenicus, Bishop of Ephesus) signed the articles of union, recognizing papal supremacy and the *filioque*[31] and otherwise smoothing over the doctrinal differences that had accrued in the years since the Great Schism (1054). Upon their return to the East, however, many of the signatories recanted their participation. However, Metropolitans Isidore of Kiev, the premier churchman in the Church of Russia, and John Bessarion did not. Isidore of Kiev was in fact ejected from his throne in 1444 and imprisoned but was able to escape. (Because the See of Constantinople was still loyal to the Council at this time, the bishops of Russia decided to seek autocephaly from it in 1449. Metropolitan Jonas was elected head of that church, and, in 1589, the metropolitan see was elevated to patriarchal rank; the breach between Constantinople and Moscow had been healed by the election of Gennadius as Patriarch of Constantinople in 1453.)

Although the laity as a rule, led by the monasteries, rejected Ferrara-Florence, Isidore and Bessarion received the rank of cardinals for their efforts. It was not until the next century however, that a council of eight Ukrainian bishops met in 1596 at Brest-Litovsk, where six of them agreed to reunite their dioceses with Rome. They asked for and received papal dispensation to continue to celebrate the Liturgy of St. John Chrysostom and to continue all other Orthodox ecclesiastic traditions, including allowing priests to marry and the first communion to be given following baptism. Those who were unwilling to conform to the union were persecuted. However, the great majority of the laity were unaware of the differences in the fine points of doctrine that separated East from West, and most continued to believe that they were still in communion with Moscow and the rest of the Orthodox world.

This tenuous union resulted in much confusion among the tens of thousands of Carpatho-Russians, Ukrainians and Galicians who immigrated to North America to work in the coal mines and to farm the prairie provinces of Canada. The older German, Irish and Polish immigrants were confused by the fact that, to all appearances, they were clearly Orthodox. Roman clergy were horrified by the fact that many of the Uniate priests were married. The stage therefore had been set for a reconciliation between the Orthodox hierarchy and disaffected American Uniate clergy.

The spark that lit this revolt can be traced to one man: Fr. Alexis Toth, a widowed Uniate priest who immigrated to America in 1889 at the behest of St. Mary's Greek Catholic Church, a Ukrainian Catholic congregation in Minneapolis, Minnesota (like the Orthodox, many Catholic parishes were being independently established by the various Catholic immigrant groups). As per normal ecclesiastic protocol, Fr. Alexis presented his credentials to Archbishop John Ireland of Minneapolis. What transpired however was most unfortunate. According to Toth's own recollection of the event in question, Archbishop Ireland was outraged at the fact that he had been a married man and questioned his credentials as well as the entire canonical regularity of the Uniate branch of Catholicism in general.[32] Indeed, harsh words were exchanged and, in Toth's own recollection, it quickly degenerated into a heated argument.[32]

The bitterness that resulted from this exchange led many of the trustees of St. Mary's parish to question the continued viability of their trustee parish's independent status. Archbishop Ireland had made it clear to Fr. Alexis, among other things, that he had not given the Ukrainians permission to build a parish in the first place.[33] Indeed, the archbishop told Fr. Alexis there was a Polish priest in Minneapolis who was "sufficient... for the Greeks [i.e. Ukrainians]."[34]

Almost immediately, a correspondence was set up between other Ukrainian Catholic parishes in hopes that, by banding together, they could better fight the impending threat of the loss of their property that Archbishop Ireland intimated.[35] One trustee of St. Mary's, John Mlinar, traveled to San Francisco to meet with Bishop

Nicholas, was cordially received and returned to Milwaukee with a "generous donation of icons." [36] Father Alexis started corresponding with Bishop Nicholas, and in less than two years, he and all 361 members of St. Mary's "were received 'back' into the Orthodox Church [that] their forefathers had left three centuries earlier." [37]

This lone act of reunification did not end there. Father Alexis became a tireless preacher of reconciliation with Orthodoxy and traveled great distances to Ukrainian parishes; by the time of his death in 1909, 65 independent Ukrainian churches totaling some 20,000 souls had become Orthodox. [38] Unfortunately for Rome, the continuing pastoral insensitivity expressed by American Catholics only exacerbated the "return to the fold." Examples of this stubbornness included the publication of the papal decree *Ea Semper* in 1907, which mandated Uniate priestly celibacy. By 1916, an additional 98 Ukrainian and Carpatho-Russian parishes numbering some 100,000 faithful had left Catholicism to embrace Orthodoxy. [39]

Of course, this is not to say that all Uniates welcomed the solicitation of Bishop Nicholas. Many openly chafed at "russification" and opted to stay with Rome. Indeed, many of the Carpatho-Russian/Ukrainian parishes that had opted for return to Orthodoxy remade themselves (as it were) into Russian parishes. Criticisms of "pan-Slav nationalism" and not Orthodox piety reverberated in many circles, Latin Catholic as well as Uniate. [40] Be that as it may, the tide to Orthodoxy, coupled with generous subsidies from San Francisco, proved to be unstoppable. For his efforts, Fr. Alexis Toth was canonized a saint in 1994 as "Confessor and Defender of Orthodoxy in America." [41]

Immigration Patterns

Among the Orthodox immigrant groups, Russians and Ukrainians tended to migrate to the coal mining regions of the Midwest, whereas the Greeks tended to settle in the cities of the East

Coast and the Midwest. The Serbs who gravitated towards the American West also took up coal mining, but the majority ended up in the steel industry of the Midwest.[42] It was the steel industry in fact that attracted a great proportion of Slavic immigrants in general, and their influence is still felt throughout hundreds of towns of the upper Midwest. Paradoxically, because of the sparseness of the native white population of the mountain West, Orthodox immigrants who migrated there quickly became a significant portion of the population. Because they were obvious and not considered "white," violence against them was endemic and their work, perilous.[43]

The Russians present a more complicated picture in that the definition of "Russian" is rather broad. Church records from that time talk about "Uhro-Russians," "Carpatho-Russians" and "Galicians" (from Poland), some of whom were Catholics of the Eastern Rite (as discussed above). The "Great Russians" would not come over in large numbers until after the Bolshevik revolution. As already discussed, the Russian population of Alaska, for example, never numbered more than 700, and their penetration into San Francisco was never as numerous as their subsequent arrival by the tens of thousands through New York following the First World War after the fall of Russia to communism.

Regardless, the overall shift in population therefore was to the East Coast of the United States, especially since New York City became the primary point of entry and dispersing for the newly arrived. San Francisco, by contrast, was the main point of entry for Chinese and other Asians, none of whom were Orthodox. This demographic shift therefore necessitated a relocation of the diocesan seat a second time, from San Francisco to New York City. It was Bishop Nicholas's successor, Bishop Tikhon Bellavin, who received permission from the Holy Synod of Russia to move, which he did in 1902, at the same time receiving a rise in rank to that of Archbishop.

The Lebanese were an interesting anomaly in that, in striking contrast to the typical Orthodox immigrant from Southern and

33

Eastern Europe, they tended to be self-employed merchants back in their homeland and had every intention of plying their commercial skills in the United States. Surprisingly, more than a few were professionals. Unlike most of their co-religionists from the Balkans, they entertained no illusions of returning to their homeland and as such usually immigrated with their families intact. They tended to congregate in large numbers on the East Coast as well as in the farm belt. Wherever they settled, they practiced mercantile occupations, preferring self-employment rather than industrialization. Due to a variety of factors, including especially the absence of a nationalistic loyalty to the "old country," they were able to assimilate more quickly into the broader American culture, a fact that has repercussions today *vis a vis* the other ethnic jurisdictions which tended to concentrate on nationalism. Moreover, relations between Lebanese Orthodox and Catholics (or "Maronites," the "first Uniates"[44]) were cordial in contrast to the relations between Slavic Uniates and the Orthodox Slavs. This may well have eased Lebanese assimilation into the broader American culture.

The Romanians were likewise exceptional in that other factors besides purely economic ones drove them to the United States and Canada. Romanians outside of the Kingdom of Romania proper actually experienced religious persecution at the hands of the Austro-Hungarian rulers of Moldava, Transylvania and Banat. The religious and cultural freedom of the Romanians was suppressed by the process of "magyarization," which forced them to speak Magyar and de-Latinize their surnames.[45] They immigrated and became concentrated primarily in the Midwest and the prairie provinces of Canada. Like the Greeks, the Romanians set out to form their own trustee parishes independent of the Russian Orthodox Church and actively recruited priests from their homeland. The first ethnic Romanian parish was founded in Saskatchewan in 1902, and the second one, two years later in Cleveland. By 1920, 12 parishes were found in the Midwest and another six in rural Saskatchewan.[46]

Besides dominating the coal-mining industry, many of the Ukrainians turned to farming, especially in the prairie provinces of Canada.[47] Though the overwhelming majority of Greeks settled in the large urban areas, significant numbers of Cretans settled in the Mountain West where they pursued shepherding, coal mining and rail-splitting, whereas others from the Aegean islands settled in the Gulf Coast where they pursued maritime activities such as fishing and sponge-diving. Their dominance in the fishing trade caused some localities in New England to authorize legislation specifically targeted against them.[48] The Serbs were heavily represented in mining on the West Coast. The first Serbian parish was founded in 1892 in a mining camp located in Jackson, California, although the majority would later be concentrated in and around the Chicago metropolitan area.

The Albanian immigrant experience was essentially no different than that of the Bulgars, Serbs, Greeks, Russians and Ukrainians: mostly illiterate young men in search of economic opportunity. Several paradoxes stand out, however, in comparison to the other Orthodox, one being that the Albanians had never had a national church of their own, and another that the liturgies of the Church had never been celebrated in their language, this, despite the fact that Christianity had been present in Illyria (Albania) since the second century A.D.[49] Sadly, the primary reason was that the Church in Albania had for the most part Greek bishops who, having lost the spirit of Cyril and Methodius, limited the Orthodox faith to its Greek cultural expression. They refused to translate the Gospel and the liturgical texts into Albanian; any nationalists who tried to rectify the situation often found themselves excommunicated. The majority of the Albanian immigrants concentrated in Massachusetts. As such, the first Albanian-language liturgy was celebrated not in Albania but in Massachusetts! Later, when the Albanian Orthodox Church was officially banned by the rabidly atheistic government of Enver

Hoxha between the years 1960-1985, it operated in exile among the Albanian faithful in Massachusetts.[50]

The Bulgarians were among the latest Orthodox arrivals to the United States. Beginning to arrive in significant numbers in 1903, they tended to assimilate more easily into older, more established Slavic parishes.[51] As far as migratory patterns, they moved to the larger urban areas of the East Coast. Often, they were misidentified as Greeks in the popular press (much to the chagrin of both groups), a fact that may have been due to the Macedonian issue, which is still a sore point between Bulgaria, Yugoslavia and Greece. Still, once their numbers started growing, they followed the Greek and Romanian custom of establishing their own ethnic parishes, complete with priests from Bulgaria and Macedonia. The first such parish was established in 1907 in Madison, Illinois.[52]

All of these migration patterns played a role in the establishment of concurrent and rival dioceses being set up in North America. Some of these rival dioceses would be intra-ethnic as well as inter-ethnic: by 1936, for example, there were four independent Antiochian archdioceses in the United States and Canada, and in the 1920s, a renegade Greek archdiocese headed by a schismatic bishop would threaten the stability of the Greek jurisdiction.

Except for the Lebanese and Arab Orthodox Christians, who, it must be said entertained few illusions about returning to the "old country," Orthodox immigrants made the journey to America for the purpose of making a little money and returning as quickly as possible to their point of origin. The amount of monies remitted to their families back in their Balkan homelands by these enterprising young men is easily calculated in the hundreds of millions of dollars, a staggering sum given the times.[53]

Regardless of ethnic origin, the alienation that the typical Orthodox immigrant felt from the dominant old-stock American, coupled with the desire to return to their respective homeland, produced indifference among most Orthodox immigrant groups to adjusting to American mores and culture. This aloofness very often aggravated the old-stock Americans; violence and other forms of mistreatment of Orthodox as well as other immigrants was not uncommon. Often, if the immigrants were shunned it was almost a blessing compared to actual violence. Out of fear, immigrants banded together into mutual aid societies based on ethnic ties. Many of these societies had officious names with grandiloquent titles for the various officers.[54] Despite their almost comical self-importance, these societies gave a sense of belonging to impoverished Orthodox immigrants who had absolutely no sense of belonging to the greater culture that, for the most part, did not want them here anyway. Although the majority of these societies were transitory, some would later go on to play a significant role in the creation of parishes, albeit ones concerned with perpetuating national identity rather than Orthodox unity (much less evangelism).

Despite the xenophobic nature of many of the immigrant communities who saw themselves as Greeks or Serbians or Russians in exile, it is unfair to conclude the Orthodox Church was unwilling to plant roots in the New World. The Russian Archdiocese of the Aleutians and North America sought to shepherd the Orthodox immigrants pouring into North America. Those immigrants who came to the United States looking for a home more quickly adapted and melted in to the United States. They also were more open to the creation of an American Orthodox Church.

The willingness of the Archdiocese of the Aleutians and North America to move its headquarters first from Sitka to San Francisco and then from San Francisco to New York indicated the Russian Archdiocese viewed Orthodox immigration as a permanent reality on the North American continent. They hardly would have gone to such lengths had they determined that the immigrations were of a transitory nature. Likewise, some of the almost half a million or so Orthodox immigrants who came to America knew that there would be no going back and sought a permanent Orthodox hierarchy.

Most of course viewed this reality along ethnic lines, but a few were more than willing to entertain the idea of a "pan-Orthodox" vision under the auspices of the Russian Orthodox Church. Unfortunately, events half a world away would alter the international political landscape and set Orthodox Christianity in North America adrift in a chaotic sea of competing ethnic realities.

CHAPTER 3

THE CALM BEFORE THE STORM: 1898-1918

Social Services, Institutions and Ecumenical Outreach of the Russian Archdiocese

In 1905, the Diocese of the Aleutians and North America was upgraded to archdiocese, and Bishop Tikhon was likewise elevated in rank to archbishop. In many ways, the Archdiocese of the Aleutians and North America conducted affairs as befitting any other major American religious denomination. Despite the penury of its flock, it offered a panoply of social services, including an orphanage, a bank and a philanthropic society that had offices on Ellis Island for assisting new arrivals with gifts of food, clothing and even shelter.[1] Even after the removal of the diocesan seat from Sitka, Alaska still received a considerable amount of attention in the area of social services, operating 17 parish schools and four orphanages. By 1887, the number of parochial schools had grown to 43, leading the Alaskan Territorial governor to complain that the Orthodox Church was spending more on education than the federal government, a fact that did not please the hordes of Protestant missionaries who were trying to "Christianize" the native Aleuts.[2]

Between 1905 and 1918, the archdiocese was subdivided into four more dioceses: San Francisco, Chicago, Pittsburgh and Sitka, as well as New York City, all of whom were under the presidency of Archbishop Tikhon in New York. (In addition, there was an auxiliary bishop for Canada also). Since these other bishops reported to New York rather than to Moscow, this meant that, for all practical purposes, the American archdiocese was well on its way to becoming an autonomous church. By 1918, the American archdiocese included the Russian contingent (which was the largest), numbering 306 churches and chapels, 242 priests and deacons and "a reader in almost every parish;" the Arab mission with 32 churches; the Serbian mission with 36 churches; and the Albanian mission with three churches. The entire American archdiocese therefore comprised 461 churches/chapels, 309 priests and deacons and almost 600,000 faithful.[3]

A church of this size demanded strong and visionary leadership. Archbishop Tikhon Bellavin (1898-1907), the major transitional figure in the history of the American church, provided exactly what was needed. Saint Tikhon, a towering cleric in the tradition of the first permanent bishop, St. Innocent, was multilingual (in Greek as well as Russian and English), a tireless traveler and an advocate of various far-sighted reforms. In addition, he clearly conceived of the day in which the American archdiocese would achieve autocephaly (being independent and self-governing) from the mother church in Russia. It was under his pastorate, for example, that the Holy Synod gave permission for Orthodox clerics in America to commemorate the President of the United States in the litanies of the Church rather than the Czar of Russia.[4]

As a measure of his breadth of vision, St. Tikhon advocated close ties with the Episcopal Church in the United States and endeavored to receive permission from the Holy Synod of Russia for *The Book of Common Prayer* (with a few modifications) to serve as the rubric for converts who wished to join the Orthodox Church by permitting them to worship with the more familiar "Western Rite." The Western Rite, already in the English language, provided a bridge for American Protestants into the Orthodox Faith as well as a common language for the ethnic Orthodox immigrants. It was under his auspices that the Episcopalian Isabel Hapgood published her translation of the Orthodox liturgies in 1906. In her preface, Hapgood acknowledges the Holy Synod of Russia as a major benefactor in defraying the cost of publishing. A footnote indicates the funds for this project originated with Czar Nicholas II.[5] Hapgood makes clear the hands-on relationship St. Tikhon had with the publication of the First Edition (1906) of the Service Book, and in the subsequent Second Edition (1922) she writes: "The first edition was prepared and published under his supervision, while he was at the head of The American Mission, as Archbishop of the Aleutian Islands and North America."[6]

Another indication of the permanence of Orthodoxy in America was the founding of a seminary in Minneapolis, Minnesota, in 1905 by Archbishop Tikhon. It later relocated to Tenafly, New Jersey, in 1912 under the leadership of Tikhon's successor, Archbishop Platon (1907-14), where it was consecrated in honor of his patron saint (St. Platon's Seminary). Classes were conducted in both English and Slavonic, and it continued to function until 1923.[7] Nor were women ignored; the "Russian Women's College" was established in 1916, although it was unaccredited.

In order to foster better communication within this vast archdiocese, the Russian hierarchy encouraged several publications, including the short-lived *Slavonian* (1871); the *Oriental Church Magazine* (1878-1883), published by a convert priest, Nicholas Bjerring; and the official monthly publication, *The Russian-American Messenger*, inaugurated in 1897, which was published in both Russian and English.[8] In addition, an Arabic-language newspaper was published entitled *al-Kalimat* (*The Word*) under the auspices of Bishop Raphael Hawaweeny and is still published today (albeit only in English).

The Ethnic Auxiliary Dioceses

Though many strides were made toward creating an American Orthodox Church, many troubling issues still demanded attention. The existence of independent, self-generated trustee parishes clashed with the canonical ecclesiastical structure of parishes under the control and oversight of a bishop. In Alaska the bishops had overseen the conversion of the Aleuts and the creation of parishes. But the massive immigration of Orthodox Christians to the

United States and Canada created a problem never faced before. The Orthodox immigrants in effect brought their parish with them and, in some instances, brought their village priest from "back home" with them. It was not the bishops but the immigrants themselves who created their trustee parishes.

The immigrant problem confronted the bishops with at least three issues: language, nationalism and ethnicity (culture). Most immigrants did not speak English. It has been said that one always makes love and prays in his native language; it would take at least three generations before the immigrants could do either in English. In an immigrant family, at first only those who worked outside the home, usually the men, learned English. Inside the home, immigrants understandably used their native language.

In order to bring the Orthodox faith to America, the bishops learned English and conducted the liturgical services in English. But in order to oversee the immigrant parishes, the bishops needed to conduct immigrant services in the native languages of the different parishes. Since ultimately the liturgical language of the American Orthodox Church would be English, it was foolish to make a long-term investment in creating a priesthood trained in the various native languages of the immigrants. In the short-term, the Russian bishops permitted the ethnic parishes to recruit priests from the "old country," as long as they provided their credentials to the archdiocese and submitted to the authority of the Russian bishops. The Russian bishops, for their part, took their mission to all Orthodox immigrants seriously. Among the Greek immigrants, for example,

> Bishop Nicholas organized churches wherever he could, having as his ultimate objective the uniting of all members of the Orthodox faith...under the jurisdiction of the Russian church. He worked with Greeks in New York, Chicago, San Francisco, New Orleans, Galveston and elsewhere. Priests were brought to the United States to

> minister to Greek communicants...the Greeks of San Francisco are known to have celebrated [Greek] Independence Day on at least one occasion in the customary manner with the Russian bishop officiating.[9]

Below the surface, however, tensions lurked. Fueled by nationalistic pride and an intense spirit of independence, people recently freed from political regimes in their homelands were not eager to surrender their national identity in becoming an American or even in becoming an American Orthodox. Among the Greeks, Greek Independence Day was a source of great pride. (Even in the United States in the 21st century, the Greek flag is still found in parish halls, and the Greek national anthem is still sung at many ceremonial events, including national Clergy-Laity congresses.) It is not surprising therefore that relations between many of the Greek parishes and Archbishop Tikhon were uneven at best. In 1902, for example, Tikhon had celebrated the liturgy in a Greek trustee parish in Chicago entirely in Greek and was warmly received. When he attempted to do the same thing two years later in a Greek trustee parish in New York City, he was "pointedly asked to leave by its angry trustees."[10]

Despite this unfortunate incident, Tikhon felt that the best way to enforce jurisdictional unity was by dividing up the archdiocese into ethnic auxiliary dioceses. Although the canonicity of such a solution is problematic at best, he realized that the insular nature of the various Orthodox immigrant groups would be best accommodated by such an arrangement. For one thing, even though many of the parishes (whether independent or not) were pan-Orthodox in composition and worshiped in a polyglot of Slavonic, English, Arabic and Greek, most Orthodox—if given the chance—preferred to hear the liturgy in their native tongues. This was usually achieved when a critical mass of a particular ethnic group was reached within the original multi-ethnic parish. The language issue was therefore the driving issue that accelerated the institution of more ethnic trustee parishes.

Indeed, the growth of such ethnic parishes was explosive: between the years 1900 and 1910, US census figures show an incredible 25,000% increase in the number of Orthodox adherents, making Orthodoxy the fastest growing denomination in the United States.[11] The rapid proliferation of Greek trustee parishes (140 between the years 1906-1914 alone) and the continuing conversion of the Uniates accounted for much of this phenomenon. Because of the great language barriers, in Tikhon's opinion, the best way to acculturate the new immigrants as well as to prevent outright schism was to consecrate ethnic bishops to minister to their respective flocks with himself as head of the archdiocese. He therefore envisioned an ethnic Arab diocese headquartered in Brooklyn, a Serbian diocese in Chicago and a Greek diocese probably in San Francisco or Pittsburgh.[12]

Although Bishop Tikhon realized that the concept of ethnic bishops was canonically problematical (it had, in fact, been condemned as a heresy by the Patriarchate of Constantinople in 1870), he felt that the critical situation in North America warranted a relaxation of canonical norms.[13] The idea may never have come to fruition had it not been for Fr. Raphael Hawaweeny, the first Orthodox bishop consecrated on American soil. Hawaweeny was literally the right man at the right time: a reformer and visionary much in the mold of Tikhon himself.

A revolutionary with a marked independent streak, Raphael Hawaweeny was not afraid of ruffling anyone's feathers. In his homeland, he had been an ardent Arab nationalist who had agitated for the independence of the Patriarchate of Antioch that, together with Alexandria and Jerusalem, had long been a dependency of Constantinople. He became fluent in Greek and, despite his outspoken nature, was awarded a full scholarship to attend the patriarchal school of Halki; he was one of the few Arabs allowed to do so. (In the Orthodox faith, priests can be married but the bishops are not. As a general rule, Arab men were dissuaded from entering the priesthood unless they were married, thereby precluding the possibility of ever attaining episcopal rank.)

Upon graduation, he was ordained to the diaconate and returned to Syria. In 1888, he entered the Kiev Theological Academy in Russia. Since he did not yet know Russian, he took his entrance exams in Greek. He became fluent in Russian and was released to the Russian Orthodox Church, where he headed the Syrian mission in Russia. Additionally, in 1893 he became part of the faculty of Kazan Theological Academy located in Kazan, Russia. There he taught Arabic studies and anti-Islam polemics. A tireless reformer, he reduced the mission's debt and enabled several other young Arab men to attend the academy in Kazan on scholarship.[14]

While in Russia, Hawaweeny had received a petition from the Syrian Orthodox Benevolent Society of New York in 1895 that requested an Arab priest for the growing Lebanese population of that city. Hawaweeny made it clear to the Arabs that he was part of the Russian Orthodox Church; if he came, he came as a Russian Orthodox priest, and they would become a Russian Orthodox parish. The parish agreed. He arrived later that year and presented his credentials to Bishop Nicholas. In short order he established six more Arab parishes across the United States and Canada. In 1898, he received permission from Bishop Nicholas to compile in Arabic a book of liturgical services. In 1904, Nicholas's successor, Archbishop Tikhon, consecrated him as the auxiliary Bishop of Brooklyn, the first Orthodox bishop consecrated on American soil. From 1905 to 1915, he established another 22 Arab parishes.[15] Although his primary jurisdiction was over the Arab contingent of American Orthodoxy, his linguistic virtuosity allowed him to mediate between the internecine squabbles that had plagued many of the multi-ethnic parishes. All told, he made three major evangelistic trips throughout the United States and Mexico, consecrating parishes, ministering to the diverse American flock, establishing the aforementioned *al-Kalimat* journal and legitimizing civil marriages.

One of Bishop Raphael's strong points was his practicality. On many of his journeys, he noted that more than a few Arab Christians worshiped in non-Orthodox churches. He exhorted his flock to desist from this practice and to instead observe the liturgical cycle at home as much as possible. To this end, he published a book in Arabic entitled *True Consolations in the Divine Prayers*, a compendium of prayers for corporate liturgical worship as well as personal prayers that could be recited in a private, family setting. It was translated into English in 1938 by Fr. Seraphim Nassar under the title *Divine Prayers and Services* (popularly known as "the five-pounder"), is still published today and remains the backbone of English liturgical services for the Antiochian Archdiocese in North America. Moreover, he encouraged the use of English in the liturgies of the Church, rightly fearing that to do otherwise would result in the alienation of the younger generation from the faith.

His reputation became known in his homeland of Syria. When that patriarchate was finally freed from Greek control, he was asked to take over control of the dioceses of Beirut and Zahle. He turned down both positions preferring to remain in the United States and serve the Arab and non-Arab immigrant communities.[16] His untimely death in 1915 led to the succession of Fr. Afthimios Ofiesh as auxiliary bishop for the Arab Orthodox. It was from the auxiliary diocese of Brooklyn that the later Antiochian jurisdiction would trace its descent with Ofiesh as its first independent hierarch.

Bishop Raphael described himself as a "Syro-Arab by birth, a Greek by primary education, an American by residence, a Russian at heart and a Slav in soul." Although his dream of an emancipated Antiochian patriarchate came to pass, he was not an expatriate fighting the battles still raging in some "old country;" though a son of Antioch, he became the boast of America. In Bishop Raphael the spirit of the American Orthodox Church was clearly visible. Less than a hundred years after his death, St. Raphael, "The Good Shepherd of the Lost Sheep in America," was consecrated a saint of the Orthodox Church in May of 2001 at St Tikhon's Seminary in New Canaan, Pennsylvania, a monastery he himself had consecrated in 1906.

Hoping to replicate the success of Hawaweeny, Tikhon tapped Fr. Sebastian Dabovich to be the Serbian auxiliary bishop of Chicago in 1905, a year after the elevation of Hawaweeny to the episcopate. However, due to repeated delays (and Archbishop Tikhon's promotion as Archbishop of Yaroslavl in 1907), the creation of the Serbian Auxiliary Diocese was put on indefinite hold. This led to resentment among the Serbs, and it was for this reason that many of the Serbian parishes agitated for secession from the Russian archdiocese. The Patriarch of Serbia refused to acknowledge their schism, and reconciliation between New York and the disaffected Serbs was reached. In the interim, Dabovich had returned to Serbia, and the candidate of choice of most Serbian-Americans was now Fr. Mardary Uskokovich. He was sent to Belgrade for ordination, but Patriarch Dimitriye of Serbia decided to make him head of the famous Rakovitsa Monastery instead.[17]

In his place, in 1924 Dimitriye sent Bishop Nikolai Velimirovich, one of the premier ecclesiasts of the 20th century, to take up the mantle of auxiliary bishop for the Serbs. Bishop Nikolai, like Bishop Raphael Hawaweeny before him, was a renaissance man of wide education and culture. Speaking seven languages, he made a name for himself as the "Serbian Chrysostom." With wide-ranging interests he preached on a large variety of topics, including the mystical theology of the Orthodox Church, in venues such as Westminster Abbey.[18] He elevated the liturgical consciousness of the laity by insisting on frequent participation in the sacraments and Bible study. However, after the devastation of the First World War (which had ravaged Serbia more than most other countries), Bishop Nikolai felt his primary duty was to his homeland. The short time he spent in the United States was at the behest of raising funds for his war-shattered diocese. He thus undertook a whirlwind mission of speaking engagements for which he received honoraria and raised the awareness of the American people about the plight of the Serbs. All told, he spent a total of two years in the United States and returned to Serbia, where he continued his voluminous output of writing. During World War II, he was imprisoned along with Patriarch Gabriel at Dachau by the German occupying forces. He returned to the United States after the war and taught at St. Savva Seminary in Libertyville, Illinois, for the few years that it was open. In some Serbian monasteries today, Nikolai is venerated as a saint even though he has not been formally canonized.

Saint Tikhon's plan of multiple ethnic dioceses under the oversight of the Russian archbishop worked with Hawaweeny in part because Hawaweeny was already attached to the Russian Orthodox Church. No such Greek, Romanian or Serbian cleric existed. The success among the Arab immigrants thus proved difficult to replicate among the non-Arab Orthodox.

The Role of the Laity: The All-American Sobor* of 1907, Parish Councils and the Subordinated Clergy

Despite the tardiness of establishing Serbian and Greek auxiliary dioceses, the Russian-American archdiocese continued to function as a full-fledged member of the American religious scene. Under Tikhon, it acculturated quickly to American norms of democracy and paved the way for lay participation with the first-ever "All-American Sobor," or council, held in Mayfield, Pennsylvania, in 1907.[19]

For the first time since the seven ecumenical councils, laymen were allowed to sit in council with clergy of all ranks and decide matters of import to the Church as a whole.[20] Given the fact that, during the previous millennium, lay participation had in fact dwindled, the liberating effect of this sobor cannot be overestimated. It anticipated the historic "All-Russian Sobor" by a decade and put into practice several of the ideas for which reformers in Russia had for several years been agitating. Although the All-American Sobor was a rather smooth affair, the careful preparations that Tikhon had undertaken years before ensured that the laity would be under sufficient supervision by the clergy.[21] As such, no major doctrinal or canonical disputes erupted, and it served as a template for future councils.

The situation in most trustee parishes was not promising. The relationship between laymen and priests, the professionalism exhibited by some of the clergy and the adherence to canonical norms were uneven at best. That the laymen had created the parish endowed the laity with a sense of power that was simply unknown in the Old World.

For immigrants, the parish was a microcosm of the Old World:

> Absence from his ancestral home, the fear that he might never see it again, the thought of losing his nationality and of dying in a strange land, caused [the immigrant]...to embrace his religion with a fervor he never had...He attended church because it reminded him of home. Neither a coercive government nor ecclesiastical decrees could have compelled these pioneers to maintain and administer their church communities with the turbulent aggressiveness that characterized them.[22]

Parish was synonymous with *ghetto* (in its original sense), which, in turn, was synonymous with *the community.* One was a member of the community by virtue of being born into it. One was a member of the parish because one was a member of the community. As the only building owned by the community, the church functioned as the city hall, town hall and sometimes taverna for the ethnic community. That people also worshiped there was a necessary nuisance for some.

The lay boards of directors were concerned with details of parish governance that astounded immigrant priests who previously had only to answer to their bishops. No issue having to do with the parish was too minor as far as these laymen were concerned, and it was obvious from the beginning of his tenure that the priest was an employee first and foremost. His spiritual leadership role was a distant second at best. Priests and bishops could protest all they wanted, but since no priest of a trustee parish received a salary from the Russian archdiocese, they were powerless to protest lay management of the parishes.

Nationalism was also a potent stimulant to ethnic insularity: all of the Balkan immigrants, whether Albanians, Bulgars, Greeks, Romanians or Serbs, lived in a time of intense nationalist fervor in which the borders of each of these countries were still unsettled. Many of these people viewed themselves as expatriates living in a diaspora. This refusal to become American caused them to be identified as hyphenated-Americans by the native-born Americans and aggravated tensions between immigrants and the old-stock Americans.[23] Many parishes served not only as outposts of foreign nationalism but also as "training grounds" for foreign militias during the various internecine Balkan wars that broke out in the early 20th century. The Balkan nations had only recently received liberation from the Turks. Literally thousands of Bulgars, Greeks, Serbs and Albanians returned to their homelands to fight in the many conflicts that erupted in those lands. Volunteer units of Greek young men, for example, often trained under the direction of retired officers of the Greek army in the basements of their respective churches.[24] Nor were the Greeks alone: Bulgars, Serbs and Montenegrins "were purchasing weapons, training and organizing to further the ambitions of their respective countries."[25] The trustee parish therefore became a venue for politics, xenophobia and militarism at the expense of spirituality.

Immigrant priests represented a problem to the local parishes. The trouble of course was that some of the priests who came over were of dubious canonical standing. It was not unknown for an imposter or a disgraced monk to misrepresent himself as a priest. Often, these men were vouched for by relatives who assured their fellow parishioners that they were in fact canonically ordained.[26]

The immigrant press regularly magnified scandals and brought to light charges of embezzlement by "con-men" clergy and lay boards of trustees as well, often working in tandem. Even among canonically ordained clergymen, abuses were not uncommon: it was not unknown for churches to be closed on Sunday because the priest had traveled to another city to perform a sacrament simply because he would receive more money in doing so.[27] Accusations of simony were not unfounded. The lack of clerical professionalism among some of these men led many laymen to accuse the hierarchy of sending men "who would be unable to qualify as messenger boys, coachmen, money-lenders, or gravediggers."[28] Many of these men made no effort to acculturate themselves to North America and had no desire to do anything but the bare minimum, foregoing religious education for the young and otherwise ignoring the spiritual needs of their flock.[29] Their combined lack of spiritual erudition and priestly discretion led to the abeyance of the sacrament of confession.

The financial survival of the trustee parish depended upon adopting a dues-paying club mentality whereby every member was responsible for a set figure to be paid annually. In addition, priests received small honoraria for performing sacraments; sometimes, this would be the only way they could subsist.[30] Other, even less savory, methods of funding parishes was tried. In Chicago for instance, Greeks from Sparta wanted to assess a 25-cent tax on "Halstead Street Greeks," who were from the Tripoli region of Arcadia, in order for them to attend their (Spartan) church.[31] As can be expected, a generalized outrage broke out when the Spartans tried to enforce this rather novel approach of church finance.

The priest shortage was so severe that it became lucrative for abuses and other canonical irregularities, mostly within the trustee parishes. One of the most famous took place in Canada, where in 1902, a self-styled cleric named "Metropolitan Seraphim" arrived in Winnipeg, Manitoba, offering to ordain Orthodox priests within his "Independent Greek Orthodox Church." Eventually, his "diocese" claimed more than 30,000 followers and 50 "priests."[32] Archbishop Tikhon tried to rectify the situation by sending a certain Fr. Constantine Popov to Winnipeg. Popov was physically threatened by the "Seraphimites" and only narrowly escaped with his life. Eventually, Seraphim's diocese collapsed, and his parishioners "scattered to various Orthodox and non-Orthodox bodies." Although Seraphim was never heard from again, canonical order in Canada was severely compromised as a result of his malfeasance.[33]

In essence, the lay boards of directors of the trustee parishes set themselves up for this type of fraud. For many of them, their fear of Russian hegemony or the loss of their control over the parishes they had created outweighed the fear of con-men or defrocked priests plying their confidence games. Given a choice of canonical oversight by the Russian bishops or independence, many, perhaps most, chose independence even if it meant hiring unqualified priests. After all, a fraudulent or otherwise incompetent priest could be fired on the spot, without recourse to the bishops and the lengthy procedures normal to Orthodox ecclesiology.

Despite the resentment that many of these groups exhibited (especially by the Greeks) towards Russian hegemony, they had not the stomach to affect a schism within the Russian archdiocese. By 1909, the uneasy truce ended. Many Greeks, fearful of pan-Slavism, staged massive protests against a bill pending in the New York state legislature that would have amended the religious-incorporation laws, effectively bringing their trustee parishes under Russian control. [34] With the headquarters of the Russian archdiocese in the state of New York, the archdiocese operated according to the laws of New York Due to their vociferous opposition, Governor Charles Evans Hughes vetoed the bill. Archbishop Platon, reacting with disdain towards the Greek-led opposition to the bill, accused the Greeks of being guilty of "self-sufficiency...in all matters of religion and faith." The defeat of the bill meant that effective control over any and all future trustee parishes was essentially over. Although the Greeks were free of Russian administrative control, they still were under Russian canonical authority as far as the Churches of Greece and Constantinople were concerned.

The secession of the 19 Serbian parishes in 1913 was the closest any national group came to achieving this aim. The schism was short-lived and reconciliation was effected. The Russians, for their part, agreed to be more solicitous of Serbian complaints and promised to devote four pages in the Church's monthly newsletter, *The Russian-American Messenger*, to Serbian concerns.[35]

The Calm Before the Storm

Despite the problems of the trustee parishes, the Russian-American Archdiocese under the leadership of Archbishop Tikhon and Bishop Raphael Hawaweeny met the challenges of multi-ethnic diversity head-on. To a man, these hierarchs were committed to evangelism and unity and were solicitous of the pastoral needs of one of the most diverse flocks in all of Orthodoxy. Tikhon's successes in North America brought him to the notice of the hierarchy of the Russian Orthodox Church. He soon was given greater responsibilities in Russia. In 1917, he was elected Patriarch of Russia, the first patriarch in fact, after a nearly 300-year hiatus. It was in fact as patriarch that Tikhon would have his greatest impact on the American church and on Orthodoxy in general.

CHAPTER 4

THE BOLSHEVIK REVOLUTION

The Collapse of Unity

Given the impediments that faced Orthodoxy in North America, from the hostility of the Baranov regime in Alaska to the penury of the overwhelming majority of Orthodox immigrants to the New World, the success of the Archdiocese of the Aleutians and North America is all the more impressive. What had begun with eight solitary individuals in 1794 had grown into a continent-wide phenomenon embracing immigrants from Bulgaria to Byelorussia. Thanks to the visionary outreach of men such as Ss. Juvenal, Herman, Innocent and Raphael, American Orthodoxy was well on its way to becoming a viable denomination. Why, then, did it fail?

The major reason of course was the Bolshevik Revolution, which caused the near destruction of the Church of Russia. Other reasons include changing demographic patters in the United States and reformist impulses that resulted in the acquisition of a Protestant-like ethos that disdained hierarchy.

The Challenge to Unity: The Living Church

Reformism had in fact been sweeping the Church of Russia for several years in an effort to breathe some life into a sclerotic and ossified hierarchy. Many priests and theologians, for instance, had long advocated for reforms such as celebrating the liturgy in the ordinary, everyday speech of the Russian people. Others suggested a shortening of the services and even a married episcopate. All of these reformers looked to increased participation by the laity in the life and governance of the Church. Known in Russia as "renovationists," many of those holding these views eventually created a schismatic sect that became known as the "Living Church." Although this movement would later be execrated as merely a communist front, initially it attracted many sincere bishops, priests and laymen.[1]

In and of themselves, many of these reforms were unobjectionable.[2] To be fair, there had been a growing ferment throughout many parts of the Orthodox world for needed reforms. Father Raphael Hawaweeny, for example, had been a prime advocate of the restoration of Arab hegemony over the sees of Antioch and Jerusalem. Even the trustee parish of North America was, in the ideal, a welcome innovation in that it solidified lay participation in the affairs of church governance.

The growing radicalism of the renovationists, moreover, reflected the radical political ferment that was brewing in imperial Russia, especially following the outbreak of World War I in 1914. The religious and political reform movements often looked to each other for mutual reinforcement. The United States and, specifically, the growing Russian immigrant community were not immune from these forces. The American Socialist Party, for example, actively recruited Russian immigrants and successfully competed with several parishes for the loyalties of their flocks.[3] Nor were the clergy immune to these revolutionary attitudes; several of these reformist Russian priests in America coalesced around the leadership of one Fr. John Kedrovsky, who, in 1918, openly added his voice to the growing chorus of criticism against the leader of the American archdiocese at that time, Bishop Alexander Nemolovsky. Kedrovsky openly advocated replacing Alexander with a more egalitarian ecclesiastical administration, one organized "without reference to royal regimes or (episcopal) decrees."[4]

St. Tikhon and the All-Russian Sobor of 1917-1918

The reality, however, was more complex. Of course, compared to many Protestant denominations, the Russian Orthodox Church appeared hidebound and reactionary. In reality, however, men of vision had been able to implement an ambitious evangelistic and social program both in Russian and in North America. Visionaries such as St. Innocent, a widowed priest, had been elected to the episcopate, and it was under his tenure that evangelism would receive further impetus and support. This was repeated in 1907, when Archbishop Tikhon was assigned to the Archdiocese of Yaroslavl, then of Vilnius, and then finally in 1917, as Metropolitan of Moscow in 1917. Reformists impulses were given another boost with the abdication of Emperor Nicholas II, when the Church had an opportunity to convene an "All-Russian Sobor" that included bishops, priests and prominent lay theologians. The purpose of this council was to discuss reforms and plan for the future of the Church under the liberal-democratic regime of Alexander Kerensky.

The model for this council was the All-American Sobor of 1907. As had been the case in America 10 years earlier, Metropolitan Tikhon was the driving force behind the All-Russian Sobor. And as at the All-American Sobor, Tikhon served as the presiding officer of the All-Russian Sobor. The most significant reform of the All-Russian Council was the abolition of the synodal form of church governance that had replaced the patriarchate during the reign of Czar Peter the Great. Tikhon, already Metropolitan of Moscow, was elected on November 5, 1917, to the newly reestablished office of patriarch; but the patriarch was subject to the Sobor in much the same way constitutional monarchies are subject to their ruling parliaments. Although the imperial government had fallen, Tikhon's election was received with much pomp and rejoicing by the faithful. The rejoicing, however, would be short-lived as the political situation degenerated considerably with the fall of the Kerensky regime and the murder of the emperor and his family.

The American archdiocese was represented at the All-Russian Sobor by the primate, Archbishop Evdokim Mischersky, himself a member of the renovationist wing of the Russian church. Not knowing how long the council would take, Evdokim appointed as his vicar, Bishop Alexander Nemolovsky, his auxiliary bishop for Canada.

The Church in Russia Under Attack

In October, 1917, the Bolsheviks took over Russia. The Russian Orthodox Church found herself facing political forces committed to creating an atheistic state. The Bolsheviks actively sought the destruction of all church life and the elimination of all religious belief within the former Russian Empire. For the first time since the days of Constantine the Great, the Church had no political patron, no rights and suffered the full-scale confiscation of all her properties. Churches were closed on a massive scale; priests, nuns and bishops were sent to Soviet concentration camps, suffering all manner of degradation, torture and even death.

The Church in Russia was fighting for her life and, as such, there were no funds and even less opportunity for overseeing the American archdiocese. The cessation of monies from Moscow meant that priests could no longer be paid and the debts of individual parishes could not be met. Many American parishes faced the imminent danger of foreclosure. Faced with the overall financial collapse of the American archdiocese, Bishop Alexander (acting in his capacity as Archbishop Evdokim's vicar) decreed in 1918 that all archdiocesan parishes would become independent legal entities, free of the control of the archdiocese. By archdiocesan decree, every parish became, in effect, a trustee parish. Thus the centralizing work of all of Alexander's predecessors, beginning with Nicholas back in the late 19th century, had therefore come to naught in one fell swoop. Alexander paid a high price for this move as many agitated for his removal from office. It was against this backdrop that Fr. John Kedrovsky and other liberals found some justification for their audacious reformist program. Be that as it may, Alexander was simply out of his depth and was replaced in 1922 by Metropolitan Platon, the man who had previously served as head of the American archdiocese (as successor to Archbishop Tikhon).

In fairness to Alexander, perhaps the best man who could have created a united American church was in Russia fighting for the life of the Russian church. For his part, Tikhon had more than enough on his plate in Moscow. America was essentially left to its own devices.

As for the immediate situation in Russia, Tikhon tried to stay as neutral as possible, even going so far as refusing to give his blessing to the White Army resistance. He displayed great courage against the Bolsheviks, however, when he publicly anathematized them for the barbarous murder of Czar Nicholas II and his family. (The All-Russian Sobor endorsed the anathema, and it has never been revoked.) This boldness against the Bolshevik government was repeated with even more vehemence upon the first anniversary of the October Revolution:

> While you were seizing the power, you asked the people to trust you, and made promises to them. But have those promises been fulfilled? You gave a stone instead of a loaf, and a serpent instead of fish (Mt 7:9-10). You have substituted a soulless international concept for our Motherland. You have divided the people into enemy camps and plunged them into a fratricidal war of an unprecedented cruelty. You have openly replaced Christ by hatred...Mark the anniversary of your rule by liberating those imprisoned by you; by ceasing bloodshed, violence, destruction and oppression of religion...Otherwise all

righteous blood shed by you, shall be required of you (Luke 11:51)...[5]

Tikhon's Anniversary Declaration was in many respects the high point of open Christian resistance to the new regime. From then on, the state would win all the major battles and the Church would only be allowed strategic retreats. Although it was not possible to see at the time, Tikhon's greatest achievement was the immediate survival of the largest Orthodox Church in the world. When all was said and done, he kept the Church in Russia from being exterminated outright.

Be that as it may, it was at this time that the renovationist movement had been consolidated into a discreet religious sect known as the "Living Church." Because of the surprising resilience of the counter-revolutionary forces of the White Army, as well as the generalized outrage caused by the brutal murder of the Romanovs, the Bolsheviks retreated from their original atheist platform of complete eradication of belief and decided to openly support the Living Church. Not only would this new sect serve as a wedge against the official Russian church, but it would show Western intellectuals that the Bolsheviks were not against religion *per se*.

Tikhon was imprisoned for an entire year and, according to many credible reports, subjected to torture. To effect his release, he was forced to negotiate "reforms" in the Russian Orthodox Church with clergy of the Living Church, who by now, it must be said, were nothing more than Soviet puppets. Among the concessions he had to make to the schismatic clergy was a vague promise to apologize for any past actions of the Church of Russia, hoping that with this humiliating concession, he could somehow salvage a remnant for the future.

Despite these concessions, it became clear to the vast majority of believers within Russia that the Living Church was compromised by its association with the Bolsheviks. Although the new sect and its sponsors were able to beguile many in the West for a period of time that the communist government was essentially reformist, the reality, at least as far as the Church was concerned, was the opposite. It was in fact nothing but a brutal lie. Consider these facts, for example: before the revolution, Russia had a total of 54,000 churches and chapels, 1,500 monasteries and 61 seminaries serving 115 million Orthodox Christians. By 1939, only 100 churches remained, and all of them for "show" purposes only.[6] The legitimacy of the Living Church was ultimately undermined within the Soviet Union by the great majority of believers who saw them for what they were. In time, the Soviet government abandoned the Living Church and concentrated on co-opting the Patriarchate of Moscow instead. Nevertheless, Tikhon's forced concessions to the Living Church that he had made before the collapse of the Living Church would have disastrous consequences for Orthodox unity in America.

The Karlovtsi Synod

Upon release from prison, Tikhon was placed under house arrest and given warders who harassed him at every turn. Despite his political compromises with the state, over 10,000 priests, nuns and bishops were massacred under the most horrible circumstances. The wholesale destruction of churches and the massive slaughter of ordinary Christians continued. On the surface, he was allowed to organize ecclesiastical affairs as before; however, few of his orders were carried out. Realizing that the Soviets were not negotiating in good faith, Tikhon made perhaps the most fateful decision of his life: he issued a proclamation (Ukase no. 326) on November 20, 1920, that gave permission for the Holy Synod to reconstitute itself in any way it could upon his death and do what it could to preserve the Russian Church wherever it was possible.

It was, however, an "open question" if Tikhon meant for this synod-in-exile to operate outside of Russian territory;[7] in fact, the situation within the Soviet state was certainly quite fluid *vis a vis* the borders and the surprising resilience of the White Army. Moreover, this ukase provided for the creation of temporary synods of bishops who had been cut off from Moscow because of the exigencies of war *and only in those dioceses that had already been part of the Russian Orthodox Church.* The creation of a synod-in-exile that would have jurisdiction over areas that had never been part of the Russian church was not canonical and not envisioned by Tikhon. Yet this is precisely what transpired.

The impetus for the creation of such a synod had already begun to take place in 1920, before the issuance of Tikhon's proclamation, when certain exiled Russian bishops had ensconced themselves in Constantinople under the protection of the ecumenical patriarchate. For reasons that are not entirely clear, they were asked to leave; in the following year, they asked for and received permission from the Patriarchate of Serbia to relocate there. In 1921, therefore, 15 exiled Russian bishops met in the Serbian town of Stremski Karlovtsi, under the protection of the Serbian monarchy, for the express purpose of administering Russian dioceses outside of Soviet control.

On the surface, the Karlovtsi synod appeared to be operating under the parameters issued by Tikhon himself (although he never issued them publicly but communicated them to only a few aides), and in fact they presented themselves as essentially a "temporary body," designed to last until the "restoration of normal conditions" in Russia.[8] The reality proved to be something quite different. The Karlovtsi bishops repudiated many of the reforms begun by Tikhon and the All-Russian Sobor of 1917, among them lay participation and the patriarchal form of church administration. They saw themselves as the supreme Russian synod and came up with the novel idea of "émigré dioceses," ecclesial districts not contiguous with Russian territory but nevertheless subordinate to them. (This, despite the fact that the concept of an "émigré" diocese had never been part of the Orthodox faith.) Such a high-handed view of their own stature was a rebuke to the Serbian church that sheltered them. Indeed, the Holy Synod of the Serbian Orthodox Church ruled shortly thereafter that the Karlovtsi bishops operated only "under the protection and supervision of the Serbian Church"[9] and were nothing more than an auxiliary diocese created for ministering to Russian exiles living in Serbian territory. Constantinople and Belgrade each respectively, offered moral support to the exiled Russian bishops, but their support was never an endorsement of the self-elevation of the Karlovtsi bishops, especially given the fact that "no patriarch can grant any rights to bishops who are not part of his own patriarchate."[10]

In an effort to end the Karlovtsi movement, Tikhon issued Ukase no. 398 the following year (May 5, 1922). This edict dissolved the synod-in-exile. Perhaps in order to soften the blow, he appointed two of the refugee bishops as metropolitans: Eulogius Georgevsky was given authority over all Russian parishes in Western Europe, and Platon Rozhdstvensky was reappointed as Archbishop of New York. Both men took their new positions but still continued to view themselves as part of the exilic synod. The remaining 13 continued on as before. Tikhon's ukase, therefore, was ignored. Still, no schism had taken place.

Tikhon died, if not a martyr at least a confessor, on January 12, 1925. Before his death, convinced the Bolsheviks would not permit his successor to be chosen, Tikhon named his own successor. He appointed three men as *locum tenentes* or guardians of the patriarchal throne. Two of the men were themselves in prison at the time of Tikhon's death. The third, Metropolitan Peter of Krutitsy, became Patriarch *locum tenens* in April, but by December 1925, Peter was arrested and exiled to Siberia. Metropolitan Sergius took over the leadership under the strange title "Deputy to the *locum tenens*."

Sergius proved to be more pliant to the Soviets and in fact became a puppet for the Bolsheviks. He supported Soviet foreign policy and lent the prestige of the Church to Soviet endeavors. In most respects Sergius compromised the Russian Orthodox Church. In retrospect, the accommodations made by Tikhon were strategic retreats when compared to the out-and-out capitulations of Sergius. In spite of Sergius, Tikhon's strategy of long-term survival for the Church prevailed. The Church refused to yield for 70 years; it triumphed in the end. For this reason alone, St. Tikhon is remembered as one of the great hierarchs of the Orthodox Church. Because of his spirituality and the torments he underwent, he was canonized a saint in 1995.

The Karlovtsi synod became known as ROCOR (the Russian Orthodox Church Outside of Russia or the "Church Abroad"). Despite its official dissolution by Tikhon, ROCOR continued as before. They justified their continuance on the grounds that Tikhon was not a free agent, and many of his decrees were very carefully worded documents that allowed some ambiguity in interpretation.

For one thing, the more strict understanding of Ukase no. 398, i.e., the complete dissolution of the Church in Exile, was not possible. The reality in Western Europe would not allow them to simply up and disband. Hundreds of thousands of Russian refugees flooded every one of the major European countries, and unlike America, which at least had an official archdiocese, none of the non-Orthodox European lands were equipped to deal with spiritual needs of the Russian Orthodox immigrants. The reality of course was different in the Orthodox Balkans, where Russian refugees could submit to the local Church authorities; but even here there were linguistic and cultural problems. The Balkan churches tried to address the issues of Russian immigrants and used the offices of the exilic synod in order to do so.

It was within this tumult that the Church Abroad was born. Fighting for her life, the Russian Orthodox Church as a whole had little time for theological speculation or renovation. The situation for the refugees in Europe was so desperate that complex doctrinal battles about the role of the laity that had been brewing in the United States were of no concern. The situation was different in America, where the Church had already anticipated the reforms of 1917 with its own clergy-laity council 10 years earlier. The Church of Russia now had three semi-autonomous branches: the Moscow Patriarchate, the Karlovtsi Church in Exile, and Russian-American archdiocese in New York.. Despite the overall chaos, the three branches of the Russian Orthodox Church still continued to recognize each other as one Church. The American branch, for its part, continued to recognize the authority of the Moscow patriarchate. Although canonically more correct, this recognition would have disastrous effects upon the American archdiocese, legally as well as ecclesiastically.

The American "Metropolia"

With the coming of the Bolshevik Revolution, Tikhon's plans for ethnic auxiliary bishops had been put on hold. Platon, his successor in America, had every intention of following through with this plan, but the turmoil of the post-World War I period caused it to collapse. One reason of course was that subsidies from Moscow had dried up. For the first time, the American archdiocese was left to fend for itself.

With the embargo of funds from Moscow, Bishop Alexander Nemolovsky, the successor of Evdokim (who had left to attend the All-Russian Sobor of Moscow in 1917), tried valiantly to hold the parishes of the American archdiocese together. Because of mounting debts, however, he was forced to make a virtue out of necessity and thus reluctantly encouraged the parishes to attain trustee status and mortgage their assets in order to finance their operations and pay off their creditors. Thus, parishes that were not trustee parishes were forced out of necessity to act as if they were.   It is indeed ironic that his predecessors' attempts at exercising control over the growing numbers of trustee parishes, beginning with Bishop Nicholas and extending through the tenures of Tikhon, Platon and Evdokim, came to naught.

The traditionalist wing of the Church reviled Alexander's handling of the financial crisis, but it was the radicals of the Living Church, led by Fr. John Kedrovsky, who used the financial chaos to force Alexander from office.   By 1922, his pastorate was no longer viable, and he was forced to resign in favor of Metropolitan Platon of Odessa and Kherson, the former Archbishop of New York and then-member of the Karlovtsi synod.   With the ascension of Metropolitan Platon as the head of the American archdiocese, unofficially the American branch of the Russian church became known as the "Metropolia," and the heads of the Metropolia would be known as Metropolitans of All-America and Canada.

The Russian Archdiocese of the Aleutian Islands and North America was a dependency of the Church of Russia and had every intention of abiding by the resolutions of the All-Russian Sobor, striving to put them into practice, "adjusting them to local conditions."[11]   The Russian Church Abroad, on the other hand, repudiated these reforms.   In doing so, the Karlovtsi synod of bishops not only reverted to the pre-1917 system of synodal leadership, but said in effect (though not yet officially) that the synodal Church-in-exile was the *only* legitimate Russian church. Later, the Karlovtsi Church Abroad questioned the legitimacy of any Russian diocese that did not see eye-to-eye with them.[12]

Though he was a member of the Karlovtsi synod, Metropolitan Platon, in defiance of that body, recognized the reforms of the Sobor of 1917-18.   The uncompromising position of the remaining 13 bishops of the Karlovtsi synod put it and the American branch of the Russian Orthodox Church on a collision course.   With the two branches of the Russian Church outside of Russia disagreeing with each other over being patriarchal or synodal, the other ethnic parishes in the United States saw no need to unite with the newly elevated Metropolitan of All America and Canada.

The Creation of Ethnic Exarchates

The inability of the Russian branches to resolve their differences had repercussions for the ethnic parishes in the United States. Between 1918 and 1930, the Greek Archdiocese of North and South America, the Syrian-Antiochian Archdiocese of New York and all North America, the American Carpatho-Russian Orthodox Greek Catholic Church, the Serbian Eastern Orthodox Diocese in America, the Bulgarian Eastern Orthodox Church of America, the Romanian Orthodox Church in America, the Ukrainian Orthodox Greek-Catholic Church of America, *et al.* came into being, essentially as "exarchates" or dependencies of the various Old World patriarchates.[13] The original Orthodox Church of America, the Russian Archdiocese of the Aleutians and North America, changed its name to the Russian Orthodox Greek Catholic Church of America ("Metropolia" for short).

Clearly, the ukase of 1920, as interpreted by the Karlovtsi synod, had disastrous consequences for Orthodox unity. For 2,000 years, canon law acknowledged there could only be one church per nation. It was therefore impossible to have "overlapping dioceses" or multiple jurisdictions within one nation. But in the Untied States, for the first time in Church history, parallel dioceses existed in the same nation, often with more than one bishop per city, a direct rejection of the canonical tradition that states that the territorial principle is absolute.[14]

Each of the ethnic dioceses set up in North America was now viewed as a dependency of a foreign government that had no territorial claim on the United States (unlike Alaska, which at least had been part of the Russian empire). To make matters worse, Metropolitan Anthony, president of the Karlovtsi synod, declared that, "Neither the Sobor nor the Synod of Bishops is bound by any territory."[15]   Ostensibly, Anthony's assertion was to enable the bishops of the synod to meet in any hospitable land and set up a temporary headquarters until the restoration of normality within Russia occurred.   However, even within this context, Anthony's assertion that the Russian church was not bound by "any" territory was arrogant to the extreme and a rejection of the canonical tradition of the Church, which affirmed that every Orthodox Church was bound by the boundaries of the nation in which it existed.

Even as the Metropolia was on its way to full independence from an Old World patriarchate, the other Old World patriarchates tightened their grips on their newly acquired exarchates in America. In essence, the Old World patriarchates committed the same error as the Russian Church in Exile: they extended their church boundaries outside the boundaries of their nation.

With the Orthodox patriarchates rejecting the principle of canonical unity, it took little time for Orthodoxy in the United States to disintegrate into an ethnic jurisdictional nightmare.   The hyper-independent nature of the American culture and the fact that churches in the United States are not state-supported encouraged the proliferation of ethnic dioceses.   Several other factors played key roles in the fragmentation of American Orthodoxy.   Ethnic tribalism was a major factor, but we cannot overlook individualism, lack of state support and the decimation of the Church of Russia.   In addition, the fact that Orthodox parishes had to receive their letters of incorporation from the various states made them something radically different on one level than what was found in the Old World.   In the final analysis, they were now legal corporations and their boards of directors were civilly liable for any acts of malfeasance. This meant that, in contrast to St Paul's admonition against taking differences within the Church to secular authorities (I Cor. 6:1-7), parishes now had almost no choice *but* to resort to the judicial system for any redress of grievances.

Ironically, one of the first plaintiffs to take advantage of the secular courts was the Living Church, which sued the Metropolia for control of the Cathedral of St. Nicholas in New York City, the actual cathedral of the American primates. The Living Church was backed by the Communist Party who hoped, by gaining control over the Cathedral itself, in time to control all Russian parishes in the United States. There was an additional urgency felt by the Soviets in that Metropolitan Platon, the primate of the American Metropolia, was one of the most implacable foes of the Soviet Union. It was impossible to prove to an American court system that did not understand the Orthodox faith that the Russian patriarchate had been hijacked by the radicals of the Living Church and that the Living Church was a Communist front. Additionally, given the fact that Platon had received his appointment in New York by the Moscow patriarchate and not from the Karlovtsi synod, a *prima facie* case could be made that he was legally subordinate to Moscow.

Facing a choice between the Russian patriarchate and the Metropolia, the New York court had no legal reason to rule against the patriarchate. When the Supreme Court of New York ruled in favor of the Living Church, Platon had no choice but to relinquish control of the Cathedral to his nemesis, "Archbishop" John Kedrovsky. The shock waves this sent throughout American Orthodoxy were incalculable. It made the prospect of American Orthodox unity seem not only impossible but, under the circumstances, undesirable.

Although Platon was forced by the ruling of the Supreme Court to vacate his cathedral, all was not lost. The good relations that had been cultivated with the Episcopalians beginning with Archbishop Tikhon were bearing fruit: the Episcopal Church magnanimously donated their former cathedral in New York City to the Metropolia to replace the confiscated St. Nicholas Cathedral. Moreover, the ruling itself also caused every other Russian Orthodox Christian living in the United States to realize that their property was not safe from communist hands. More to the point, it forced many to think the unthinkable: autonomy from Moscow itself.

The Road to Autonomy

Despite the very real need for autonomy, the Metropolia faced serious canonical obstacles that would have to be overcome if autonomy was to be achieved. There were, to be sure, five Russian-American dioceses in existence in North America (the bare minimum needed for an autonomous church being three). On the other hand, the multiplicity of ethnic parishes, all vying for themselves, made independence canonically impossible. An autocephalous church cannot arise in a nation unless all of the parishes in question agree to unite. Of course the existence of rival parishes and dioceses in the first place was a new problem in the history of Orthodoxy, as it had never spread by immigration but by evangelism. The American experience, beginning as it did with the first trustee parish in 1864, was therefore incompatible with normal Orthodox ecclesiology.

The plight of the American parishes and the Moscow patriarchate became all the more grim when Patriarch Meletius IV of Constantinople normalized relations with the Living Church in 1923. With these two victories under its belt (the first being the confiscation of the Metropolia's cathedral), the Living Church, acting at the behest of their communist overlords, forced Patriarch Tikhon to issue another ukase (Jan 16, 1924) dismissing Platon from his office and ordering him to return to Moscow to face an ecclesiastical court to answer charges that he "engaged in public acts of counter-revolution."[16] For Platon, this was nothing more than a prospective death sentence.

Needless to say, the majority of the American church ignored this decree. To his credit, the language used in Tikhon's ukase was sufficiently vague, implying that his removal would not take effect until his replacement had actually arrived.[17] Platon's replacement would be Fr. John Kedrovsky, who in the interim had been consecrated as "archbishop" by the Living Church, the same man who in many ways had set these events into motion when he led the rebellion against Archbishop Alexander.

To be sure, Kedrovsky's tenure ultimately went nowhere, and the same could be said of the Living Church in Soviet Russia. Regardless, panic swept through the Metropolia. If the Supreme Court of New York could rule in favor of the Soviet state and confiscate the greatest church in the American archdiocese, then what guarantees did the other, smaller parishes have, many of whom were already heavily mortgaged?

Platon, whose goal had been to reverse the increasing decentralization that his predecessor (Alexander) had encouraged once the normal funding from Moscow had dried up, now found himself accelerating the trend of decentralization in order to get his parishes free from Soviet control gained via the American courts. The Metropolia took this desperate action hoping that, in doing so, the Living Church would not be able to go after each of the individual parishes, which now numbered over 350. This move worked. By being trustee parishes, the parishes were free from any Soviet threat. Unfortunately, their freedom now made unity impossible. The prospect of canonical unity in the United States had been destroyed.

PART II

THE CHURCH AS GHETTO:

THE CREATION OF THE EXARCHATES

1918-1960

CHAPTER 5

MOSCOW AND THE CHURCH ABROAD

The Exilic Synod and Pressures on the American Archdiocese

After Patriarch Tikhon's death, the Karlovsti synod made use of Tikhon's proclamation (Ukase no. 326) issued on November 20, 1920, that gave permission for the Holy Synod to reconstitute itself in any way it could upon his death and do what was necessary to preserve the Russian church wherever possible. The Karlovtsi bishops became, in effect, the new holy synod. They went about repudiating the patriarchal form of church government as well as most of the provisions of the All-Russian Sobor of 1917, such as lay participation in any level of church administration, including the election of bishops.[1]

The reality of the situation inside Russia made the Church Abroad an ecclesial force to be reckoned with. With the death of Tikhon, who was the first Russian patriarch in 300 years, the Karlovtsi synod understood itself to be the proper successor and therefore the guardian of the Russian church and all its dioceses. This of course included the Russian-American archdiocese. However, Metropolitan Platon, having been appointed to New York by the orders of Patriarch Tikhon even though he was a member of the exilic synod, did not consider North America to be subordinate to Karlovtsi. This was confusing to say the least. Platon continued his membership within the Karlovtsi synod for the time being in order to better "coordinate" activities with the other metropolitan districts of the Russian church, especially those outside of Russia proper.[2]

In 1926, however, Platon withdrew from the exilic synod. The repercussions were immediate. The émigré bishops' opinion of their body had now grown to such an extent that they felt they were the only legitimate Russian ecclesial body; with this outlook, they "suspended" Platon from his office, forbidding him from celebrating divine services. Platon found himself in the almost comical position of not only being suspended by the Bolsheviks' Living Church, which now claimed the mantle of the Russian patriarchate, but also "defrocked" by Moscow's mortal enemy, the exilic synod.

As negligible as these interdicts were, Platon had to fight challenges to his authority within his archdiocese in the interim as well. One of the diocesan bishops, Bishop Stephen Dzubay of Pittsburgh, had declared himself to be the true diocesan hierarch in October of 1922.[3] Platon, however, was able to muster the necessary support and neutralized this attempted coup. Despite this success, the remainder of Platon's tenure would be one marked by challenges brought about either by the patriarchate or the Karlovtsi bishops. The challenges brought about by the Karlovtsi bishops were more vigorous, however, due of course to their freedom from Soviet control.

Needless to say, Platon's suspension was recognized by nobody outside of the Karlovtsi synod. Regardless, the Karlovtsi bishops enjoyed some degree of popularity within the United States, partly due to their unwavering hostility towards the Soviet regime. They were able to use this prestige to set up rival parishes in North America and, in time, would eventually set up their world headquarters in Jordanville, New York. (After Karlovtsi, they relocated to Munich and then Berlin, where they remained during the Second World War.)

For the Metropolia, the reforms of 1917, coming as they did on the heels of the All-American council of 1907, only intensified the degree of lay participation in the life of the American church. As far as the Americans were concerned, there was no turning back, and woe to any future jurisdiction that held otherwise. This independent spirit was reflected in 1919, when Bishop Alexander Nemolovsky, Archbishop Evdokim's temporary replacement for North America, was elected ruling bishop by both clergy *and* laity in Cleveland (pending Moscow's approval of course). Although Alexander's tenure ended badly, the precedent had been set. From then on, the ruling bishops of the Metropolia would be elected by clergy and laity convening as one body in subsequent sobors.

Old World Controversies and the Erosion of Unity: The Balkan Question

First-generation immigrants, regardless of their land of origin, each brought with them the social, political and religious turmoil raging in their particular homeland. The immigrants therefore unwittingly brought with them the chaos that engulfed Europe following the First World War. Since a significant percentage of immigrants had no intention of staying in the United States, this type of arch-nationalism was somewhat understandable. The rabid nationalism that wracked the Balkan nations rallied these young men to return to serve their homelands when wars broke out as they inevitably did.

Much of this nationalism was political rather than military. Among the Greeks, for example, entire communities in North America were split at this time between the royalists who supported King Constantine I and the republicans who supported the prime minister, Eleutherios Venizelos. Tensions between these two groups often erupted in outright violence, and entire parishes were split based only on political matters *back in the homeland.* One Venizelist faction in Brooklyn, New York, for example, broke away from the predominantly royalist parish of St. Constantine's in order to establish a more "liberal" parish named in honor of St. Eleutherios, the patron saint of their hero.[4] The Greek immigrants not only fought among themselves, they also fought with immigrants from countries that neighbored Greece. Intramural squabbling between Bulgarians and Greeks over the identity of Macedonians poisoned relations between these two immigrant groups. Albanian nationalism likewise inflamed passions between this group and the Greeks.

The other Old World patriarchs did not fill the vacuum created by the loss of oversight by the Patriarch of Moscow. None of the autocephalous churches had the resources to interfere in North America. It was under these circumstances that the ecumenical patriarch, for example, issued the Tome of 1908 that placed the Greeks of North America under the jurisdiction of the Church of Greece. This was essentially a dead letter, as the Church of Greece had no intention whatsoever of alienating the Romanov dynasty by exercising any authority at all over the American Greeks. It was nothing more than a face-saving gesture as the Patriarch of Constantinople's Ottoman overlords forbade him from having anything to do with Greeks outside of Greece.

The other Old World synods had their own reasons for not choosing to send ethnic bishops, mostly because they could not afford to do so. Nonetheless, the events of 1918 forced the hand of almost all of the autocephalous churches. It was for this reason that the ethnic jurisdictions were created, with either canonical bishops at their heads or vicars who reported directly to Old World synods.

One other event further eroded Orthodox unity in America. After the communist revolution and the fall of the czar, hundreds of thousands of Russian refugees flooded Western Europe and the Americas. The Russian-American archdiocese, already engaged in strong efforts to assimilate the hundreds of thousands of non-Russians under its aegis, now found itself inundated with Russian immigrants to America. The Metropolia, unable to do both things at once, took over the care of the Russian immigrants. Thus, non-Russian Orthodox immigrants were encouraged to seek oversight from bishops from their respective "Old Countries" almost by default.

The swelling of Orthodox ranks in America by these refugees exacerbated the already growing ethnic squabbling between the various immigrant groups. Without having an American Orthodox Church to spearhead liturgical reform, inroads in the use of English in the liturgies of the Church and in its publications came to a sudden halt. The ministry of each ethnic jurisdiction was directed to the newly arrived immigrants (often called "Fresh-Off-the-Boat" or FOBs by their peers who had already assimilated as Americans) who did not speak English.

The flood of Russian immigrants into America thus hampered the efforts of the Russian-American Metropolia to oversee the birth of the American Orthodox Church. On the other hand, the influx of Russian refugees into Europe strengthened the hand of the Karlovtsi bishops. The average Russian refugee, finding himself in Munich or Paris, had no time for the trans-Atlantic disputes between New York and Karlovtsi and certainly no understanding of the independent streak that animated the American church. As far as the refugee knew, Patriarch Tikhon's ukase of 1920 empowered émigré bishops to establish dioceses. The refugees' own experience within Russia prior to 1917 was that laymen had no say in the administration of the Church. With refugees unquestionably filling its parishes, the Church Abroad grew stronger, especially in Western Europe.

The Church Abroad and its Challenges to the Metropolia

In the meantime, the Moscow patriarchate continued to compromise with the Communists. Because Metropolitan Platon considered himself under the authority of the Patriarch of Moscow (though, after 1926, the throne was vacant), the Church Abroad, being as it was opposed to the Communists and the Living Church, considered Platon's position to be traitorous; this, despite the fact that Platon was an unwavering opponent of the Communist party. The Church Abroad continued to apply pressure on Platon and his successors to come under their authority. Certain diocesan bishops in America, who viewed the Church Abroad as a legitimate counterweight to Metropolitan Sergius and/or the remnants of the Living Church, often sided with the Church Abroad against Metropolitan Platon and his successors.

Examples of this infighting appear on parish levels as well. In 1948, for instance, certain disgruntled parishioners tried to have their priest removed. The matter eventually went before the secular courts for settlement. In *The Russian Orthodox Church of the Transfiguration et al* vs. *Rev A Lisin et al*, the Superior Court of Los Angeles ruled in favor of the Church Abroad. For guidance, the Superior Court looked to the ukase of 1920 and agreed that Tikhon's edict did, in fact, allow for the creation of a new authority, "…for the whole Church throughout the world outside the boundaries controlled by the Bolsheviks."[5] Although this case was decided some 25 years after the events in question, the intervening years seemed to legitimate in the public eye the views of the émigré synod *vis a vis* the political situation. The findings of the Superior Court, therefore, when viewed in this light, are not controversial. The Superior Court ruled that the American church was "merged" with the Church Abroad and thus could not initiate rulings on its own without going through the proper canonical (i.e., Church Abroad) channels. This was yet again another stunning defeat for the Metropolia.

The Canonical Status of the Russian Orthodox Church Outside of Russia

In spite of the vitality of the Church Abroad in the face of the horrible Soviet repression, the question of the canonicity of the Church Abroad remained. Although it was created by patriarchal decree, it was subsequently dismissed by another patriarchal decree just two years later. Strictly on this basis alone, the exilic synod was a canonical body only during 1920-1922. After the second decree, it lost its canonical status, or so it would seem.

For one thing, the Church Abroad questioned the validity of the second decree. Although on its face it is rather explicit in its condemnation, it is an open question as to whether Tikhon was compromised when he issued it. In addition to issuing the second decree, for example, Tikhon also appointed Platon to be primate of the Metropolia: was his appointment therefore equally null and void? (We begin to see, for example, the legal difficulties that Platon had entered into when he accepted appointment to New York during this chaotic period.)

Obviously, no resolution to its canonicity is to be found in the diktats of Tikhon, as the extent of his freedom and competence during his short patriarchate (1918-1925) cannot be known with any degree of certainty. There are, however, relevant canons of the Church that deal with the formation of synods. In this respect the Church is very clear: only "ruling" bishops can comprise a synod. Of the 15 bishops who met in Karlovtsi in 1921, only one, Eulogius, was still a bishop of an intact diocese. The rest had abandoned their dioceses in order to flee to safety. None of the canons of the Church provide for the formation of "synods-in-exile." There are also no canons that allow for dioceses without any territorial limitations.[6]

Moreover, the rationale for adopting a synodal form of church government lies in Russian *political* history rather than in Russian *church* history. The synodal form of ecclesial government was in fact the creation of Peter the Great in the 17th century. Peter had borrowed the idea from the nations of Western Europe that had so entranced him during his travels. In Peter's eyes, the proper role of the Church was as a department of state, and to this end he allowed the office of patriarchate to lapse. The senior ecclesiarch of Russia was from then on known as the Metropolitan of Moscow, who was viewed as part of a holy synod. To ensure imperial oversight of the Church of Russia, Peter appointed a layman to oversee all meetings of the synod, an officer known by the Germanic title of "*ober-procurator.*" Although this officer could not enter into deliberations with the hierarchs, his presence essentially put the bishops on notice that the state bureaucracy was watching. In time, the *ober-procurator* would be responsible for all hierarchical appointments.

After a nearly 300-year hiatus, the Russian church abandoned the synodal form of governance when it restored the patriarchate with the election of Tikhon in 1917. With his independence as patriarch cut short by the Bolshevik Revolution, Tikhon did not have the necessary time to sink the roots of the patriarchal form of governance deep into the Russian consciousness. In this vacuum, the Church Abroad found it easy to revert to the synodal form that had preceded Tikhon's election.

Russian Orthodox Christians therefore found themselves members of one of three Russian Orthodox Churches: those living in Russia were members of the Moscow patriarchate, a church for the most part controlled administratively by the Communists; Russian refugees living in Europe found themselves members of the Church Abroad; and Russian immigrants to America were members of the Metropolia. The confusion was only exacerbated by the fact that the Americans continued to look to the Patriarch of Moscow as the legitimate head of the Russian church overall, even when noxious diktats were issued at the behest of the Soviets. This situation was unsettled, to say the least.

The Moscow patriarchate found itself powerless to stop the rise of the Church Abroad. Neither Tikhon's decree that dissolved the Karlovtsi synod[7] nor the even more strident denunciations of Tikhon's successor, Metropolitan Sergius, *locum tenens* of the Moscow patriarchate, proved effective. Indeed, Sergius's condemnations only strengthened the hand of ROCOR, coming as they did from an individual regarded by many as nothing more than a Soviet puppet, and an altogether enthusiastic one at that.

The "Heresy" of Sergianism

Sergianism received its name from Metropolitan Sergius, *locum tenens* of the Patriarchate of Moscow and successor to Tikhon in 1928. Sergius, probably acting under extreme pressure, issued a declaration shortly upon his ascension to the throne that the Church of Russia would be loyal to the Soviet state in all matters having to do with foreign policy.[8] From a historical perspective, Sergius's passivity in the face of communist aggression stands in stark contrast to the witness of the Church throughout her history when facing similar persecution. Sergius's accommodation with the communists was particularly troubling when set along side his predecessor's public anathema and epistles directed against the Bolsheviks.

To be fair, Sergius faced a regime dedicated to eradicating theism in any form. In order to ensure the survival of the Church, he compromised the administrative integrity of the Church of Russia. He certainly stretched the boundaries of *oikonomia* in his canonical compromises, but whether he compromised its *theological* integrity is another question. A fair assessment would be that, like the Patriarchate of Constantinople under the Ottoman occupation, theology and doctrine remained intact, even though unfortunate practices such as simony were allowed to flourish. The Church of Russia for all intents and purposes now found herself forced to commit the same type of compromises that helped precipitate the secession of the Russian metropolitan district from Constantinople some five hundred years previously.[9]

The so-called heresy of Sergianism may therefore be viewed in the same context that canonical Orthodox churches viewed the state of the ecumenical patriarchate during the Ottoman control of the Phanar: as long as there was no blatant heresy being preached by the Russian church, then any canonical compromises, though unfortunate, could be overlooked in the spirit of *oikonomia*. Theologically speaking, a state of grace still existed and the sacraments of the Church continued to be efficacious. In this same spirit, it could be said that, in the long term, Sergius had successfully fought off the Communist-inspired assault via the so-called Living Church. Had the Living Church succeeded it *would* have preached heresy from the patriarchal throne and by so doing would have compromised the theological integrity of the largest Orthodox Church in the world, perhaps rendering its sacramentality null and void.

The First Steps Towards Autonomy

According to canon law, an autonomous church can arise if there are at least three "duly appointed ruling bishops."[10] As mentioned above, among the 15 bishops that created the Church Abroad, only Eulogius Georgevskii was a ruling bishop of an intact diocese. Not only were the majority of bishops who met in Serbia no longer ruling bishops, but, contrary to the claims of the Church Abroad, the boundaries of the dioceses of any autonomous church are strictly delimited by territory, again, as per canon law.[11] Indeed, any Christian who flees from one land to another is duty-bound to submit to the authority of the Church of the country where he seeks refuge.[12] The émigré bishops had first met in Constantinople in 1920 and then a year later at Karlovtsi; they were thus under the protection of the Church of Constantinople and then later of Serbia. Therefore, their allegiance was to either of these two patriarchates.

The four years (1922-26) that Metropolitan Platon remained part of the Karlovtsi synod while at the same time being primate of the American archdiocese staved off any encroachment onto American territory by the Church Abroad. During this period, the American archdiocese recognized the synod of the Church Abroad and all its provisions "subject to certain 'adjustments.'"[13] Although initially the Metropolia recognized the claims of the Church Abroad, it confusingly continued to behave according to the protocols of the

Sobor of 1917. In 1924, for instance, it convened an All-American Sobor in Detroit, consisting of bishops, priests and laymen, all of whom were empowered to elect the metropolitan and resolve issues and controversies within the American church. These councils met regularly and on occasion overruled the Provisional Statutes of the Karlovtsi synod, particularly their rules regarding the transfer of priests within a diocese and from one diocese to another.[14] Furthermore, the Metropolia established a "Metropolitan Council" of laymen and clergy that was consonant with the Sobor of 1917. The creation of the Metropolitan Council directly violated the Provisional Statues of the Church Abroad that considered any synergistic council of laity and clergy to be anathema.

The Metropolitan Council may have been the breaking point as far as the Karlovtsi synod was concerned. In 1926, just two years after the Detroit sobor was convened, the Church Abroad ordered Metropolitan Platon to dismiss the council and revoke the resolutions of the Detroit sobor. Platon refused to do so.[15] The Church Abroad duly dismissed Platon and stripped him of his liturgical functions. Metropolitan Platon and the overwhelming majority of the Metropolia resolutely ignored the Church Abroad. Platon, for his part, continued on as Metropolitan of All America and Canada until his death in 1934, whereupon he was succeeded by Theophilus Pashkovsky, the Archbishop of San Francisco.

Matters continued in this vein for the next decade. Each succeeding convocation of the All-American Council caused a knee-jerk response from the Karlovtsi synod decrying the findings of the sobor in question, which the Metropolia, in due course, ignored. The independent nature of the Russian-Americans and especially lay participation never ceased to be a bone of contention for the Church Abroad. In 1935, for example, the Provisional Statutes of ROCOR were amended to address specifically the issue of laymen serving in council along with clergy and bishops (to the detriment of the laity). Indeed, the Church Abroad went to great lengths to call the sobor of

1936 a "general Diocesan Convention" rather than a sobor. At the Sobor of 1937, some of the American bishops who were appointed by the Church Abroad requested that the resolutions of that particular council be submitted to the latter body for approval, "but the All-American Sobor [of 1937] rejected this suggestion," choosing instead to submit them for "informational" purposes only and not for "approval."[16]   This was a direct rebuke of Section III of the Provisional Statutes of 1935 of the Church Abroad that arrogated only to the synod of the Church Abroad the power to make changes and amendments.[17]

These intramural disputes continued until 1946, when the Seventh All-American Sobor, which met in Cleveland, dissolved all its ties with the Church Abroad and turned instead to Moscow seeking recognition for "full autonomy."[18]   This overture to Moscow was "considered ineffective" by the Superior Court of California in its 1948 ruling, because the American church bypassed the "normal" approval process that stated that the American church was "merged" with the Church Abroad (as mentioned earlier). As far as the civil government of the State of California was concerned (and thus the entire United States unless challenged in another venue by the Metropolia), the independence of the Metropolia from Karlovtsi was invalid, since, in the words of the earlier court ruling, the Metropolia was "an integral part of the Church Abroad, subject to its jurisdiction, government, and laws."

The Metropolia and Moscow

Of course, the issue of autonomy had already been broached as early as 1924, when the Living Church had won the right to confiscate the cathedral of St. Nicholas in New York City. At the All-American Sobor in Detroit (1924), they declared the Metropolia to be "...a 'self-governing church,' being organized in accordance with the resolutions of the Moscow Sobor of 1917..."[19]   The delegates declared this resolution to be effective immediately. They asked Metropolitan Platon to remain as head of the new American church, a request that he honored. It is from this date, therefore, that an effective autonomy can be detected for the Metropolia.

The *locum tenens* of the Russian church, Metropolitan Sergius, declared this action "null and void, since it was made without the consent of the Moscow Patriarchate."[20] Sergius's declaration only hardened the resolve of Platon and his flock. Although schism was still not officially proclaimed, the effect was the same. Platon chose to make it official when, on June 3, 1933, he issued a "Message" in which he suspended all relations between New York and Moscow and declared the American church to be "autonomous" for the time being. For Sergius this was the final straw: Platon was declared a schismatic and (yet again) stripped of his offices and summoned before the Court of Bishops to be charged with violations of several of the Church's canons.[21] Platon understandably refused to attend any court convened in Moscow.

It was becoming increasingly obvious to the Metropolia— which was caught between the compromised Moscow patriarchate on the one hand and the stridently anti-laity Church Abroad on the other—that autonomy was not only necessary but desirable as well. Unfortunately, no other Orthodox immigrant group was of this mindset. Any talk of autonomy, much less unity, would have to wait until the final days of the 20th century.

CHAPTER 6

THE GREEK ARCHDIOCESE

Constantinople Becomes Istanbul

On April 7, 1453, Muslim forces attacked Constantinople by land and sea. Less than eight weeks later, the last remnant of the Roman Empire ended on May 29, 1453, and the Ottoman Turkish Empire began. The largest church in Christendom, Hagia Sophia became a mosque. It was the end of the Christian Empire, but it was not the end of Christianity in the East.[1]

The Turks permitted Christianity (along with Judaism and Zoroastrianism[2]) to exist within its Islamic empire as second-class citizens. Each group existed as a self-governing unit within the empire. Eastern Orthodox Christians became known as the *Rum millet* (the Roman nation) wherever they were found within the boundaries of the Ottoman Empire. Because the office of the Byzantine emperor (*basileus*) had been abolished, many of his secular, administrative duties had been allocated to the Patriarch of Constantinople, who was now known as the *ethnarch*, or national leader of all Eastern Christians. The patriarch had now become, for all intents and purposes, the "civil emperor" of all Christians within Islam. As such, he was held accountable for the behavior of Christians not just within the Patriarchate of Constantinople, but for all Christians within the Ottoman Empire *in toto*.

As vacancies occurred in the patriarchates of Antioch, Jerusalem and Alexandria, the Patriarch of Constantinople named his own men, who were invariably Greek-born, as replacements. With the reduction of the ancient sees of Antioch, Jerusalem and Alexandria to mere dependencies, the ecumenical patriarch became *de facto* the "religious emperor" of Orthodox Christianity as well.[3] In addition, the autocephalous churches of Serbia and Bulgaria were likewise reduced to being dependencies of the now, much more massive, Patriarchate of Constantinople. As for the offices of the patriarchate itself, they were relocated to the Phanar district of Constantinople, where they remain to this very day. Despite the loss of the majority of its resources within Constantinople, the enhancement of the status of the ecumenical patriarchate created a papist mentality that had heretofore been suppressed by the Emperor of Byzantium during the entire Byzantine era (A.D. 320-1453).

The resurgent Islamic state of the Ottoman Turks began to weaken in the late 1800's. It was during this time that the Balkan churches—specifically, the Churches of Bulgaria, Greece, Romania and Serbia—began reasserting their independence from Constantinople. During World War I, the Ottomans sided with Germany and were defeated by the Allied Powers. Ironically, at this same time, the Orthodox Church in Russia (which had been autocephalous since 1488 and had never been part of the Ottoman Empire) came under attack from the Bolsheviks while the ancient patriarchates found themselves free of the Ottoman Turks. The birth of modern nation-states and the new political realities of the 20th century not only shaped the histories of these emerging nationalities, but also shaped, and continue to shape, the history of the immigrants and the church they brought with them when they immigrated to the United States.

The Greeks in America and the Tome of 1908

Regarding those Orthodox Christians formerly under his control, the ecumenical patriarch adopted a hands-off approach when they immigrated to the United States. Once in the United States, they were canonically under the oversight of the Russian Orthodox Church. Even before the Bolshevik Revolution destroyed the unity of the Orthodox faith in North America, the Patriarch of Constantinople reversed his policy towards the Greeks in North

America by issuing a *tomos* (or edict) in 1908. Though he had never exercised any ecclesial authority in the Americas before, in this tome he declared that the Greeks were to be under the care of the Church of Greece, even though the Greeks of America had already been under the pastoral care of the Russian archdiocese. The issuance of this tome left the impression to many that the ecumenical patriarch still thought himself "emperor" of the Orthodox Church.

All appearances aside, the tome of 1908 was nothing of the sort; indeed, the need for an ethnic Greek bishop to minister to the growing Greek-American population was evident even to the Russian hierarchy. As mentioned previously, both Tikhon and his predecessor Nicholas had actively recruited Greek priests such as Fr. Ambrosius Vrettas, who served as the pastor of a Russian church in Chicago, to serve in the Russian archdiocese. (Another Greek, Fr. Michael Andreades, had served as vicar of the Western states.) The concerns of Greeks and other non-Russians had long been taken into consideration by the Russian hierarchs who had, in fact, sent more than a few Greek young men to the Russian seminaries in Kazan and St. Petersburg, often on scholarship.

The tome itself, therefore, should not be viewed as a deliberate provocation to Moscow. More to the point, the Patriarchate of Constantinople was not an independent agent, and their "divestiture" of the American parishes was due to the insistence of the Turkish government, which wanted them to have no association with nationalistically minded Greeks living abroad.[4] Heretofore, neither the Church of Greece nor Constantinople had expressed any concerns whatsoever about the Americas.

By contrast with its late interest in the United States, the Phanar aggressively acted against the establishment of autocephalous churches in the Balkans, which they condemned as schismatic. That two of these churches, Bulgaria and Serbia, had been independent in times past meant nothing to the Greek-controlled Phanar. The ecumenical patriarch reacted vociferously against their claims of autocephaly, going so far as to deny that a state of intercommunion existed between these offshoot daughter churches and the mother church of Constantinople. (Within relatively brief periods, the interdicts against these churches were lifted.)

That these nations had succeeded in gaining their independence was of little consequence: as long as the Turkish government had the patriarchate within its borders, the Turks still had some authority over the foreign policies of these now-independent Orthodox kingdoms. Every ecumenical patriarch knew that, as far as the Balkans were concerned, he still had some authority, and he gave it up only grudgingly. The tome of 1908 was a belated effort to exercise some control over the Greeks in North America. But like the interdicts that Constantinople had placed on the national churches of Bulgaria, Greece and Serbia, the tome of 1908 was a fiction. Neither the Church of Greece nor that of Constantinople had any real authority or resources to manage the affairs of the Greeks in the Americas, at least as long as the Church of Russia was alive and well.

Additionally, the Greek monarchy (which was closely related to the Romanov dynasty) had its own political reasons for not wanting to meddle in church affairs in America. Relations between the two royal houses were always cordial and, given the expansionist aims of Greece, the military might of Russia would be needed if for no other reason than to keep the Turks worrying about their northern border. Such cooperation between the two nations was manifested in many ways throughout the period. In 1913, for example, Czar Nicholas II, at the request of the Greek government, sent a contingent of several hundred Russian marines to Mt. Athos (which had only been acquired by Greece the year before) in order to remove forcibly 600 renegade Russian monks from the monastery of St. Panteleimon who had succumbed to a novel heresy.[5]

With the collapse of the czarist government however, the newly reinstated Patriarch of Russia, Tikhon, was in no position to worry about America, regardless of his own experiences there or how fond his own recollections of that land. It was for this reason, therefore, that on July 4, 1918, the Holy Synod of Greece, acting under the presidency of the newly elected (and controversial) liberal-reformist Metropolitan of Athens, Meletius Metaxakis, passed a resolution establishing the "Archdiocese of America."[6] On August 22, 1918, Meletius arrived in New York City with the intention of enthroning the archimandrite Chrysostomos Papadopoulos as "Bishop of the Greek Orthodox Church in the United States." He declined the honor, and Meletius was forced to find another candidate.

Meletius's choice at that point was Bishop Alexander of Rodostolou, a suffragan bishop in the Archdiocese of Athens, who shared many of his own liberal and pro-Western views, but unfortunately none of his energy, tact or organizational skills. Meletius's meddling in American affairs was detrimental in another respect in that Alexander (like himself) was an ardent supporter of the liberal Prime Minister of Greece, Eleutherios Venizelos. (Meletius himself gained his office upon the forcible removal of the incumbent, Metropolitan Theoclitus.) His appointment of Alexander was therefore viewed by many of the Greeks in the United States, who were royalists, as a direct provocation. Alexander, who had a brittle, abrasive personality and governed with an officious air, did not endear himself to the masses, and his politics alienated many of his flock even more.

The idea of a "Greek Archdiocese of America" may have been an oxymoron in the first place, given the parameters that the Holy Synod of Greece had erected. Indeed, the Church of Greece committed a major blunder by appointing a primate for America who was beholden to the political leaders of another country, especially one whose political climate was as turbulent as Greece's.[7] Canonically, of course, this was impossible as well: the same criticisms that Constantinople and Belgrade had leveled against the

Church Abroad, with its insistence on creating independent Russian dioceses within Orthodox lands, could be made against the Church of Greece in its attempt to cleave the Greek independent parishes from the Metropolia.

In short, the newly created Greek Orthodox Archdiocese of North and South America, tied as it was to politics in Greece and based on its own inherent contradictions, was going to implode unless it severed all ties with Greece. The absurdity of the situation became apparent with the restoration of Constantine I to the throne in 1920. Constantine had been restored by a plebiscite that trounced an overconfident Venizelos and forced his exile in turn. Theoclitus, the previous Metropolitan of Athens, was likewise restored to his episcopal throne and Meletius joined his patron in exile, which further complicated his plans for the organization of the Greek churches in America. In fairness to Meletius, it should be noted that he saw the need for a united American Orthodox Church.

The Associates of Canonical Hellenic Clergymen

Bishop Alexander realized that the downfall of his patron necessitated taking matters into his own hands. He invited "many, if not most" American priests to New York City to organize the "Association of Canonical Hellenic Clergymen," whose "stated objectives were to preserve the doctrines of the Greek Orthodox Church and to proclaim the independence of the members of the association."[8] The Holy Synod of Greece took a dim view of this and summoned Alexander to appear before it in Athens. Alexander refused, arguing, "he could not communicate with 'a degraded clergyman' [without suffering] the penalty of his own degradation, in accordance with Canon 11 of the Holy Apostles."[9]

Instead of leaving matters at that, Alexander took a further step that would have far-reaching consequences as to the issue of foreign control of the American church: he instructed all his priests that he would not enter into any relationship with any ecclesiastical regime based in Greece and that, henceforth, the ecumenical patriarchate was the only "body with which he would communicate regarding his jurisdiction."[10] In effect, Alexander single-handedly overturned the tome of 1908. In freeing the Greek-American church from Greece, Alexander made its status contingent upon the good graces of the Phanar. The Association of Clergymen endorsed Alexander's actions, and their executive committee cabled the *locum tenens* of the ecumenical patriarchate, Metropolitan Dorotheus of Proussa, that they would only recognize him as their sole "canonical officer."[11]

Although Alexander had the endorsement of the Clergymen's Association, this does not mean the overwhelming majority of the Greek-American clergy as a whole supported the action. While "many" priests had been invited to come to New York in order to establish this organization, "most" priests had *not* been invited. Royalist priests were purposely left out of the equation in order to ensure that the association itself would be nothing more than a pliant rubber stamp.

While in exile, Meletius returned to the United States (as would his patron Venizelos in due time) and was welcomed by the Venizelists as a conquering hero. To his credit, Meletius judiciously issued an encyclical in which he emphasized that he had no intention of "disputing the legality" of Constantine's restoration but would not relent in his condemnation of the "anti-canonical new Holy Synod" and his summary dismissal at its hands.[12] Regardless of this olive branch that he offered (albeit one from a position of weakness) to the royalists' government, Meletius redoubled his efforts along with his protégé Alexander to strengthen their respective positions within the Greek-American jurisdiction. The Holy Synod of Greece responded by declaring both men and any who followed them to be schismatics.

Mutual recriminations ensued, and the situation became even more tangled when Bishop Germanus Troianos of Sparta, a royalist, arrived as a legate of the Holy Synod of Greece in order to instill some order in an increasingly chaotic situation. In his role as synodical Exarch of the Church of Greece, he hired and fired priests and in general served as a rallying point for the royalist forces as well as for many that were tiring of Alexander's ineptitude. His presence, however, caused many intra-parish schisms that resulted in much litigation over parish property.[13]

Germanus was no mere *provacateur*, however; he took his role as exarch seriously. In spite of acting under the auspices of the royalist-dominated Holy Synod, he came to realize that America could not be governed from afar by legates. He also stressed the need for the creation of a canonical seminary that could train American-born men for the priesthood.[14] While Meletius, Alexander and the Venizelists on the one hand disagreed with the royalists regarding external politics, their positions regarding the Greek jurisdiction were beginning to converge. The question thus became, "which group could better effect this Americanization (for want of a better word): the Venizelists or the Royalists?"

The Election of Meletius to the Patriarchate and the Revocation of the Tome of 1908

Meletius of course believed that he was eminently suited for this task regardless of his recent expulsion from the see of Athens. His entire career as bishop, whether in the Church of Cyprus or in Greece, was one of tireless and ambitious reforms. His pro-Western and liberal views likewise brought him to the attention of prominent American and Western European eminences who saw in him a kindred spirit. To his credit, he saw the need for a united American Orthodox Church, ostensibly with a like-minded individual as its head.

In 1921, he began his triumphal tour of North America, traveling extensively, maintaining important political contacts and serving as a support for his embattled protégé, Archbishop Alexander. He was instrumental in setting up the first Greek seminary (in Astoria, New York), which was named after St. Athanasius. He also strived to expand his contacts with prominent Protestant leaders, specifically those in the Episcopalian denomination. He remained in contact with Venizelos, his patron (and uncle) who likewise visited the United States while he, too, was in exile. At this point, history took an unexpected turn: in the middle of his American exile, when his power base in Greece had eroded completely, Metaxakis was elected to the patriarchal throne of Constantinople. The man who had once been Archbishop of Cyprus and then Athens was now Patriarch Meletius IV of Constantinople.

Amidst great rejoicing by Venizelist forces in the United States and with the enthusiastic support of Western religious leaders, Meletius was feted as the man of the hour. On December 21, 1921, special services were held in his honor at the Episcopal Church of St. John the Divine in New York City. Dignitaries from the Russian and Syrian churches were in attendance, as were Armenians and Episcopalians.

Meletius's reputation as a religious reformer was unmatched in Orthodox circles and his patriarchate was expected to be ambitious. Despite his popularity in progressive and ecumenical circles, the Holy Synod of Greece did not take Meletius's elevation sitting down. An ecclesiastical court in Athens decreed that Meletius had been degraded to mere "…monk [and] should be imprisoned for life in the monastery on the island of Zante."[15]

Meletius ignored this rebuke from his former church and was enthroned with much pomp on February 8, 1922. As one of his first acts, Meletius revoked the tome of 1908 (which had already been in abeyance thanks to Alexander's earlier decision) and officially transferred the Greek-American archdiocese from the Church of Greece to that of Constantinople; in other words, to himself. As to whether he had the right to do so, he felt that he was empowered by canon 28 of the Council of Chalcedon, which grants the Patriarch of Constantinople jurisdiction over all Christians in the "barbarian lands."

Although Alexander did not enjoy the same reformist reputation as Meletius, he recognized that an independent church was necessary, one that was aloof from the convulsions of the recent past. In a rare spirit of unity, all parties agreed that a united Greek archdiocese in America was in the best interests of all concerned; thus, the Holy Synod of Greece recalled Bishop Germanus and accepted the revocation of the tome of 1908.[16]

In this same spirit, Alexander saw fit to convene a second assembly of clergy in order to set up a constitution that provided for four dioceses: New York, Boston, Chicago and San Francisco. With Meletius as patriarch, approval for the constitution was guaranteed; Meletius accepted it without revision and urged Alexander to proceed with its immediate implementation. On December 4, 1922, Alexander issued an encyclical that created the four new dioceses. It appeared that *rapprochement* among the Greeks of America was likely and that the wounds of the past would begin to heal. More importantly, the Greek Orthodox Archdiocese of North and South America would be autonomous, containing at least three ruling bishops of real dioceses.

As ecumenical patriarch, Meletius did not disappoint his supporters in the West. He undertook a long-overdue modernization program at the expense of conciliarity and traditionalism. Some of the reforms were necessary and most of them were not, in and of themselves, controversial. Taken as a whole, however, his whirlwind program was a model of modernist/ecumenist audacity that plunged Orthodoxy worldwide into an upheaval, the ramifications of which are still evident today. His unilateral espousal of the Gregorian calendar, for instance, brought the Orthodox Church into the 20th century; it also was his single greatest affront to the conciliar tradition of Orthodoxy. However, his single most important decision of immediate consequence had to do with the Church of Russia. Meletius IV unfortunately normalized relations with the Living Church of Russia, giving legitimacy to a Communist front whose only purpose was the subversion of the Moscow patriarchate.

The destruction of canonical unity in America and the present circumstance of multiple ethnic jurisdictions in many ways can trace their beginnings to Meletius's recognition of the Living Church, which only hastened the effective collapse of the Patriarchate of Russia and, therefore, its daughter archdiocese in North America. As for Meletius himself, he reigned as Patriarch of Constantinople for barely a year before being forced into exile by the revitalized Turkish forces of Mustapha Kemal who defeated the Greek armies in Anatolia

After his ejection from the patriarchal throne, Meletius went in exile to Mt. Athos, the great monastic center of world Orthodoxy. From Mt. Athos, Meletius urged the Greeks in America to lay aside their differences and enact the provisions of the new charter. Meletius and Alexander knew that, unless dioceses were established and staffed with the proper canonical officers forthwith, inertia would set in and result in lassitude and even corruption, to say nothing of the inevitable interference from Greece. Accordingly, two of the three dioceses (Boston and Chicago) acted without delay. They formed diocesan councils made up of canonical clergymen and duly elected lay representatives who submitted a list of qualified candidates to the ecumenical patriarchate.[17] The Chicago diocese convened its ecclesiastical assembly in Chicago on April 18, 1923, and candidates from a list of qualified clergymen were submitted to the exiled Meletius. The Boston diocese, meeting one week after the Chicago assembly, followed the same procedure. Meletius chose from the two lists of candidates the archimandrites Philaretos and Joachim to be Bishops of Chicago and Boston, respectively.[18]

Philaretos was consecrated Bishop of Chicago in St. Constantine's Church on June 21, 1923, "in a colorful, three-hour ceremony replete with touches of the Old World."[19] As per canon law, at least two bishops were present to assist in the ordination. In addition, several dignitaries from other denominations also attended.[20] Not in attendance, however, were Syrian and Russian bishops. Though delegations of Russians and Syrians had previously participated in the enthronement services for Meletius upon his elevation to the Patriarchate of Constantinople, they apparently abstained from attending the enthronement of Philaretos. No doubt, Meletius's recognition of the schismatic Living Church had played a significant role in their absence.

The "Lowell Schism" and the Challenge of Trustee Parishes to Orthodox Ecclesiology

In the United States, Alexander's high-handedness as well as recriminations created by the calendar dispute eventually came to a head. Holy Trinity Greek Orthodox Church, a royalist-dominated church in Lowell, Massachusetts, issued a call for autocephaly that became known as the "Lowell Schism." The board of trustees of Holy Trinity took it upon themselves to create an "autocephalous" church in America. Canonically speaking, this was rather absurd, as autocephaly can only arise (among other things) if the new Church is going to include *all* Orthodox Christians within a polity, regardless of ethnicity, and not just those of one faction within one ethnic group. Moreover, nationalist sentiments that were riding high among all of the Balkan immigrants at that time assured that the emergence of a united church encompassing all the Orthodox in the United States was (under these circumstances) virtually impossible.[21]

The call for autocephaly was not a call for the creation of a single united Orthodox Church in the United States. The royalists of Lowell, acting in their own narrow interests, were declaring their independence from the political control of the "old country." At the very least, however, they recognized that the Church in America would always be at the mercy of the Old World unless it severed all its foreign ties. At almost the same time, the leaders of the Lowell Schism and the members of the Metropolia came to the same conclusion: the only way to prevent such meddling would be through autocephaly. Though the recall of Bishop Germanus Troiannos to Greece ended the Lowell Schism, it did not end the problems that led to the schism in the first place.

The Lowell Schism illustrated the canonically unsettled nature of the trustee parish in regards to its place within the life of the Church. The actions of this particular parish council, though audacious and not a little absurd, were not inconsistent within the overall American religious context. In order to worship, immigrants banded together to set up their own churches. Created by their own action rather than at the instigation of bishops, trustee parishes were legally independent corporations, set up according to the laws of the state wherein they were incorporated and independent of overseas authority. Upon their incorporation as legal entities, parishes ratified constitutions and passed by-laws that granted parish council members almost supreme authority. Under these conditions, most parish charters provided for hiring and firing a priest "at will."[22] Priests now worked for parishes rather than for the bishops. The hierarchical structure of the Orthodox Church was thus, for the first time in history, upended.

Although the Lowell Schism fizzled out, it reflected an important fact about the American ethos and its legal system. For the first time, Orthodox immigrants (in this case from Greece) had discovered what every other immigrant, whether it be the English at Jamestown or the Puritans in Massachusetts, had discovered: one could not simply transplant the Old World to the New. In America, Old World realities were no longer in effect; to the extent that they existed at all, they became transformed into novel realities influenced by the republican, frontier and egalitarian ethos that permeated Anglo-American culture. In America, and unlike Alaska, new circumstances never before faced by the Orthodox Church required discarding the old model of evangelism and church planting conducted by bishops and monastics and replacing it with a new system, an American system, of trustee parishes, driven primarily by laymen. The Orthodox faith could be exported to America, but not the *Russian* Orthodox Church, nor the *Greek, Serbian, Bulgarian* or *Syrian* Orthodox Church, for that matter. Once in America, the Orthodox faith interacting with the democratic political tradition and the legal realities of America (albeit unwittingly and without any sense of premeditation) created a new church, the American Orthodox Church. In its own context, the American Orthodox Church was as Orthodox as the Russian Orthodox Church, but was as different from the Russian church as the Russian church was from the Greek church. As much as anything else, the Lowell Schism announced the birth of an *American* Orthodox Church.

All was not bleak however: true to being an *Orthodox* Church, doctrinal schism (fortunately) did not exist. But controversies arose regarding the practice of Orthodoxy in America. The introduction of pews and instrumental accompaniment exacerbated liturgical inconsistencies from parish to parish. Moreover, building a church with pews was expensive on two counts. Not only were pews an added expense in themselves, they necessitated an increase in square-footage which could multiply unnecessarily the cost of the church edifice. The question of pews first arose when parishes bought already-existing Protestant churches that contained them. Some of these former Protestant buildings also contained organs or pianos. Given the expense expended in acquiring a formerly Protestant church, parish councils were in no mood to pay to remove either organ or pews. This phenomenon was more apparent in churches made up of non-Russians who were independent of San Francisco, although it must be said that several

Russian and Ukrainian parishes eventually introduced pews into their churches as well.

Regarding priests and their qualifications, the lay leadership had valid concerns, and many were not shy about asking pointed questions. Unlike the Metropolia, which had set up a seminary and even employed competent Greek and Syrian priests from the Old World, trustee parishes that disdained Russian episcopal oversight were entirely at the mercy of often unscrupulous clergymen.

Even with properly credentialed clergymen, the laity had many valid questions. Many resented the fact that some of the priests had no appreciation of America or the challenges facing the children of immigrants. Many complained about priests reciting the liturgy in rote, uninspired fashion, of sermons that were merely harangues about non-spiritual matters and the overall neglect of the young.[23] Many priests hoped that, as long as they taught afternoon Greek school, then the paucity of religious instruction would be overlooked. Too often, they were correct. More than a few priests were not competent to hear confessions and, on occasion, made it a far more traumatic experience than was necessary.

A few brave souls addressed the issue of English as a liturgical language. Many of the first parishes actually used English in the liturgy as a bridge between the Serbians, Syrians, Russians and Greeks who made up the typical trustee parish of the late 19th century. However, as far as entirely Greek parishes were concerned, using English was considered to be anathema. This lack of vision was reflected as well in the fact that spiritual issues as a whole were very often secondary to the political convulsions that wracked the Greek archdiocese.[24]

The political rivalries of the royalist/republican factions only heightened the dearth of catechism and spirituality. By focusing on the Old World and its political issues, by not conducting services in English, by being more concerned with being Greek than with being Orthodox, the Church alienated the younger generation from the

Church, causing many never to return. Indeed, entire "lost generations" of Greek-American youth were the legacy of such ethnic chauvinism. The continued arrival of new immigrants from Greece, however, mitigated the continued loss of American-born Greeks. Greek parishes, at least, continued to be full, and many more were established thanks to the continued immigration (which did not end until the late 1960's). In order to maintain their Hellenism, parishes insisted on securing a priest from Greece. Such a priest would (naturally) be proficient in the Greek language and Greek culture but was invariably completely out of touch with the second and third generation of Greeks who had been born in the United States.

By the 1940's, some priests recognized the low esteem in which the Church was held, not only among the young but even among more progressive immigrant elements as well. Some made tentative forays into introducing English into the liturgy, which, more often than not, caused an uproar among many of the laity. Outraged parish councils dismissed the offending priests willy-nilly. While most other ethnic jurisdictions to their credit addressed the transition to English in a largely peaceable fashion, the issue of using English was not even broached on the hierarchical level in the Greek archdiocese until the episcopate of Archbishop Iakovos Coucouzis (1959-1997). The Greek jurisdiction therefore lagged behind the other jurisdictions in matters of evangelism and retaining the younger generation.

Besides the Greek jurisdiction's obsession with Hellenism, critics complained that, under Archbishop Alexander, the archdiocese sponsored no missionary activity and did little in the way of philanthropy. His successor, Athenagoras Spirou (1930-1947), responded to the lack of philanthropy by creating the Philoptochos ("Friends of the Poor"). The indictment against Alexander is even more grievous given that he reigned as archbishop during the "Roaring Twenties," whereas Athenagoras led the Church during the depths of the Great Depression.

The Deposition of Archbishop Alexander

The respite Archbishop Alexander enjoyed in 1922 with the acceptance of the new charter and the return to Greece of Bishop Germanus did not last. Alexander was soon to be confronted with an even more formidable foe, Bishop Basil Komvopoulos. Bishop Basil, an ardent royalist, was appointed by Patriarch Meletius IV to a republican-dominated diocese (Chaldea) in 1922. In an open act of defiance to the republican patriarch, Basil refused the appointment and departed instead for the United States in 1923.[25] Basil undertook a whirlwind tour of the United States, preaching, liturgizing and rallying royalist support. A man in many ways like his nemesis, Meletius, Basil was a charismatic preacher, a superb liturgist and a born leader of men. In Lowell, Massachusetts, the focus of royalist opposition to Alexander, Basil met with the leaders of several parishes and acclaimed himself the "Autocephalous Head of the Greek Churches of the United States and Canada."[26] Unable to handle the growing crisis on his own, Archbishop Alexander asked for help from the ecumenical patriarchate, and on May 10, 1924, an encyclical was issued in both Greek and English, stating that Bishop Basil had been degraded to "the ranks of the laity."[27]

Rather than being ostracized, Basil instead became the "martyred hero" of a well-organized opposition that was growing against Archbishop Alexander.[28] One reason support for Alexander crumbled was because of his brittle personality and his arrogance. There was also an element of class warfare as well in that the majority of Alexander's supporters tended to be the more well-to-do, whereas Komvopoulos's supporters were mostly royalists who were viewed more often than not by the Venizelists as "urban peasants."[29]

Against a man of Basil's caliber, Alexander suffered in comparison. Despite his degradation, Basil gathered more support, established himself in Chicago, and even won over Venizelist parishes that had previously shunned him.[30] Next Basil went to New York, taking the battle to Alexander's own diocese. It was during this time that many questioned the wisdom of revoking the tome of 1908 and placing the church under the ecumenical patriarchate. On the other hand, the option of returning to the oversight of the Church of Greece had been closed by the laity themselves, who wished to be spared the convulsions of the Greek political scene. Moreover, autocephaly was not possible as long as the Greeks wished to be independent of their Slavic and Arabic co-religionists. From 1923-1930, a rival, renegade archdiocese existed centered on the person of Bishop Basil.

While Basil could not hope to overtake the archdiocese alone, he could (and did) make life miserable for Alexander. Fundraising dried up, causing the seminary of St. Athanasius to close its doors in 1923, after operating for only a few short years. Alexander, who suffered in comparison with his mentor Meletius in the eyes of Western clergymen, now had to contend with comparisons to the defrocked Basil from among his own people. Even his own bishops were not as forthcoming with support as they should have been and eventually turned against him.

The absurdity of a rival archdiocese required that something be done. In 1930, the ecumenical patriarchate designated Metropolitan Damascene of Corinth as patriarchal Exarch to the United States. A man of sterling qualities, Damascene represented both the Phanar and the Church of Greece, proof that both churches were serious about healing the breach in America. Damascene arrived on May 20, 1930, and paid the customary courtesy calls on the President of the United States and other dignitaries. Once the proper courtesies had been observed, he headed forthwith to New York. On May 31, 1930, he issued an encyclical to the priests and executive committees of all Greek parishes. The encyclical itself was a call to unity and to peace, "As of this day you have endured the hardships of partisanship and disunion. Now try the goodliness of peace and you shall observe the difference between peace and partisanship, love and hate, brotherly affection and fratricidal strife."[31]

If Alexander had had the political skills necessary, he would have picked up Damascene's olive branch and seized the moral high ground. Instead, he reacted petulantly to this encyclical and issued his own counter-encyclical, accusing Damascene of being a tool of the royalists and even stating that his meddling was a violation of the constitution of the Archdiocese.[32] He issued this rebuttal without consulting his brother bishops, an action that further eroded their support for him. At this point the dam burst: reports abounded of Alexander's "insubordinate spirit," and previous letters and memoranda he had sent to the patriarchate were viewed in a new light, one that seemingly underscored his prickly personality, and became grist for the mill. By now it was too late. The majority of parishes and Bishop Joachim of Boston were ready to bolt and looked to Damascene for guidance.[33] The three diocesan bishops arrived in New York to decide what to do. Joachim led the defection while Philaretos of Chicago and Kallistos of San Francisco chose to straddle the fence for the time being.

Alexander issued a second dispatch that showed signs of paranoia and desperation.[34] Beneath the surface, however, a clandestine meeting had been set up between Basil and Alexander and a surprising reconciliation had been effected between the two men. Both men embraced in the spirit of Christian unity and forgave each other the insults of the previous seven years. Despite this reconciliation between the two rivals, it was clear to Damascene that Alexander was not competent and could not remain as archbishop. Nor was Basil any better. A mass meeting was held June 17, 1930, in which all church organizations in the greater New York area were invited to attend. Damascene let it be known that similar gatherings were to be held in other metropolitan areas on the same day, and that everybody should feel free to speak openly.[35]

As a result of these mass meetings, the Phanar decided to strip Archbishop Alexander of all primatial (though not episcopal) authority without benefit of trial.[36] Upon the recommendation of Damascene, Archbishop Athenagoras Spirou of Corfu was designated to be the next primate. Athenagoras's tenure would be imperiled however if both rival bishops, Alexander and Basil, remained in America. It was decided therefore that Basil would be restored to episcopal dignity, and that both Alexander and Basil as well as the Bishops of Chicago and Boston would be given assignments in Greece. Peace came to the Greek archdiocese, and it would be up to Athenagoras to heal the wounds inflicted by Alexander's arrogance and Basil's rebellion.

To be fair to Alexander, his tenure in America had its high points. He conducted the affairs of the Greek archdiocese in America in a true synodal fashion. The dioceses he established in Boston, Chicago and San Francisco were real dioceses and functioned with great autonomy. He viewed himself in the proper ecclesiastical fashion as president of the synod and exercised no jurisdiction over his brother bishops.[37] The bishops themselves were selected in part by the laity who, together with the priests, submitted lists of qualified clergymen to the ecumenical patriarchate for consideration. In all these particulars, the traditional ecclesiology of the Orthodox Church was upheld. For all intents and purposes, the Greek jurisdiction under its first hierarch was autonomous.

In addition, like his mentor Meletius and Archbishop Tikhon, Alexander pursued a policy of amity with the Episcopalians, who graciously allowed the veterans of the short-lived St. Athanasius Seminary to matriculate at the Episcopalian Seminary in Nashbotah, Wisconsin.[38] This accord allowed the archdiocese to provide for well-educated priests during a time in which they were few and far between and many parishes still struggled with irregular and/or uneducated clergy. Had Archbishop Alexander been less officious in his dealing with subordinates, less inclined to view the throne as a patrimonial right, and less dismissive of the royalists, he might have served out his reign in peace. Instead, rancor was his lot and a rigid centralization would be the price that the Greek-Americans would pay.

The Episcopate of Athenagoras and the Challenges of Ethnocentrism and Assimilation

In order to bring peace to the Greek archdiocese, Athenagoras, overreacting to the disunity that festered under Alexander, pursued a process of centralization, degrading the three dioceses of San Francisco, Chicago and Boston and arrogating all canonical authority unto himself. Many Greek-Americans reacted vehemently to autocratic rule. In Detroit, anti-Athenagoras riots broke out.[39]

In order to safeguard unity at all costs, Athenagoras decided not to fight other battles. One battle that he decided not to engage was the issue of English as a liturgical language. For the sake of peace, he allowed the increasing use of organs in parishes. Although the use of instruments was proscribed by the canons of the Church, Athenagoras avoided conflict by issuing an encyclical of dubious credibility stating that an organ had been used in the liturgical services of Hagia Sophia in Constantinople.[40] Likewise, he often looked the other way when parish councils refused to follow the proper protocols in the design and construction of new churches. Traditional Orthodox iconography likewise continued its steady decline under his episcopate.

The major battle was between the royalists and the Venizelists, and, to his credit, Athenagoras was able to reconcile these two factions and thus stop any schism within the Greek archdiocese. This accomplishment cannot be overstated and must not be underappreciated. In-fighting between these two groups often resulted in violent fracases at parish council meetings, social gatherings and even during the liturgical services of the Church itself.[41] The unity that Athenagoras was able to effect stands in sharp contrast to the intramural fighting that went on between the Metropolia, ROCOR, the Moscow patriarchate and the multiple Syrian dioceses (of which more later). He was even able on more than a few occasions to effect reconciliation on the parish level, getting royalists and republicans to put aside their differences.

Out of this unity, Athenagoras built a permanent seminary, Holy Cross, in Pomfret, Connecticut, in 1937 and strived to normalize the finances of the archdiocese with the institution of per-capita assessment called a *monodollarion* (one dollar).[42] He instituted a ladies' benevolent association (Philoptochos) that today is one of the largest women's philanthropic associations in America. It was under his episcopate that the *Orthodox Observer,* the official journal of the Greek Archdiocese, was first published. He maintained warm relations with the leaders of Protestant denominations and even welcomed a few converts from Protestantism into the Orthodox fold, something unheard of within the Greek archdiocese prior to that time. A few of these converts entered the priesthood. One, Robert Royster, was actually ordained a bishop.[43]

More importantly, his commitment to the United States and his close friendship with President Truman started the Greek archdiocese on a process of assimilation to America that was long overdue. Under Athenagoras, the Greek archdiocese began the process of divesting itself of its fantasies of being a mere outpost of Hellenism, at least in the political sphere.

Conclusion

In all ethnic jurisdictions, the immigrant generation was not looking for visionaries. They were concerned with survival. They were poor people who sought to recreate the village church, to live a Christian life as best they knew how and to try to pass the faith on to their offspring. To their great credit, they brought their faith with them and, not waiting on the bishops, built churches for themselves. To be sure, they brought with them their Old World politics. Nationalistic convulsions coupled with the trustee parish system undermined Orthodox ecclesiology and created new ways of viewing not only fellow Orthodox, but also each other.

Because of their ethnic chauvinism, the Greek parishes clung to Old World politics and to the Greek language. It is for these reasons that administrative unity within the Greek Orthodox Archdiocese of America (as it is presently known) is of a more tenuous nature than is found in the other jurisdictions. It is also because of this disunity that liturgical integrity, as exemplified by the number of different hymnodies, is more chaotic as well. As for the linguistic expression of the liturgy, there is absolutely no consistency from parish to parish.

Men like Athenagoras, leading the American church in the manner of St. Tikhon and St. Raphael, began to tackle the most pressing issues. It would take a new generation of leaders to steer a new generation of American laity in correcting those things left undone or incorrectly done.

CHAPTER 7

THE ANTIOCHIAN ARCHDIOCESE

Unlike the Balkan immigrant, who typically was uneducated and unskilled and viewed himself as a stranger in a strange land, hoping to return to his homeland with just enough money to provide for his family, many of the Syro-Lebanese were professionals or self-employed merchants. These people brought with them their trading and entrepreneurial skills. They set up their own businesses all over the United States and Canada. Another major difference between them and their Balkan co-religionists was that they came over as families. For them, America was not some temporary sojourn but a destination.

Why did the typical Arab have this view? As the Ottoman Empire began to crumble, various Islamic groups began vying for power in an effort to create their version of a modern Islamic state. The Christian Arabs had always been a minority within the formerly Christian lands of the Near East, at least since the time of the Crusades. By the 20th century, it was obvious that demographic trends were definitely against them. Though ethnically part of the Arab culture, Arab Christians had no voice in shaping these emerging Islamic governments. Although the Turks likewise dominated the Balkans, the Islamic presence in the Balkans was miniscule by comparison, and the Christian populations of the Balkans had been able to wage successful wars of liberation throughout the 19th century. This option was not available to the Christians of the Middle East.

Like the other Orthodox immigrants, however, the Lebanese formed fraternal societies before they formed parishes. In 1895, the Lebanese immigrants formed the "Syrian Orthodox Benevolent Society," with Dr. Ibrahim Arbeely, a prominent Damascene physician, serving as its first president. It was Dr. Arbeely who wrote to Fr. Raphael Hawaweeny, then teaching Arabic studies at the Orthodox Theological Academy in Kazan (Russia), inviting him to come to New York in order to set up the first Arabic-speaking parish in North America.[1] From Kazan, Fr. Raphael went to St. Petersburg to interview with Bishop Nicholas of San Francisco, who at that time, coincidentally, was visiting Russia to recruit missionaries for America. Nicholas agreed and received Fr. Raphael into the Russian Orthodox Church on Nov 17, 1895.

As discussed in an earlier chapter, Fr. Raphael proved to be a pivotal figure in American Orthodoxy. Because of his academic and administrative brilliance, he rose to positions of leadership among all Orthodox in America in general. At the head of a large Arab delegation, it was he who greeted the future Bishop Tikhon when he arrived in New York Harbor in 1898. Father Raphael served as Tikhon's right-hand-man, acclimating Tikhon to America and its customs.[2] Hawaweeny rigidly adhered to church protocols and always respected Bishop Tikhon's prerogatives, especially when he would request Syrian priests to come to America. Both men were remarkably pan-Orthodox in outlook and ministered with diligence to all Orthodox in America, regardless of ethnicity.

Before Tikhon's arrival, however, Fr. Hawaweeny had already acquired a growing reputation as an administrator and leader. Wasting no time after his arrival to New York City, Fr. Raphael purchased the first church for his new flock in lower Manhattan at 77 Washington Street. By 1900, the population, mostly Lebanese, had expanded significantly to Brooklyn, and with this came the need for another church. An existing church was purchased in 1902 at 299 Pacific Street. (It was at this location that Fr. Raphael was consecrated Bishop of Brooklyn on March 12, 1904, thus becoming the first bishop consecrated on American soil). Archbishop Tikhon would later move the church yet again to 355 State St., where it remains the Archdiocesan Cathedral of the Antiochian Archdiocese to this day. All three of these Syro-Lebanese churches were dedicated to St. Nicholas of Myra.

Father Raphael, who had been Greek- and Russian-educated, was the right man for the time. Not only did he get along famously with Tikhon's successor, Archbishop Platon, but, because of his facility with Greek and Russian, he also was able to minister to non-Arab Orthodox Christians during his three missionary journeys throughout North America. His fluency with English accelerated the acculturation of Arab Christians to the New World, and his courage in publishing prayer books in English helped stave off the generational losses that plagued the other jurisdictions.

The Establishment of Multiple Arab Jurisdictions

Although Fr. Raphael had been consecrated bishop by hierarchs of the Russian Orthodox Church and was unwavering in his support of the Metropolia, the same pressures working against American Orthodox unity came to bear against the Lebanese population as well. With Bishop Raphael's untimely death in 1915, the Syro-Lebanese Auxiliary Diocese lost its administrative cohesiveness. His replacement, Archbishop Aftimios Ofiesh, could not provide the leadership necessary to sustain Arab unity (nor loyalty to the Metropolia, for that matter). Part of the reason was outside interference by the Karlovtsi synod of bishops as well as the ecumenical patriarchate.[3]

Between 1920 and 1936, four competing Syrian jurisdictions emerged due to this leadership vacuum. In addition to the official archdiocese headed by Aftimios Ofiesh, there were three schismatic jurisdictions headed by (1) Metropolitan Germanus Shehadi, (2) Archbishop Victor Abo-Assely and (3) Bishop Emmanuel Abo-Hatab.[4] Disillusioned, Archbishop Aftimios resigned his episcopate in 1933 and married. However, four Arab jurisdictions were not only anomalous, but unviable, and by 1936, only two remained: the

Archdiocese of New York and All North America, headed by Metropolitan Antony Bashir, and the Archdiocese of Toledo and Dependencies led by Metropolitan Samuel David.[5]

Metropolitan Antony Bashir

Bashir succeeded Aftimios Ofiesh. Among all of the Orthodox ethnarchs, he was the most successful in stabilizing his jurisdiction. A gregarious individual, he translated texts into English, tightened church administration and made the Archdiocese of New York and All North America the most financially secure of all the major Orthodox jurisdictions.[6] More importantly for the future, he encouraged the Americanization of the Church and was the first to reintroduce English into the Liturgy.[7] Although the use of English was not welcomed uniformly by all of the Arab parishes, the rapidity with which it was able to gain ascendancy within the Antiochian jurisdiction bears witness to his leadership. Bashir also took the lead in welcoming converts into the Church, ordaining many to the priesthood. Indeed, a sign of his visionary leadership was in allowing Episcopalian converts to practice the Western Rite in their own parishes should they choose to do so.

In all these particulars, Bashir not only set his jurisdiction on the path of financial security, but proactively protected the Antiochians from the convulsions that would nearly wreck the career of Archbishop Iakovos Coucouzis of the Greek Orthodox Archdiocese of North and South America in the late 1960's and 1970's. What is truly remarkable is that Bashir received the failed pastorate of his predecessor and in its place handed to his successor a viable and growing archdiocese. When Antony died in 1966, Philip Saliba succeeded him.

Metropolitan Philip Saliba

Metropolitan Philip Saliba, like his contemporary Archbishop Iakovos Coucouzis of the Greek Orthodox Archdiocese, was one of those individuals able to bridge the gap between an immigrant/ethnic past and an American future. Unlike Iakovos, however, he largely succeeded. Fortunately for Saliba, he followed in the footsteps of a visionary predecessor who had consolidated his power, made some hard decisions and thus imprinted his vision upon the Church. One problem remained, however: at the time of Antony's death, the Antiochian Orthodox Church was still divided into two rival dioceses. It was up to Philip to rectify this situation.

On June 24, 1975, Metropolitan Philip Saliba of New York and Metropolitan Michael Shaheen of Toledo (Samuel David's successor) signed the "Articles of Reunification," which merged both dioceses into one administrative whole. Upon ratification by the Holy Synod of the Patriarchate of Antioch, Philip was named primate and Michael was deemed "Auxiliary-Archbishop," a position he held until his death in 1992.[8] At present, the Antiochian Archdiocese of New York and All North America has four auxiliary bishops assisting Metropolitan Philip: Bishop Antoun Khouri, Bishop Joseph Al-Zehlaoui, Bishop Basil Essey and Bishop Demetri Khoury. The archdiocesan headquarters are in Englewood, New Jersey, but St. Nicholas on State Street in Brooklyn, New York, remains the archdiocesan cathedral.

Even before the consolidation of the two rival dioceses, Philip's leadership resulted in explosive growth for the Antiochian jurisdiction. In 1966, for example, both jurisdictions had a combined total of 65 parishes; by 2002, there were 206.[9] Part of the reason for this growth was the fact that, during the 1950's, Metropolitan Antony had addressed the twin controversies of language and evangelism. (These successes cannot be overstated, especially in comparison to

113

the Greek Orthodox archdiocese, which continues to be convulsed to this day.)

Philip continued Bashir's program and accelerated it. The use of English meant that the immigrants' children who only knew English could understand the services of the Church. It also meant that non-Orthodox could also understand the services. Philip saw the need to minimize obstacles to the acceptance of the Orthodox faith by non-Orthodox Americans. To his critics, however, the fact that Philip showed a lack of interest in monasticism or that he adopted a more Western clerical garb for daily wear and refused to wear a beard bespoke an unfortunate hastiness to conform too readily to American mores. In addition, he came out boldly in favor of a married episcopate and allowed a widowed priest to remarry.[10] Although he was given permission to exercise "pastoral discretion" in the matter by Patriarch Ignatius IV, this action was not well-received by many within the Antiochian jurisdiction and caused some priests to ask for reassignment to other jurisdictions.[11]

The Western Rite of the Orthodox Church

The history of the Western Rite is a complex one, dating back to the early Gallican, Mozarabic and Sarum rites of the Christian Church of the pre-*filioque* period (ca. third—eighth centuries). These liturgies flourished in ancient Gaul, Spain and Britain, respectively, until the Franks and Normans, who practiced the Latin rite, suppressed them. The Church of England, created by Henry VIII in the 1500's, revived the use of the Western Rite, partly in his desire to solidify his supremacy over the Church of England. Within Anglican circles, the Western Rite has served as a focal point in the tension between Anglo-Catholics who prefer liturgical worship and "Low-Church" Anglicans who have disdained ritual in general as papal affectations. In time, the debate caused by the Western Rite would open up a rich dialogue between the Anglican Communion and the Orthodox Church. In particular, a rather lively debate ensued in England between the Rev. J. J. Overbeck and various dignitaries in Moscow (and, to a lesser extent, Constantinople) on this subject.[12]

The initial approach by American Episcopalians to St. Tikhon was itself part of a broader dialogue between worldwide Anglicanism and Orthodoxy. Indeed, before the fall of Moscow to the Bolsheviks, it appeared that an official union between the two traditions (Anglicanism and Orthodoxy) would be affected.[13] This may have been part of the secret Anglo-Russian agreement of 1915, in which Great Britain gave its tacit approval for the annexation of Constantinople by the Russians. When the czarist government fell, however, negotiations between Orthodoxy and Anglicanism shifted from Moscow to Constantinople itself.[14]

Discussions thus existed between Canterbury and the East that made such inroads in America understandable. To be sure, not all Episcopalians who wished to join the Orthodox faith disdained the Eastern Rite; some had already joined the Russian church in America and even became priests. Though rare, conversions to the other jurisdictions were not unknown either. However, the fact that classes at Holy Cross were still conducted in Greek well into the 1940's severely limited the appeal of conversion to the Greek archdiocese (although here, too, there were exceptions).

In regards to the Western Rite, both Antony and Philip showed remarkable vision and flexibility that allowed the Antiochian archdiocese to look beyond itself and think in broader, American terms. Like St. Tikhon before him, Metropolitan Antony had been approached by disgruntled Episcopalians who wished to join the Church, but were put off by the ethnicity and strangeness of its liturgy. They therefore asked if they could worship in a more familiar setting. After much thought, Antony issued an edict in 1958 allowing the legitimate use of the Western Rite within churches of his archdiocese.[15] At present, 15 parishes within the Antiochian archdiocese use the Western Rite. They comprise a "Western Rite Deanery" within the Antiochian Archdiocese. Denver, Colorado, has two Western Rite parishes (one, St. Augustine's, was a former Roman Catholic Church that was received into Orthodoxy by Bishop Kallistos, the Greek Orthodox Bishop of Denver, in 1985). The largest Western Rite parish is St. Peter's in Ft. Worth, Texas.

The Evangelical Orthodox Church

During the late 1970's, several individuals associated with various evangelical groups had embarked on a quest for finding the "authentic" expression of Christianity. After many years of intense Scriptural and historical analysis, a group of evangelical Christians associated with Campus Crusade for Christ felt that all of the mainstream denominations had "fallen away" from the Apostolic Church or were of such recent vintage that they could never prove a historical link with the ancient Church. This group, headed by Peter Gillquist, Jon Braun, Jack Sparks and Gordon Walker, among others, decided to create the "New Evangelical Apostolic Order." By 1982, they had become known as the "Evangelical Orthodox Church."

According to their own literature, they "laid hands" on Gillquist and ordained him "bishop" of the Order.[16] Their continued study and historical research brought them into contact with the Orthodox Church in North America. They petitioned for inclusion in the Greek archdiocese and were sent to Constantinople, but they were rebuffed. Through various other intermediaries, they were told to contact the Patriarchate of Antioch. Back in the United States, they began discussions with Metropolitan Philip. On September 1, 1987, over 2,000 members of the Evangelical Orthodox Church were welcomed into the Antiochian archdiocese via chrismation.[17] Gillquist gave up his title of "bishop" and received ordination into the priesthood, as have some of the other original founders of the Evangelical Orthodox Church. Today, many of these men work for the archdiocese directly under Metropolitan Philip; Fr. Peter, for instance, is director of Missions and Evangelism and maintains a rigorous speaking schedule, despite a recent bout of cancer (he is presently in remission).

The Ben Lomond Affair

The title for this affair came from a parish made up largely of converts in Ben Lomond, California. Ss. Peter and Paul Orthodox Christian Church had been a sterling example of a vibrant parish by anybody's standards. At its height, it had over 800 parishioners and maintained an extensive liturgical cycle; even minor services like the Hours were well attended. They formed a major publishing house (Conciliar Press), and one of the senior priests, Fr. Luke Dingman, had established a reputation as one of the premier iconographers in North America. The senior priest of the parish, Fr. John Weldon Hardenbrook, was an established author and noted authority on several issues involving Orthodoxy. Another priest, Fr. David Anderson, also published books and produced an excellent series of videotapes on the Orthodox liturgy that is still available today. One of the parishioners, Jim Buchfuehrer, became publisher of *The Christian Activist*, a very popular journal of Orthodox opinion (which was edited by Frank Schaeffer). Ben Lomond became known for its intellectual ferment, the excellence of its publications, and as a bastion of traditionalism within Orthodox circles in America.

As to the controversy itself, few facts are known. To date many of the principals in the case are forbidden to talk. But the basic issue appears to have been the growing "conservatism" of Ss. Peter and Paul, a parish that had experienced explosive growth due to conversions, a lively liturgical cycle and dynamic leadership. None of this is controversial in and of itself; nonetheless, several of the parishioners and clergy felt that the local Antiochian bishop, Joseph Al-Zehlaoui of Los Angeles, was pressuring them to relax their liturgical schedule. According to these same sources (admittedly second-hand), Metropolitan Philip was "alarmed" by their increasing conservatism as well.

While it is true that the overall tenor of Philip's pastorate has not been known for conservatism, in reality what probably took place was a clash of temperaments. The Ben Lomond church was essentially an American-born convert church. As Bishop Joseph Al-Zehlaoui and Metropolitan Philip were not born in America, it is therefore possible to assume that an American democratic ethos clashed with a more autocratic Arab one. Soon a whispering campaign within the archdiocese began that suggested Fr. Hardenbrook was operating the parish according to a "cult of personality," and that unless the assistant clergy were brought to heel, the parish as a whole would lapse into "hyper-Orthodoxy."

In order to safeguard the traditionalist thrust of the parish, several parishioners made discreet overtures to the bishop of Los Angeles for the Orthodox Church in America, Tikhon Fitzgerald (himself an adult convert to Orthodoxy). The hope of many of these people was that the entire parish—along with all its properties—could transfer to the jurisdiction of the OCA. This, of course, presented a dilemma for Bishop Tikhon who, though sympathetic to many of their concerns, was unwilling to encroach on another jurisdiction's territory. Tikhon, for his part, chose not to interfere in the matter.

It was during this time that the archdiocese informed some of the priests that they were going to be transferred. Suddenly, the entire matter erupted openly, and events started spiraling out of control. Vitriolic attacks against Philip appearing in the electronic media did not help the situation.

Many parishioners attributed the success of their parish and its auxiliaries to the leadership of Hardenbrook. Many felt if his leadership cadre were broken up, the momentum would dissipate. Unlike most ethnic parishes, there were no blood-ties between the vast majority of parishioners who had come over to Orthodoxy from diverse Christian backgrounds and traditions. The friendships they had forged with each other and their clergy were the ties that bound them together and made the entire operation work. In essence, it was all they had. In the absence of being an ethnic community, they had become a church family. A significant percentage of the parish felt that if any or all of their clergy were transferred and replaced by outsiders who were unaware of the internal dynamics of the parish, then the continued vitality of Ss. Peter and Paul could not be guaranteed. Joseph Al-Zehlaoui and Metropolitan Philip, used to working with ethnic parishes that often survived *in spite* of their priests, had no reference point for working with a community that existed *because* of their priests.

The refusal of the priests to accept reassignment only intensified the resolve of Philip and Joseph. In no time, an all-out scandal rocked the Antiochian archdiocese and American Orthodoxy in general; epithets were thrown back and forth and the situation quickly spun out of control. On February 11, 1998, an "emergency meeting" of the deacons at Ss. Peter and Paul in Ben Lomond, California, took place.[18] The next day, a general parish meeting transpired with Fr. John Hardenbrook and a representative from archdiocesan headquarters. At this meeting, Frs. Hardenbrook and Luke Dingman, the two most senior clergymen, were relieved of their duties. Several members of the parish, who were loyal to Fr. Hardenbrook *et al*, tried to prevent the seizure of their church by the archdiocese and pursued the matter in civil court. In August of 1998, the Superior Court of California ruled against those elements within the community stating that the parish and all its assets belonged to the archdiocese.[19]

Moreover, Hardenbrook's support among his clergy was not monolithic: Frs. Andrew Beck and George Washburn, along with eight deacons, refused to support him. This disunity made it easier for Philip to accuse Hardenbrook of insubordination. Soon the clergy were summoned to appear before the Holy Synod of Antioch in Damascus, Syria. In a last-ditch effort to resolve the situation and thus head off a tribunal, a clandestine meeting was set up at the last minute between Metropolitan Philip and Fr. Hardenbrook. According to several sources, Philip tried to be conciliatory and scaled back his requests for their immediate transfers, but the Ben Lomond clergy refused to back down from their position. Fr. Hardenbrook was summoned to Damascus, defrocked and excommunicated.[20]

In the immediate aftermath, Fr. Gordon Walker, one of the original leaders of the Evangelical Orthodox Church, became interim pastor until Fr. David Barr assumed the role of senior pastor.[21] The affair resulted in the interruption of Conciliar Press and its flagship publications *Again Magazine* and *The Handmaiden* for the better part of a year. By then, the Ben Lomond Affair had ended for all intents and purposes. (Conciliar Press and its journals are once again being published.)

Conclusion: The Antiochian Archdiocese Becomes Autonomous

Among all of the ethnic jurisdictions, the Antiochian archdiocese provides possibly the best template for the acculturation of the Orthodox Church to the American context. In spite of the Ben Lomond controversy and the admitted liberalism of Metropolitan Philip Saliba regarding certain canonical provisions, the far-sighted actions taken by Metropolitan Antony Bashir in the 1950's and followed by Philip placed this jurisdiction firmly within the American camp and helped accelerate the dissolution of Old World control. With the resolution of the Ben Lomond controversy in favor of the archdiocese, Philip enhanced his reputation within his jurisdiction and among his fellow hierarchs.

Philip's own demeanor towards his fellow hierarchs in Damascus, however, was not unlike that of the inner core of the dissidents at Ben Lomond. Over the years, he has repeatedly called for autonomy from Damascus, and, when challenged by Patriarch Ignatius IV of Antioch about the American church's "maturity," he has not been shy to respond with counter challenges. Because of Philip's boldness towards Damascus, he was able in 2001 to force the issue of autonomy for the Antiochian jurisdiction in North America. The patriarchate, bowing to the inevitable, relented and granted the Lebanese autonomy in 2002.

The Lebanese jurisdiction, for all its criticisms, continues to exhibit vitality, growth and stability. Under the firm hands of Antony and Philip, and in the opinion of some clergymen from the other jurisdictions, the Antiochian jurisdiction is closer to becoming a truly American Orthodox Church than any of the remaining ethnic exarchates.[22]

CHAPTER 8

THE OTHER JURISDICTIONS

The Russian Archdiocese of the Aleutians and North America was the permanent, settled Orthodox Church in America. Its missionary activity was well-known among its faithful, and it was not averse to moving its hierarchy wherever it was needed most: first in Sitka, then San Francisco, and finally in New York. The bishops of the Archdiocese of the Aleutians and North America initiated steps to meet the immigrants' spiritual needs, and as a result, a tentative spirit of unity existed between all Orthodox immigrant groups. In time, some of these immigrant groups, especially the Greeks, Romanians and, to a lesser extent, the Serbs, resented Russian hegemony; fearing "pan-Slavism," they took whatever steps they could to set up ethnocentric parishes. Others, such as the Bulgarians, the Albanians and the Lebanese, were more comfortable operating within the framework of the Russian hierarchy.

Despite the Russian bishops' willingness to minister to each of the immigrant groups, cultural and linguistic barriers ultimately proved hard to overcome for almost all Orthodox immigrants. The first few pan-Orthodox parishes were shining examples of what could have been, but the catastrophic events of the post-World War I period destroyed the Orthodox unity that existed during the late 19th century. Thereafter, separate ethnic jurisdictions became the norm in North America.

One of the distinguishing hallmarks of many of the jurisdictions that reverted to Old World control was that, when their respective patriarchates fell to Soviet domination after World War II, they became convulsed in the same types of controversies that plagued the American archdiocese of the Russian Orthodox Church in the inter-war period. Like the Metropolia,[1] they had to make a decision as to whether to accept Soviet control through patriarchal surrogates or seek outright autonomy. Because of their much smaller size, all of the Balkan exarchates (excepting the Greeks) decided that autonomy was not the answer; instead, they sought unification under the ecumenical patriarchate or with the quasi-autonomous Metropolia. The Ukrainians, many of the Carpatho-Russians, the Byelorussians and a fraction of the Albanian parishes chose the Constantinople option and became part of the Greek archdiocese; whereas the Bulgarians, Romanians, Serbs and the greater part of the Albanians chose to incorporate with the Metropolia.

Both the Greek Orthodox Archdiocese of North and South America (as it was known before 1996) and the Metropolia resurrected St. Tikhon's idea of ethnic auxiliary dioceses in order to accommodate diverse ethnic groups so that they could maintain their unique cultural perspectives. In the Greek archdiocese, these ethnic bishops had jurisdiction only over their respective ethnic groups, whereas in the Metropolia, the various ethnic auxiliary bishops were actually ruling bishops of regional dioceses as well.

The Albanians

The experience of the Albanian Orthodox is unique among all other groups in one significant respect: the liturgical services of the Church had never been celebrated in the language of the Albanian people, this despite the fact that Christianity had penetrated into ancient Illyria from the second century.[2] Throughout Albanian history almost without exception, Greek bishops had controlled the Albanian Orthodox Church, and all liturgical services were conducted in Greek.[3] Perhaps because of this, Albania therefore became evenly divided between Orthodox and Catholics and, with the Ottoman conquest, between Christians and Muslims. In total numbers, Orthodox have historically compromised 20% of the Albanian population.[4] When the nationalist fervor that raged throughout the Balkans in the 19th century finally inflamed the passions of the Albanians, those Albanians who were Orthodox sought to "recreate their church as an 'Albanian' rather than 'Greek' body."[5] This was rather difficult to do, since the majority of the hierarchy were Greeks who treated their Albanian co-religionists with varying degrees of contempt. The Greek hierarchy, for example, routinely excommunicated Albanian nationalists.[6]

The ethnic tug-of-war between the Greeks and the Albanians continued among these immigrant groups even when they settled in the United States. The tension between the two groups often came to a head, particularly in Massachusetts, where the vast majority of the approximately 25,000 Albanians had immigrated. One such incident occurred in 1906, when a Greek priest refused to bury an ardent Albanian nationalist.[7] The outrage that ensued caused the Albanians to petition the Metropolia to establish a separate Albanian mission under the protection of the Russians along the lines of the Syro-Arab and Serbian auxiliary dioceses. Metropolitan Platon acceded to this request and ordained Fan (Theophan) Noli, a former cantor, to the priesthood in 1908.[8] Noli went on to found five more Albanian parishes in Massachusetts, each under the auspices of the "Albanian Orthodox Mission in America."[9]

Noli himself proved to be one of those rare figures in American Orthodox history, not unlike Innocent Veniaminov, Raphael Hawaweeny and Nikolai Velimirovich. Noli was not only known for his administrative skills, but for his erudition, learning and leadership skill. Noli also enjoyed a remarkable secular career as Albania's legate to the League of Nations, and following his elevation to the episcopate in 1923, he actually became the Prime Minister of Albania.[10] In 1924, he was overthrown in a coup, and after a brief period of exile in Germany, returned to the United States to study at Harvard University. His interests were likewise varied: besides translating Orthodox services into English, he translated the works of Shakespeare into Albanian.[11] Because of his efforts, the first Albanian-language liturgy was celebrated in the early part of the 20th century not in Albania, but in Massachusetts. From 1932 until his death in 1965, he led the Albanian Orthodox Church in the United States under the auspices of the Metropolia.

The Albanian Orthodox presence in America today is divided into two branches. One of these is under the Greek archdiocese and is led by Bishop Illia Katre, a widowed priest who was consecrated as bishop in June of 2002. The Greek-led jurisdiction has only two parishes, one in Boston and the other in Chicago. The other, more numerous Albanian branch is a diocese under the Metropolia. At present, this branch, which has 12 parishes, is headed by Metropolitan Herman, the primate of the OCA, who occupies this capacity as *locum tenens.*[12]

The American Carpatho-Russian Orthodox Greek Catholic Diocese

This group is distinct from the earlier Carpatho-Russians who had been evangelized by Fr. Alexis Toth during his ambitious evangelistic mission that lasted from 1891 to 1909. Although roughly 100,000 Uniates had rejoined the Orthodox Church thanks to Fr. Alexis's missionary work, there remained many Uniates who had not chosen to do so. However, the Catholic Church did not learned from their previous insensitivity. Following a rather harsh papal bull issued in 1929 that sought further to erode their traditions,[13] about 25,000 Carpatho-Russians located in and around the Johnstown, Pennsylvania, area petitioned the ecumenical patriarch for admission into the Orthodox Church.[14] They were received into the Church of Constantinople in 1938. In 1950, they were incorporated in the Commonwealth of Pennsylvania.[15]

They chose the Greek-dominated Church of Constantinople instead of the Russian-dominated Metropolia because they feared that the same "russification"[16] that had happened to many of the earlier Carpathian and Ukrainian Uniates would also happen to them.

(It should be noted that the earlier group of Uniates had enthusiastically embraced "russification."[17]) The ecumenical patriarchate, to its credit, did not force "Hellenization" upon them, allowing them a great degree of liturgical freedom. The Carpatho-Russian diocese today comprises 76 parishes and one seminary, Christ the Savior Orthodox Monastery (founded in 1940), which is based in Johnstown, the diocesan seat. It is headed by Metropolitan Nicholas of Amissos.

The Bulgarians

The Bulgarians were among the last of the second wave of immigrants to the United States. Because of their Slavic origins, they were able easily to assimilate into predominantly Russian parishes. However, they soon followed the example of the Greeks and the Romanians and began setting up trustee parishes wherever their numbers would warrant it. Many of these people considered themselves "Bulgaro-Macedonians" (or some such variant), and the first independent, Bulgarian trustee parish created in the United States, in Madison, Illinois (1907), was incorporated as a "Bulgaro-Macedonian" parish.[18]

During this period, Bulgarian nationalism was directed against immigrants from Greece and Serbia and did not manifest itself as agitation against the Russian archdiocese. Unlike the Serbs who threatened schism (and had, in fact, effected it for a brief interlude), the Bulgarians appeared to be quite content within the framework of Russian hegemony. This is all the more remarkable when we consider that Archbishop Tikhon and his successors had no known plans for a Bulgarian auxiliary bishop (and had, in fact, already begun an Albanian mission). The Bulgarians probably would have remained happy with the *status quo* except for the trauma of 1918, which cut adrift the American archdiocese from all support from Russia.

At that point, the Holy Synod of Bulgaria informed the Bulgarian trustee parishes that they were now under their jurisdiction and that they were to be administered by a legate, Fr. Kresto Zenava.[19] However, following the conquest of Bulgaria by the Soviet Union in the post-World War II era, a majority of the Bulgarian parishes petitioned the Metropolia for admission into its jurisdiction. Fearful that the Patriarchate of Sofia was a puppet of the Communist government, many anti-communist Bulgarian-Americans sought refuge in the Metropolia. Not all chose this option, however. Therefore, two different Bulgarian dioceses emerged: the Bulgarian Eastern Orthodox Church, which is the patriarchal church, and the Bulgarian Diocese of the OCA. The patriarchal church is headed by Metropolitan Joseph and has nine parishes,[20] while the Bulgarian branch of the OCA has 19 parishes and is headed by Archbishop Kyrill, Bishop of Pittsburgh.[21]

The Romanians

The Romanians (who are not Slavs, but Latins), alone among all Balkan immigrant groups, actually suffered cultural and religious oppression by their Hungarian Catholic overlords. The Romanian view of Orthodox identity in America closely mirrored that of the Greeks, who similarly feared the specter of "pan-Slavism" and Russian hegemony. Like the Greeks, therefore, they regularly sent for priests from Romania and viewed their parishes as ethnic outposts. Also like the Greeks, irredentist pressures clouded the picture considerably as the majority of Romanian immigrants were not from Romania proper but from the "unredeemed" areas of Moldava and Banat. Thus, their contacts within the actual Kingdom of Romania were sporadic. The immigrant Romanian parishes had to rely on itinerant priests, not unlike Methodist "circuit-riders," who would travel from parish to parish in order to serve their spiritual needs.[22]

Another characteristic of the Romanian migration to North America was its "transitory nature."[23] Significant percentages of the immigrants returned to Romania once Moldava and Transylvania were integrated into Romania proper. Unlike the Greeks who, because of their massive numbers, had achieved a critical mass that allowed them to incorporate dioceses and seminaries, the Romanian sojourn in America was far more unsettled. Twenty-five years elapsed between the founding of the first Romanian parish and the first convocation of Romanian parishes, which took place in Detroit (1929). Unlike the Greeks, however, the Romanians boldly proclaimed their newly formed diocese to be an "autonomous missionary episcopate" reporting directly to the Holy Synod of Romania.[24] As head of this autonomous episcopate, the Romanians elected an abbot named Fr. Polycarp, an assistant to the Metropolitan of Transylvania.

Polycarp's pastorate began in 1936, and for the next three years, he inaugurated a whirlwind of activity. The mood for his pastorate was set in his inaugural speech to the Romanian-Americans: "I accept you as I found you, but from now on, we shall have order and discipline."[25] From 1936 until 1939, he established a periodical that is still published today (*Solia*), visited as many parishes as possible, established women's and youth auxiliaries and purchased a diocesan center near Jackson, Michigan.[26] Polycarp was not without his detractors, and the Romanian immigrant press regularly assailed him. When all was said and done, however, he stabilized the Romanian jurisdiction. He was in Romania when World War II broke out, however, and was unable to return to the United States to complete his mission.[27]

At the end of World War II, the Romanian jurisdiction in America became the first flash-point in the Cold War when, in 1947, the newly established Communist government forced Polycarp into retirement and abolished the Romanian jurisdiction (of course, the Americans refused to heed this edict).[28] Polycarp had done his job well: finding a diffuse agglomeration of parishes, he had molded them into a cohesive jurisdiction that was unified enough to stand up to the Communist government. Bowing to the inevitable, the government relented in their attack on the Romanian jurisdiction and recognized its existence. Rather than try to control it overtly, they tried to subvert it indirectly through the appointment of a pliant bishop named Antim Nica. The ever-stubborn Romanian-Americans refused to recognize his authority and physically prevented him entry into the diocesan center and even their parishes.[29]

The Romanian government decided to end this stand-off by dismissing Nica and had a Romanian-American priest, Andrei Moldovan, consecrated bishop of a "new diocesan structure...named 'The Romanian Orthodox Missionary Episcopate in America.'"[30] This time, the Americans decided to fight the Romanian government. The litigation was protracted and costly.[31]

By 1951, all but two of the eighty-plus Romanian parishes in the United States and Canada were ready to make a complete break with Bucharest. They chose as their head one Viorel Trifa, an established lay theologian who unfortunately was a controversial figure in pre-war Romania. Among the more egregious accusations leveled against him was that he was responsible for fomenting anti-Semitic violence.[32]

In addition to his controversial past, Trifa's ordination as archbishop was not without canonical difficulties. For one thing, he was consecrated as archbishop by the "Ukrainian Orthodox Church of the United States of America" (which is not to be confused with the Ukrainian Orthodox Greek Catholic Church of America). This body is not in communion with the other Orthodox jurisdictions and is "in conflict with some recognized teachings of the Orthodox Church."[33] Moreover, additional canonical questions were raised by the very fact that one autonomous Orthodox church cannot consecrate a bishop for *another* jurisdiction that belongs to another already-existent Orthodox church.[34] (This is not to say that bishops from one jurisdiction cannot *participate* in the consecration of a bishop from another jurisdiction.) As such, Archbishop Valerian's pastorate was not viewed as canonical in the strict sense of the word until the majority of the Romanian parishes requested entry into the Metropolia in 1960, when Valerian's consecration was normalized.[35] Despite these difficulties, Valerian was, by all accounts, a dynamic leader who continued Polycarp's mission, expanding the number of parishes, convening annual congresses, inaugurating an English-language catechism and improving the diocesan center (known as the *Vatra*) significantly.[36]

Unfortunately, no matter how successful his career, Archbishop Valerian could never escape the questions about his past. Many Jewish groups continued to accuse him of anti-Semitism, which he consistently denied but which the Communist government of Romania was only too willing to aid and abet.[37] In the American press, for example, he was regularly labeled as the "Nazi Archbishop," which only heightened tensions between the Romanian jurisdiction and American Jews. In fact, some radical Jewish groups fire-bombed Romanian churches in New York.[38] He received death threats and was forced to go into hiding.[39] Rather than continuing to fight protracted legal battles, he "...voluntarily resigned his American citizenship in 1983 to spare the episcopate further financial and public difficulty."[40] He died in exile in Portugal in 1987.

In the interim, the patriarchal branch of the Romanian church had grown from two to 14 parishes and became known as the Romanian Orthodox Archdiocese in America and Canada. It was headed by Archbishop Victorin, who died in 2001, and is currently led by Archbishop Joseph. Like all other non-Greek jurisdictions, the Romanians petitioned for merger with the Metropolia, and as such, two distinct Romanian jurisdictions exist at present in North America. The Romanian Orthodox Archdiocese in America and Canada (the patriarchal church), headed first by Archbishop Victorin (who died in 2001) and now by Archbishop Joseph, has its headquarters in Chicago, Illinois.[41] The larger group, consisting of some 83 parishes, is part of the OCA and is lead by Bishop Nathaniel of Detroit.[42]

The Russian Patriarchal Church of America

The remnant of the Living Church, which was used by the Soviet government to harass the Metropolia, particularly through the use of civil litigation, became known as the Russian Patriarchal Church of America. Once the usefulness of the Living Church to the Soviet state came to an end, the Communist government gave all of that Church's properties and assets to the remnant of the Patriarchate of Moscow. This gesture of seeming good will included all former Living Church assets in North America. The confiscated Cathedral of St. Nicholas thus became the nucleus of the Russian Patriarchal Church in North America.

The Russian Patriarchal Church is an exarchate in the truest sense of the word, essentially no different from the Antiochian, the Greek or the various other patriarchal churches in North America. As such, it receives its orders directly from the Patriarchate of Moscow, but unlike the other exarchates, it has not maintained relations with the other jurisdictions. (It is not, for example, a member of the Standing Conference of Canonical Orthodox Bishops in America [SCOBA].) This may be due to the lingering ill-will that existed between it and the Metropolia in the aftermath of the post-World War I period. At present, the Russian Patriarchal Church of America has 30 parishes and one monastery; its administrative head is Bishop Merkury of Zaraisk. Relations between it and the OCA are certainly improving and have been since the OCA received autocephaly from Moscow in 1970. As to why Moscow did not turn over this jurisdiction to the OCA, however, remains unclear. Relations between the Russian Patriarchal Church of America and ROCOR are non-existent.

The Serbians

The Serbians likewise have two independent jurisdictions: the Serbian Orthodox Church in the United States of America, headed by Metropolitan Christopher (which is the patriarchal Church), and the Serbian Orthodox Diocese, which is under the auspices of the OCA. In contrast to the Albanians, Bulgarians and Romanians, however, the patriarchal church is larger and far more dynamic, consisting of some 40 parishes and two monasteries.[43]

The Serbian diocese actually was the first to go into schism from the Russian archdiocese in 1916, when all 19 Serbian-dominated parishes petitioned for merger with the Patriarchate of Belgrade. This was due in part to the tardiness with which the Holy Synod of Russia acted with their (and Archbishop Tikhon's) request for the installation of a Serbian auxiliary bishop. The hope was that Fr. Sebastian Dabovich would fill this role. Since Fr. Raphael Hawaweeny had already been consecrated in 1904, the Serbs could not understand why Tikhon's wishes were not acted upon expeditiously. During the chaos of the Great War and the immediate aftermath, there was no way this could be resolved. Matters became complicated further when, during the war, Dabovich returned to Serbia to serve as a chaplain in the armed forces, never to return. Therefore, another candidate had to be found.

The hopes of the Serbian-Americans settled on Fr. Mardary Uskokovich, and he was sent to Belgrade to receive ordination as bishop. Patriarch Dmitrij, however, ordained him as Abbott of Rakovitsa monastery and sent instead Bishop Nikolai Velimirovich, one of the premier theologians of the day. Some maintain that Bishop Nikolai was the first head of the Serbian diocese in America;[44] however, the reality is Nikolai came to America to undertake a whirlwind lecture tour to raise funds to help his ravaged diocese in Serbia. A gifted speaker and renowned theologian, he toured over a hundred cities.[45] From 1921 to 1926, he traveled off and on between Serbia and America, laying the groundwork for the eventual organization of the Serbian Orthodox exarchate in America. In 1926, Bishop Mardary actually came to take control of the Serbian exarchate. He established the short-lived St. Sava's Seminary in Libertyville, Illinois, and taught there for three years upon his return to America. (During the Nazi occupation of Yugoslavia, he had been interred in Dachau along with the Serbian patriarch.)

In some ways, the Serbians in America served as a flashpoint in the debate on Orthodox unity during the waning years of the Clinton administration. It was because of the NATO bombing campaign against Serbia that thousands of Orthodox Christians of various backgrounds began asking pointed questions of the various ethnarchs who appeared impotent in their petitions to the White House. Many Orthodox—not just Serbians—were angered, for example, when the bombing campaign was allowed to continue during Pascha, which was perceived by many American Orthodox as a slap in the face. (Why, for example, was a previous bombardment of Iraq suspended temporarily during the Muslim holy month of Ramadan?) A fortunate side-effect of the Kosovo crisis was a heightened consciousness of non-Orthodox Americans about the history of the Serbs in particular and their relationship within the Orthodox world in general. Although American Orthodox leaders were powerless to stop the bombing, they were able to at least start a dialogue with fellow Americans who were evenly divided as to the wisdom of America's involvement with the NATO operation itself

The Ukrainians

The Ukrainian branches of the Orthodox Church in North America are perhaps the most settled in that the two jurisdictions were the first to actually follow political boundaries. That is to say that Ukrainian parishes in the United States are under the jurisdiction of the Ukrainian Orthodox Church in America, whereas Canadian parishes fall under the Ukrainian Orthodox Church of Canada. The American branch is an exarchate of the Patriarchate of Constantinople and is headed by Metropolitan Constantine. The archdiocesan seat is in Pittsburgh, Pennsylvania.[46]

The American branch itself is the result of a merger between two competing jurisdictions, one headed by Bishop Vsevolod of Skopelos and the other by Archbishop Constantine. When both merged into one church, Vsevolod became subordinate to Constantine but retained his diocesan seat in Chicago. A third bishop, Archbishop Antony, is "President of the Consistory" and is in charge of the seminary located in South Bound Brook, New Jersey, where the actual administrative headquarters of this jurisdiction are located.

Many of the Ukrainians came from a Uniate background. The present chaos that exists within the Church in Ukraine characterized the Ukrainian Church in North America to an extent. For example, at present there are three Orthodox Churches competing for supremacy within Ukraine, one of which is loyal to the Patriarchate of Moscow. (In addition, there are two parallel Roman Catholic jurisdictions, one Latin-Rite and the other Eastern-Rite.) In the United States, the largest Ukrainian body was the "Ukrainian Orthodox Church of the United States of America," the same body that ordained Archbishop Valerian Trifa of the Romanian jurisdiction and that was not in communion with the other Orthodox exarchates (as already discussed above). The situation, however, in North America has become more settled since Valerian's ordination and is far more stable than what presently exists in Ukraine.

Both Ukrainian jurisdictions are among the largest of the ethnic exarchates: 106 parishes and five monasteries in the United States and 74 parishes in Canada.[47] The Canadian branch is headed by Metropolitan Wasyly, Archbishop of Winnipeg and the Central Diocese. In addition, there are two other dioceses: Edmonton

(Archbishop John) and Toronto (Bishop Yurij).[48] Like its sister-church in the United States, the Canadian branch is an exarchate of the ecumenical patriarchate. Interestingly enough, it maintains its services completely in Slavonic.

The Russian Orthodox Church Outside of Russia (ROCOR)

The Russian Orthodox Church Outside of Russia, which is the ecclesial body created by the bishops of the Karlovtsi synod, contributed much in the way of Orthodox spirituality to the American scene. Indeed, the beauty of its churches, its fidelity to pre-1917 liturgical practices and the voluminous output of its press in Jordanville made it stand out as a vibrant spiritual presence. This is reflected, by way of example, in the deep spirituality of some of the hierarchs who served in America, the most famous being St. John Maximovitch, Arch-bishop of San Francisco (formerly of Shanghai, China).

Like many of the ascetic saints of the Church, Maximovitch was known for his convictions, courage and personal piety. Stories abound of his concern for ordinary people in all walks of life as well as miraculous cures that had been effected in his presence or through his intercession. Though Russian-born, he was of Serbian extraction and was small of stature and physically unattractive. Despite his physical presence, he possessed a charisma that drew many to him. Whether in Russia or as a refugee in China, his reputation as a living saint grew.

Though primarily a spiritual man, he proved to be an able administrator as well. Upon accepting the ROCOR diocese of San Francisco, he proceeded to build a stunning cathedral, Our Lady, the Joy of all Who Sorrow, with only meager resources (and not without court challenges). It was at classes held in this cathedral that one of the most dynamic Orthodox theologians of the late 20th century, Fr. Seraphim Rose, converted to the Orthodox faith. The former Eugene

Rose, who died in 1984, was a former Buddhist who had earlier translated the *Tibetan Book of the Dead*. A polymath fluent in Chinese as well as Tibetan, he learned Russian and became one of Maximovitch's most fervent disciples. Upon receiving ordination, he took the monastic name Seraphim and retired to Platina, California, after the death of his mentor. There he established a skete[49] known as the St. Herman of Alaska Brotherhood and began publishing many profound books on esoteric Orthodox topics, including his most controversial book, *The Soul After Death*. Today, this tiny skete publishes several highly regarded books on Orthodoxy, the most recent being *Genesis, Creation and Early Man*, a posthumous compendium of lectures, notes and manuscripts left by Fr. Seraphim and compiled into book form by Fr. Damascene Christensen, the present director of the Brotherhood.

Although ROCOR has been unwavering in its hostility to the Soviet government and the Moscow patriarchate (which it views as a Soviet puppet), since the fall of the Berlin Wall, its *raison d'etre* has evaporated. The present hierarch of ROCOR, Metropolitan Laurus, who was elected in 2001, is perceived by many to be amenable to reconciliation with Moscow (and through it, the rest of Orthodoxy).

Presently, ROCOR is comprised of 44 parishes in the United States. It maintains 13 monasteries, a stunning testament to its deep commitment to monasticism, and a seminary at Jordanville, where Bishop Nikolai Velimirovich taught for a few years after the closure of the Serbian seminary of St. Sava in Libertyville, Illinois. (It should be noted that ROCOR is only in communion with the Church of Serbia, which offered it its good offices in 1920 and was the site of its first synod, at Sremski Karlovtsi.)

Conclusion

With the loss of the oversight of the Russian Orthodox Church via its Archdiocese of the Aleutians and North America,

Orthodox Christianity in North America scattered to the four winds. The newer, "second-wave" Orthodox immigrants did not come as missionaries, but they did bring their faith with them. They also brought with them ethnic pride and an intensified nationalism. Many resisted becoming Americanized. They set up "Greektowns" and "Russian Hills" in many of the major American cities and even in smaller, agricultural settings. They also resisted being united under the oversight of the Russian-American archdiocese. It took at least three generations before they stopped being hyphenated Americans and became just Americans. It took even longer for them to stop being hyphenated Orthodox and become, instead, just Orthodox.

PART III

THE FIRST STEPS TOWARDS UNITY:

SCOBA, LIGONIER AND THE EMERGING ORTHODOX CONSCIOUSNESS

1960-1994

CHAPTER 9

THE POST-WAR, COLD WAR AND SCOBA: 1945-1970

The First Steps Towards Unity: Dog-Tags and the Federation of Orthodox Churches

Once the Roaring Twenties lost their roar, the various ethnic jurisdictions faced, along with all other Americans, the Great Depression. Because of the ravages of this economic crisis, ecclesiastical unity was not a priority. Americanization, when it progressed at all, was within ethnic lines, and Orthodox Christians were even more fragmented from each other than ever. With the onset of the Second World War and the conscription of thousands of Orthodox young men into the armed forces of the United States, the ethnic ties that bound the second generation to their parents' homelands started fraying rather quickly.

Prior to Pearl Harbor, Serb- and Greek-Americans keenly followed events in Europe as their homelands were overrun by the Axis powers. The valiant resistance displayed by these two nations in the face of overwhelming odds did much to erase years of shame that the second generation had felt as "greenhorns." The draft, however, concentrated the minds of those young men on issues more immediately at hand. The close bonding that Americans of all ethnicities felt in the foxholes forged a growing American consciousness in the second generation of Orthodox Americans that their fathers had never known. One of the glaring anomalies that became evident to these young men was their classification as "Protestant" on their dog tags. Even Jews and Catholics were identified by their religion, and this was taken as a slap in the face to men who loved their new homeland and were shedding their blood for it.

Orthodox priests who wished to serve in the Chaplain Corps were likewise refused benefits afforded to the other recognized clergy. One such priest, the Rev. John H. Gelsinger of the Antiochian archdiocese, was denied Class IV-D benefits by the Selective Service.[1] It was outraged laymen rather than the hierarchy who decided to do something about this glaring inequity. Before the federal government would entertain their complaints, however, it was obvious that the many jurisdictions had to speak with one voice. This unfortunately would not happen during the war; nevertheless, the issue remained. Into this fray stepped George E. Phillies, an attorney from Buffalo and former Supreme President of AHEPA (the American Hellenic Educational and Progressive Association, the largest Greek men's fraternal organization in the United States, which had been founded in 1922 in Atlanta, Georgia, for protection against the Ku Klux Klan). Phillies made an effort to unite the various jurisdictions.[2] He formed the Federation of Orthodox Churches.

Although the Federation met with stiff resistance, they realized that if they had something concrete to show for their results, then an easier case could be made for unity. The immediate task at hand therefore became the reclassification of Orthodox servicemen as "Eastern Orthodox" rather than Protestant. To achieve results quickly, they decided that it would be easier to lobby state legislatures rather than petition Congress. Soon, legislatures all over the United States were enacting resolutions calling for the recognition of the "EO" classification.[3]

In addition to the more immediate need of the proper recognition of Orthodox servicemen and chaplains, Phillies undertook an ambitious campaign to make amendments to the Religious Corporation Law of March 20, 1943, outlining methods that were to be employed by incorporating Greek churches in New York State.[4] A two-pronged strategy was thus being pursued, both intended to heighten a pan-Orthodox consciousness. Although the

Federation ultimately failed in its original goal of uniting all the ethnic jurisdictions, the pressure on various state legislatures to recognize the "EO" classification ultimately succeeded. Senator Leverett Saltonstall of Massachusetts introduced a bill to that effect, and on June 6, 1955, Secretary of Defense Charles E. Wilson issued a directive ordering the inclusion of "EO" ("Eastern Orthodox") on the dog tags of Orthodox servicemen.[5]

The Standing Conference of Orthodox Bishops of America

The first real steps towards canonical unity were undertaken in 1960 when the newly installed Greek Archbishop of North and South America, Iakovos Coucouzis, took it upon himself to end the self-imposed isolation of the Greek archdiocese. In meetings held with the various other ethnic bishops, he helped set up the Standing Conference of Orthodox Bishops in America (SCOBA), whose stated goal was the eventual unity of all jurisdictions into one American Orthodox Church.[6]

The steps leading towards the formation of SCOBA had already taken place on a liturgical basis in several instances in the 1940's and 50's. In November of 1941, for example, Bishop Macarius of Brooklyn (Metropolia) had celebrated the Divine Liturgy with Archbishop Athenagoras and assisted in the ordination of a Greek bishop.[7] This was the first of many other examples of joint services between bishops of the Metropolia and the Greek archdiocese: (1) in January 1949, Archbishop Athenagoras (GOA) celebrated his last liturgy in America before departing for Constantinople with Bishop John of San Francisco (Metropolia);[8] (2) in July 1957, Archbishop Dmitri of Philadelphia (Metropolia) celebrated with Athenagoras's successor, Archbishop Michael, at Valley Forge, Pennsylvania, during the World Congress of Boy Scouts;[9] and (3) in December 1960, Bishop John of San Francisco performed the funeral service of the Grand Duchess Olga

Alexandrovna (the sister of the late czar) with the assistance of Bishop Athenagoras Kokinakis (GOA) in Toronto.[10]

Other examples include representatives from each of the ethnic jurisdictions attending the installation of hierarchs in their respective cathedrals, which occurred rather frequently during the late 1940's and throughout the 1950's.[11] In addition, St. Vladimir's Seminary in Crestwood, New York, was often the site of pan-Orthodox meetings and provided training for future priests from every other jurisdiction. Since Holy Cross still conducted classes in Greek, many Greek-American young men who were not fluent in Greek, chose to attend St. Vladimir's Seminary for their training.

As far as the American hierarchy was concerned, the only thing that remained was the creation of a formal vehicle to discuss unity. Given the decrepit nature of the vast majority of Old World patriarchates at this time, it is a wonder that the formal unification of jurisdictions did not take place. In retrospect, this appears to have been a grave mistake on the part of the hierarchy, as America had a fresh burst of energy in 1960. The torch of leadership passed to the vigorous John F. Kennedy, who challenged America's youth with the words of the Roman orator Cicero, "Ask not what your country can do for you; ask what you can do for your country."

By 1960, momentum towards unity had started growing for a variety of reasons. The immigrant generation was dying out, and the ethnic ties that bound the second and third generations of Orthodox Americans to their ancestral homelands was almost gone. In the case of the Slavic-Americans, the Iron Curtain had seen to this. Likewise, the Arab Christian component of Syria, Lebanon, Jordan, Iraq and Egypt rapidly lost ground *vis a vis* the Islamic population. Furthermore, American foreign policy was very often at odds with these peoples' homelands;[12] this made it increasingly difficult for many Orthodox Americans to identify too strongly with the policies of the "old country."

It would have required decisive leadership to achieve the bold move of Orthodox unity. The newly installed Greek Archbishop of North and South America, with his tenure just begun, was in no position to undo the work of Athenagoras, who had labored mightily to prevent the fissure of the Greek archdiocese, or his successor, Archbishop Michael, who had solidified Athenagoras's gains. It was for this reason that Iakovos decided to take the half-measure of calling for a "standing conference" rather than an all-out call for unity.

The Metropolia and the Cold War

For the Metropolia, the need for independence from Moscow had been a long time coming. The first rupture of course occurred when Patriarch Tikhon was forced to remove Metropolitan Platon from his post in the 1920's for his anti-Soviet stance. (Tikhon's edict however was carefully worded so as to allow Platon to remain in office indefinitely.) Tikhon's successor, however, the infamous Metropolitan Sergius, issued a more severe edict in 1927, when he demanded written pledges of loyalty to the Soviet government from every Russian clergyman anywhere in the world. [13] This was reiterated by Patriarch Alexis I of Moscow in a letter to the American exarch of the Moscow patriarchate in the United States dated July 12, 1944, which stated that "the demand for utmost loyalty to the Soviet regime was 'not a political, but ecclesiastical [!] condition.'"[14] Realizing the impossibility of enforcing such an onerous condition on Russian-Americans, Patriarch Alexis softened the wording somewhat in a ukase dated February 16, 1945, to the effect that all that the "American Orthodox Church [had to do was]...abstain from political activities against the USSR and that it give appropriate orders to all its parishes [to this effect]."[15] Regardless of the wording, the intentions of the Moscow patriarchate were clear. More importantly, the competence of that same office was even clearer:

the Patriarch of Moscow was nothing but a puppet of the Soviet regime, a fact that was by now obvious to everyone.

Besides the theological speciousness of such an edict (Rom. 13:1-3), the political situation made it completely unviable. Indeed, it heightened the political situation given the cold war. Simply put, being an American and Orthodox placed every member of the Russian Orthodox Church in America in an untenable position; this fact alone gave every American citizen "more than enough reason to repudiate it."[16] Metropolitan Platon's earlier Message of June 3, 1933, demanding independence from Moscow, acquired even more urgency as the years went by and the general odiousness of the Soviet regime increased. The Metropolia henceforth continued to function as an autonomous church *de facto* and pursued whatever avenues it could to get its independence recognized *de jure*.

Ironically, Alexis I used the same arguments against autocephaly for the American diocese that had been used against Russian autocephaly 500 years earlier. Even as he issued these edicts demanding loyalty from dioceses outside the borders of his own country, Alexis busily prepared for the half-millennial celebration of the autocephaly of the Patriarchate of Moscow from Constantinople, an event precipitated by conditions not unlike what Moscow was attempting to enforce upon America.[17]

In 1948, Alexis invited the heads of all autocephalous churches to Moscow to commemorate this event; all of them attended or at least sent representatives. The message sent by the other patriarchates by their presence at the 500-year anniversary of Moscow's autocephaly was essentially the same message that the Metropolia had been sending to Alexis: secession is not only legitimate but sometimes necessary.[18]

The impetus for Russian independence from Constantinople mirrored almost exactly the conditions faced by the Metropolia in the United States. In 1448, the only way that the Russian metropolitan district could maintain its identity and the purity of its faith was by breaking off contacts with the Uniate-controlled Patriarchate of Constantinople, which, it should be remembered, demanded fealty to the findings of the Council of Ferrara-Florence of 1439 and the forced union that it required. The Muscovites went even further and exiled Metropolitan Isidore of Kiev for his championship of this same council. By 1448, the Muscovites elected one of their own, Metropolitan Jonah, as administrative head of the Russian church, and by 1589, this see had received patriarchal status.

Half a millenium later, Alexis remarked, "The Russian Church saw the possibility of preserving the Orthodox faith only by remaining completely independent of the fluctuations of the Greek Church."[19] What had been true for the Russian church centuries earlier had now become true for the Russian metropolitan district in America. The strictures of Leninism on the Moscow patriarchate itself created not only the necessity of ROCOR, but also the necessity for independence of the Metropolia from Moscow.[20]

Regardless, the Moscow patriarchate continued its heavy-handed relationship with the Metropolia. It demanded reunification with Moscow in a ukase dated February 16, 1945, and downgraded its American parishes (the remnants of the Living Church) from the status of exarchate to that of mere diocese in 1954.[21] In essence, the situation that had transpired in and throughout the 19th century. It also placed the Metropolia under interdict yet a third time in 1947 (the first two times were in 1933 and 1935), forbidding its bishops from celebrating all divine services.[22] Needless to say, these interdicts were resolutely ignored.

In the meantime, the Metropolia continued convening "All-American Sobors" at regular intervals, ignoring for all intents and purposes both Moscow and the Synod Abroad. The third All-American Sobor (Detroit) had declared that the Metropolia was "self-governing" and acting in accord with the reforms mandated by the All-Russian Sobor of Moscow held in 1917.[23] By the time of the convocation of the ninth All-American Sobor held in 1955, the reforms of the All-Russian Sobor of 1917 had achieved statutory form and comprised for the most part the very charter of the Metropolia itself.[24]

The Metropolia Becomes Independent

As the first, authentic Orthodox presence in North America, the Metropolia had the right to demand the subjection of all other ethnic jurisdictions. Moreover, unlike all of the other exarchates, it had several independent, canonical dioceses within its jurisdiction. Not only had the Metropolia been established according to normal ecclesiastical protocols, it had experienced a normal type of growth and had been recognized by several patriarchates as the authentic Orthodox presence in North America.

The requirement to have canonical dioceses headed by ruling bishops had been met decades before. When it first demanded independence in 1924, it had at least three ordained bishops and five dioceses: Metropolitan Platon of New York (1922), Bishop Stephen of Pittsburgh (1916) and Bishop Theophilus of Chicago (1922); San Francisco and Sitka were vacant. This of course is the absolute minimum for autonomy. By 1933, however, it had added two more dioceses: Baltimore (Antonin) and Canada (Arsenius), which had been upgraded from auxiliary status. It thus had a total of eight sitting bishops, including Theophilus (San Francisco), Benjamin (Pittsburgh) and Leonty (Chicago).[25] In due time, more dioceses would be added, including Philadelphia, Brooklyn, Detroit, Boston, Dallas, San Francisco and the District of Columbia, for a total of 11 dioceses. What had begun therefore as a missionary diocese headquartered in Sitka had now grown into a continent-wide American church with diocesan seats in many of the major metropolitan areas of North America.

The Metropolia stood in stark contrast to the other ethnic jurisdictions that had become almost papal in their structure. Though calling themselves archdioceses, most had eliminated all dioceses and diocesan bishops. In reality they each had become one large diocese with all authority centralized in an archbishop or metropolitan. The ethnic jurisdictions were also legal entities incorporated under the laws of the various states in which they were headquartered. Very often, their articles of incorporation very clearly spelled out policies, procedures and hierarchical structures that could not be abrogated at whim, despite the best intentions or canonical requirements. Immigrant bishops quickly learned that charters could bind their hands, and deviations from those charters could make them civilly liable. Unlike the Metropolia and her bishops, who had been spitefully treated by Sergius and his successors, the other jurisdictional heads, normally seeing eye-to-eye with the patriarchal synods in their respective homelands, had received better treatment. On a merely political basis, the other ethnic jurisdictions were not anxious for autocephaly.

With the passing of time, relations between Moscow and New York thawed considerably. The Metropolia recognized the claims of Moscow as a legitimate church; it did so in opposition to ROCOR, indeed, *because* of ROCOR and its many tactless pronouncements against Moscow. Even during the height of tensions (1945-46), the Metropolia officially treated the Patriarch of Moscow with respect and went through the normal channels to request "full autonomy," letting it be known that it wished for Alexis to remain the American church's "spiritual father."[26] Under pressure from the Soviets, however, Alexis refused to grant the Americans autonomy even though he recognized the autocephaly of Russian-controlled churches within the Soviet bloc, such as Czechoslovakia and Poland.[27]

The Soviets had found they could use the Russian church for their own ends. In the early Stalinist period, Stalin sought the extinction of the Church. The German invasion during World War II forced Stalin to request the Church's moral authority in order to help repel the Nazi invasion.[28] The extent of Stalin's capitulation to the Church was staggering: not only were churches allowed to reopen, but patriarchal elections were held and, following the conquest of Eastern Europe, Catholic and Uniate parishes (many of which were formerly Orthodox) were turned over to the Moscow patriarchate. It was increasingly obvious that, despite close communist supervision, the Church of Russia was being revitalized.[29]

This revitalization came at the expense of the Metropolia at least during the late Stalinist period. In a *quid pro quo* with the Soviet state, the Church of Russia maintained the Cold War with the American Metropolia; in return (and because it was within Soviet interests), the Russian church had as free a hand as possible in dealing with European and Arab-controlled patriarchates. With its growing strength, the Church of Russia pressured many of the other ancient patriarchates to sever relations with "groups in the West [i.e. ROCOR] it regarded as schismatic."[30]

Despite the repeated interdicts issued by Sergius and Alexis I against the American church, ROCOR had little success at cultivating the Metropolia. Its heavy-handed insistence that the laity had absolutely no role to play in Church affairs alienated the vast majority of Americans. What should have been an invaluable ally against Communism instead became an implacable foe for the Metropolia. Given the fact that ROCOR controlled more parishes in the United States than did the Patriarchate of Moscow and had even set up their world headquarters in Jordanville, New York, the Metropolia bided its time and accepted ill treatment from Moscow.

In the mid-1950's, the ukase of 1945 that mandated written loyalty oaths from American parishes and forced reunification was repudiated by Moscow. By the 1960's, the Metropolia, along with every other Orthodox Church, was perfectly willing to recognize the claims of Moscow as a legitimate Orthodox Church. ROCOR of course adamantly refused to do so. This gesture of good will on the part of the Americans led to complete reconciliation between the Metropolia and the Church in Russia.

In 1970, the Metropolia was granted, by virtue of its status as a fully canonical daughter church, autocephalous status by the Holy Synod of Russia.[31] Metropolitan Ireney Bekish became the first "Metropolitan of All-America and Canada" of the Orthodox Church in America (OCA). Almost immediately, the new church received recognition of its canonical status by the Orthodox Churches of Bulgaria, Finland, Georgia, Poland and Czechoslovakia as well as Russia. The Greek-controlled Churches of Constantinople, Cyprus, Greece, Alexandria and Jerusalem withheld recognition, however, whereas the Patriarchates of Antioch, Romania and Serbia "adopted a wait-and-see attitude."[32]

Despite its non-recognition by the Greek-controlled churches, the OCA adopted a deferential attitude towards the other ethnic exarchates in North America. The very name of the newly independent entity, the "Orthodox Church *in* America" (as opposed to "*of* America"), spoke volumes about their desire for the eventual inclusion of all ethnic jurisdictions into one national church. Regardless, Ecumenical Patriarch Athenagoras, feeling betrayed, reacted vehemently to the OCA's autocephaly, and it was only because of the special pleading of Archbishop Iakovos Coucouzis that he did not declare the OCA to be schismatic.[33]

One cannot overestimate the role SCOBA played. The unity that existed within SCOBA helped shape the relationship of the OCA to the other ethnic jurisdictions. Because of Iakovos's personal intervention, the ecumenical patriarchate did not declare the OCA to be in schism. In spite of meddling by the Old World, SCOBA knew that autocephaly for the OCA was but the first step towards there being an American Orthodox Church. For the first (and perhaps last) time, the American ethnarchs—led by Iakovos—shared a single vision. They knew that if the Church in America were to survive, it had to transcend the ethnic ghettoization that the Bolshevik revolution and ethnic hubris had inflicted upon her.

The Americanization of the Church: The Language Issue

The Greek archdiocese began taking a more serious look at its self-image. Were they an immigrant church of American-born Greeks who were merely biding their time in the United States, hoping to amass a fortune and retire in Greece? Or were they what Iakovos had maintained all along, American Orthodox of Greek descent, the vanguard of a unified American Orthodox Church?

One way to effect a change in this self-appraisal was to reconstitute the dioceses that Athenagoras had dissolved. No more would the various bishops of the Greek archdiocese be auxiliaries to the sole bishop located in New York, but titular bishops in their own right. To the Phanar's credit, it allowed Iakovos to proceed, and a new charter was issued in 1977 that allowed for the creation of several canonical dioceses. Nine dioceses were then created: San Francisco, Denver, Chicago, Boston, New York, Atlanta, Detroit, Pittsburgh and Baltimore. Although some of these diocesan seats were parallel to those of the OCA (and thus canonically problematical), Iakovos chose not to create a "Diocese of Washington, DC," thereby averting major canonical problems with the newly installed (OCA) Archbishop of Washington, Metropolitan Ireney.

Another way of changing the worldview of Greek-Americans was by addressing squarely the language issue. Like many of his colleagues in SCOBA, Iakovos knew that, unless this issue was resolved, the Greek archdiocese would continue hemorrhaging the young from its parishes. The two jurisdictions (the OCA and the Antiochian) that had already put the issue of language behind them were enjoying remarkable growth, whereas the Greek archdiocese, though far larger, was essentially in stasis.

Demographics of course had played a part in the language issue. Russians and other Slavic-Americans (as well as the Romanians and Albanians) had had their ties to their homelands severed by the Iron Curtain. This left only the Greeks and, to a lesser extent, the Lebanese with free access between North America and the Old World. This was reflected in fact in the hierarchy as well. Not only were Greek and Arab bishops allowed to travel freely, they often were promoted to ancient dioceses oversees after serving tenures in North America. The most famous example of this of course is Archbishop Athenagoras of the Greek Orthodox Archdiocese of North and South America, who in 1948 was elected Patriarch of Constantinople and flew to Istanbul aboard President Truman's own plane. The freedom of travel that Greek bishops enjoyed allowed them to cement ties between the American dioceses, Greece and the Phanar. The Metropolia and the other Slavic jurisdictions whose headquarters were behind the Iron Curtain had no such luxury. Because of this, the Slavic jurisdictions all the more quickly acculturated themselves to the America.

The Greeks were the last of the three largest ethnic jurisdictions to ordain an American-born bishop, John of Thermon in 1972. The ties that bound the Greek-Americans to their Hellenic culture were so strong that when Archbishop Iakovos (himself Greek-born) declared that the liturgies of the Church should be celebrated in English, he was widely pilloried by many in the Greek jurisdiction. The massive erosion of support that followed this uproar caused him seriously to consider tendering his resignation. Patriarch Dimitrios of Constantinople counseled him against such a move. Although Iakovos was pressured to retract his earlier suggestion, in private meetings with priests over the years he exhorted them to try and include as much English as possible.

The reluctance to introduce English was understandable given that the majority of the priests and all of the bishops were themselves foreign-born and usually spoke English in a broken

153

fashion. More to the point, some translations being tried in the parishes were atrocious. Some of the hymns were jarring to the ears when heard for the first time.[34] Very often, those Greek-Americans who viewed themselves as Americans first or who requested the liturgy be celebrated in English were labeled *yannitseri* ("jannisseries" or race-traitors) by their compatriots, both here and abroad.[35]

Until Iakovos, no one in authority had suggested anglicizing the entire liturgy. The average first generation Greek-American had absolutely no stomach for this innovation. Unfortunately, they fought the wrong battle. While they busily defended the use of Greek, they surrendered on a number of critical fronts such as church architecture, Westernized iconography, the use of organs, mixed choirs and polyphonic hymnody. Because of limited funds and a far-flung archdiocese, hierarchs simply could not oversee the construction of each and every parish and whether it conformed to Orthodox norms. For this reason, more and more parishes installed pews and organs, whereas others bought existing Protestant churches that already had them as part of their furniture. In essence, the Greek jurisdiction felt that, as long as the Greek language was intact, everything would be fine.

One change for the better that took place was the integration of the sexes. Before the Second World War, Orthodox parishes, regardless of jurisdiction, continued the practice of men standing (or sitting) on one side and the women and children on the other. The main force driving this change, according to one source, was returning veterans who had missed being with their wives during the war.

This is not to say that Greek-Americans were going to accept the *status quo* regarding the language issue forever. As early as the 1940's, many younger Greek-Americans and even a few of the immigrant generation had questioned the continued use of Ecclesiastical Greek in the liturgical services, especially when their own knowledge of Greek was the common, everyday, demotic Greek. Of course, this same question was asked by many second- and third-generation Slavic-Americans who likewise had trouble understanding Church Slavonic, a language that more closely resembled medieval Bulgarian, rather than the Slavic languages spoken by their parents.

Following the lead of the Antiochian archdiocese in the 1950's, the Metropolia issued directives allowing the use of English in the services of the OCA. Archbishop Michael, the successor to Athenagoras, seeing the increasing apathy of the younger generation, issued an encyclical that stated the Epistle, Gospel, Creed and the Lord's Prayer could be said in both languages, as could the sermon. This was merely a stop-gap measure that ultimately pleased no one: the die-hard Hellenists thought this was the camel's nose under the tent, while those who heard these parts of the liturgy for the first time in English only wanted more.

Iakovos, cognizant of the relative ease with which the Arab and Russian hierarchs had anglicized their liturgies, overestimated his authority and underestimated the negative reaction of his people. An unlikely source, the Roman Catholic Church provided ammunition to those who opposed using English in the services.

During the early years of Iakovos's tenure, the Roman Catholic Church underwent a radical reassessment with Vatican II. One of the great reforms pushed by this council was allowing the Roman mass to be celebrated in the vernacular. When Pope Paul VI mandated that the so-called "New Rite" be celebrated all over the world, the convulsions that racked the Roman Catholic Church in America had a curious spillover into the Greek archdiocese. Angry Catholics told horror stories of electric guitar masses (as opposed to electric organs) to any and all who would listen. In reality, however, Vatican II had done more than change the language of the Mass; it had in fact radically changed the Mass itself. Many Greek-Americans, ignoring the fact that the Orthodox liturgy had remained intact even after being anglicized in the other jurisdictions, used the Catholic situation as an excuse not to use English.

In time it became apparent that the Greek language had not protected the Greek church. Because the Greek archdiocese had not taken a proactive approach, widely-divergent hymnodies—in Greek no less—were celebrated all over America, leading to a cacophony of diverse practices, precisely what the Greek-Americans (who feared the reforms of Vatican II) had said the use of Greek would prevent.[36] Parishes that used only Greek were subjected to variations in several of the hymns of the Church. Examples included parishes that commemorated the King of Greece in the Great Litany, whereas others would mention the name of the President of the United States; others mentioned both names. Still others would sing the hymn "The Exaltation of the Holy Cross" with the word *eusebeis* ("respected people") substituted for the more correct *basileusi* ("kingdom") if they were of made up of Venizelists. In several of these parishes, these changes were often done at the whim of the congregation.

The Leadership of Iakovos

Iakovos displayed his far-sightedness as well as his authoritarian bearing when he single-handedly decided to march together with Dr. Martin Luther King in 1965, forever identifying himself with the civil rights movement. The famous photograph of him standing with Dr. King graced the cover of *Life Magazine* and instantly sent shock waves throughout the Greek-American community. The courage that Iakovos displayed cannot be overstated; and the speed with which he stepped into this maelstrom bespeaks a courage that is otherwise unknown in the American Orthodox episcopate. Many Greek-Americans were horrified when they first saw the picture of their young archbishop standing next to the Rev. Dr. King, a man viewed by many of them as a communist sympathizer. In Iakovos's own recollections of this event, he received death-threats and was called a *prodhoti* ("traitor").[37] For many years after this event, he would travel with a bodyguard.[38]

The significance of Iakovos's act went beyond courage. Here was an Orthodox bishop concerning himself with an *American* issue. It was not the injustices in the "old country," but the injustices in this country that concerned Iakovos. For the Orthodox Church truly to become an American church, the bishops, priests and laity had to stop looking over their shoulders at the "old country." They had to make America their home. Iakovos practiced what President Woodrow Wilson had said to the immigrants following World War I: "While you bring all countries with you, you come with the purpose of leaving all other countries behind you, bringing what is best of their spirit but not looking over your shoulders and seeking to perpetuate what you intended to leave behind in them."[39] When Iakovos marched with Dr. King he was standing face-forward, embracing America as his country and taking up the challenges facing this nation.

Iakovos took the initiative on many fronts. He walked into St. Patrick's Cathedral in Manhattan and initiated a dialogue with the Catholic Church in America that many view as the spark that led to the historic meeting between Patriarch Athenagoras and Pope Paul VI in 1966 in Jerusalem. Among the concrete accomplishments this move engendered were the overturning of the bowls of anathema between Rome and Constantinople; the repatriation of holy relics, such as the skull of St. Andrew to Patras, Greece; and the abeyance of the Latin Patriarchate of Constantinople upon the death of the last occupant of that office in 1963.

Iakovos's penchant for going it alone caused his critics to label him a glory-seeker. Throughout his career, Iakovos took bold moves, seemingly going to the brink and then miraculously surviving. This is not to say that there were no missteps along the way: towards the twilight of his career, he officiated at the wedding of an already thrice-married divorcee with prominent social connections to the Governor of New York State. To make matters worse, the wedding was performed in the middle of Great Lent. Unlike the civil rights march, the *rapprochement* with the Catholics or his insistence on the use of English, there could have been no justification for this event, attendant as it was with so many canonical violations. Even his most die-hard supporters found themselves unable to defend this action.

Nonetheless, Iakovos always seemed to survive. Because of his vision, the aggrandizement of power within his person and the judicious use of this power, he was able to acquire tremendous capital that he used to great effect in the political arena, much to the benefit of the Greek-American lobby and the Greek government. The Greek lobby was never more powerful than it was when Iakovos was in charge. During the Turkish invasion of Cyprus in 1974, an event that galvanized the Greek-American consciousness in ways that had not been seen since October 1940, when the Greek Army had routed a superior Italian force, the influence of Iakovos and the Greek lobby on American foreign policy in regards to Cyprus was quite apparent.

The excellent relations Iakovos enjoyed with the other hierarchs of SCOBA, all of whom acknowledged him as their leader (even though he was canonically inferior to the Metropolitan of the OCA), encouraged him to take his boldest move yet: the convocation in 1994 of the Ligonier Conference at the Antiochian Village in the Pennsylvania town of the same name. Iakovos realized that the Church in America was unable to meet the challenges facing her unless she was united and truly independent.

CHAPTER 10

THE SECULARIST CHALLENGE

The Fruits of Disunity: The Secularization of the American Church

The years leading up to the Conference of Bishops at Ligonier, Pennsylvania, underscored the chaotic nature of Orthodox ecclesiology in America. The absence of a true, American Orthodox Church meant that no unified Orthodox voice addressed the issues tearing apart the nation and challenging the Christian faith, issues including abortion on demand, the fraying of the nuclear family, the war in Vietnam and the growing culture of sex and violence.

This is not to say that the Orthodox Church was silent in expositing on the major moral issues of the day; it had filed an *amicus* brief before the Supreme Court of the United States plainly stating its principled opposition to abortion at any and all times. Other encyclicals issued over the years by many of the hierarchs and by SCOBA left no moral issue untouched: birth control, the fraying of the family, homosexual partnerships, the ecological crisis, human rights and questions of war and peace. Sometimes the various jurisdictions spoke with one voice; other times a division was instantly apparent. An example of the latter was when Archbishop Iakovos repudiated the United Nation's equation of Zionism with racism, a move that angered many within the Antiochian jurisdiction.

Though the Church had not been silent, her disunity made it increasingly difficult for her to be heard. Her disunited ethnic voices—often talking past each other—amounted to little more than a whisper. Many Americans felt that the ethnic jurisdictions were following the example of Lot's wife, looking backwards to their old country, thereby forfeiting their right to be heard in America. Ethnic jurisdictions that continued to raise funds to finance schools, hospitals and orphanages in their ancient homelands but rarely, if ever, in the United States had little credibility to address American social and political issues. As such, they were usually ignored. In addition, Orthodoxy, with rare exceptions, lacked political clout.

A lack of credibility coupled with a lack of political clout muted the moral voice of American Orthodoxy, not only socially and politically, but also theologically. The issue of the Orthodox Church's membership in the National Council of Churches and the World Council of Churches became increasingly difficult given the latter body's affirming pronouncements on homosexuality, feminism and "liberation theology." Even less conservative members of Orthodoxy became uncomfortable with the prospect of ecumenism in general, fearing a dilution of the Orthodox faith. More than a few Orthodox theologians have viewed their membership within these bodies as window dressing, providing theological cover for mainstream Protestant bodies that no longer seriously believed in the basic tenets of the Christian faith.

Because the Orthodox Church looked backwards to the old country rather than forward to America, individual Orthodox believers assimilated themselves to America with little or no guidance from the Church. Part of this was understandable given the xenophobia that followed the massive waves of immigration following World War I. During this time, the Ku Klux Klan, the America Firsters and other nativist organizations became political forces to be reckoned with throughout the United States, not merely in the Deep South.[1] Many immigrants looked for opportunities to show they were now Americans. Thousands of Orthodox men of all ethnicities, for example, joined the Masonic fraternity, many rising to levels of prominence within it. Others created facsimiles of Masonry, such as the Order of the American Hellenic Educational and Progressive Association (AHEPA), a fraternal lodge dedicated to inculcating Americanism among Greek immigrant men.

Although Orthodox teaching had specifically and thoughtfully addressed this issue,[2] many clergy ignored prohibitions against membership in the Masonic order. Beginning in the early 1970's, *The Orthodox Observer*, the official journal of the Greek archdiocese, ran a series of articles and editorials courageously stating the Church's position against membership within the Lodge. Although the official position prevailed, it was roundly ignored by the majority of Orthodox Christian men who remained within the Masonic Lodge. Indeed, many clergymen hypocritically looked the other way when it was brought to their attention that many of their more affluent parishioners were members of this fraternity. On the other hand, a few Orthodox Freemasons asked an equally pertinent question: how could the Church condemn Masonry while many Greek-Americans were members of AHEPA, a Masonic-like organization? This issue and others like it came to a boil several times over the years when Archbishop Iakovos castigated AHEPA for holding their annual supreme convention during the Assumption Fast (August 1 - 15).

Because the Church failed to face America head on, she failed to provide guidance and leadership in becoming assimilated to the American culture. The issue of membership in the Masonic Lodge is an example of this failure of leadership. Left to fend for themselves, individual Orthodox did they best they could to make a place for themselves in America. What should have been a theological and an ecclesiological issue became instead a political and existential one for the local priest. Many were hypocritically told by their bishops that it was up to individual priests to use their "pastoral discretion." (Many priests feel that, within time, the issue of dual membership within Masonry and the Church will be moot as the entire cultural phenomenon of lodge membership for middle-class men is on the wane.[3] This appears to be the situation for AHEPA as well.)

The Evangelical and Charismatic Challenges to the Orthodox Church

Another issue that frayed the fabric of the Church was the growing challenge of the evangelical and charismatic movements, which made significant inroads into American culture beginning in the mid-1970's. The election of the evangelical Jimmy Carter to the presidency brought the question of being "born-again" or whether one was "saved" into the national spotlight. Many Orthodox now faced zealous evangelicals who directly asked them if they were saved. Most had no answer. When the youth asked their elders what the Church taught about salvation, more often than not, they received no answer as well. That many parish priests could not answer this question when asked by their parishioners solidified in the minds of many that the church of the Orthodox immigrant was nothing but a bastion of superstition.

If the average Orthodox did not understand salvation, how could he answer the "hard questions" that American Protestantism asked? What of icons? Are they not a violation of the Second Commandment? Why do Orthodox "worship" Mary and the saints? The traditional response of "believe, and don't question" did not work with the third- and fourth-generation Orthodox American, who more often than not was well-educated and cognizant of the piety and intelligence of his evangelical friends.

Many Orthodox began attending Bible studies and worship services with their evangelical friends. Conversion to Protestantism often followed. Frequently, Orthodox youth graduated from high school, went off to college and never returned. Ethnically they may have remained part of the "community," but they now were now only nominally Orthodox, if that.

Almost unnoticed, the ethnic Orthodox churches lost two generations: their children and their grandchildren. They sacrificed their children on the altar of ethnicity and their insistence upon conducting the services in archaic versions of their native languages. Quite simply, the Orthodox services were unintelligible even to those who spoke modern Russian, Greek, Serbian or Arabic. The enormously successful movie *My Big Fat Greek Wedding* unintentionally bore this out: the semi-senile Greek grandmother curses the Turks in Greek and subtitles are given so the American audience understands what is being said, while the baptismal service is performed in Greek without the benefit of subtitles. That part of the movie was thus incomprehensible to the audience, but the message was clear: if you do not speak Greek, we do not want you.

In comparison to the incomprehensible services provided by the average parish, charismatic and evangelical worship created an intense feeling with music forms and language that the congregation identified with; participation therefore followed from comprehension. In addition, evangelical churches offered a full menu of classes, Bible studies, support groups and recreational activities.

The joy of evangelicals and charismatic worshipers was in stark contrast to the often morose-looking faces exhibited by many of the older generation in the ethnic parishes. Though their lack of gaiety bespoke a reverence that was unknown to the non-Orthodox, to the younger generation, such seriousness was often confused with boredom. For many, it clearly was boredom. Even among the older generation, tardiness was more often the rule when it came to participation in the liturgy. Clearly, religious nominalism was the order of the day.

The seeds of this decadence within the immigrant church arrived with the immigrant generation, although it would not bear fruit for several years. As long as the Church existed inside Islam, stasis was the order of the day. Quite simply, one was Orthodox because one was not a Muslim. Often, one had no choice, save conversion to Islam. Within three generations of being in America, the rot became obvious. People did not participate in the services;

they let the chanters or the choir do the services. The congregation became an audience.

The clearest example of sacramental decadence occurred in the receiving of the Holy Eucharist. The ancient practice of the Church had been to receive the Eucharist at least every week. If one missed receiving the Eucharist three weeks in a row, he was considered to have excommunicated himself. In order to be readmitted to the Chalice, he was required to confess to the priest. One did not come to church to watch; one came to partake.

In the ancient Church, the threat of excommunication was real precisely because of the frequency of communion. By the time the immigrant church came to America, the laity had become spectators and only received Eucharist once or twice a year. No one feared excommunication any longer; for all practical purposes, they excommunicated themselves 50 weeks out of the year.

With the loss of participation in worship and in receiving Holy Eucharist (along with the abeyance of confession), many forgot the deeply spiritual nature of Orthodox liturgical life. Several of the more contemplative services that reinforced the spirituality of the Church, such as Vespers, Compline and Matins, were likewise dropped from the roster of regular Church services. In many parishes, they were held only during Lent. Although the typical Orthodox parish (of whatever ethnicity) provided a rich social life, many parishioners began asking pertinent questions such as, "Is that all the parish is for? What of spirituality or even intellectual stimulation?"

In response to the challenges offered by the charismatic movement, a Greek Orthodox priest, Fr. Eusebius Stephanou, started preaching in an ecstatic fashion sometime in January of 1972.[4] He achieved a measure of fame and became a prolific writer on the issue of glossolalia and other charismatic phenomena, and in 1978, Archbishop Iakovos gave him official approval "to preach everywhere specifically on the 'gifts of the Holy Spirit.'"[5] This accommodation with quasi-heretical practices showed just how desperate some of the ethnic jurisdictions were in their efforts to make Orthodoxy "relevant" to the American scene. Even with an ecclesiastical blessing, Stephanou's career ultimately went nowhere.

Fortunately, the American Church was not without leadership in spearheading a spiritual renewal. Taking their inspiration from Bishop Nikolai Velimirovich, three of the most famous patristic scholars in North America, Frs. George Florovsky, Alexander Schmemann and John Meyendorff (all of whom were successive deans of St. Vladimir's Seminary), led the way in this renewal. Like Bishop Nikolai, they pioneered a "Eucharistic ecclesiology," emphasizing frequent lay participation in the sacraments, particularly confession and communion.[6]

Their role in the vanguard of the "patristic revival" as well played a significant role in the consciousness of Orthodox Christians everywhere, leading many to the realization that the entire Augustinian/Calvinist moorings to which the Church in America had hitched itself were unnecessary and probably heretical. The work of these men led many to question the "Western Captivity" of the Church and its entire philosophical ethos. This in turn led not only to a theological revival but a liturgical, iconographic and architectural one as well. Orthodox text books for Sunday Schools that displayed a total dependence on Western concepts were re-edited. Orthodox understandings of eschatology and theodicy, as exemplified by the pioneering work of Fr. John Romanides, served as a corrective to the Calvinistic "blood-guilt" concepts that permeated American evangelicalism.

The Issue of Interfaith Marriages

The alienation that many Orthodox felt from their churches grew, especially in the more ethnic parishes. Many parishes just barely survived; some closed. Few young men went into the priesthood, and monasticism for both sexes was virtually unknown. The most significant factor affecting these negative trends was interfaith ("mixed") marriages.   Whereas in the 1950's, Orthodox/non-Orthodox unions were relatively rare, perhaps one in ten, by 1980 they made up about 90% of all church weddings.[7] Often the Orthodox spouse viewed his/her Church with embarrassment and welcomed the marriage as a chance to leave it in the interests of raising a family in one faith. Many of these people used the mixed marriage in order to climb the social ladder.

A surprisingly large number, however, brought their spouses *into* the Church. Although many were not welcomed and were even treated with hostility, those who overcame these hurdles developed a deep appreciation of Orthodox spirituality.   These conversions followed the type practiced in the earliest days of the Russian migration to Alaska: Russian-Siberian men marrying Aleut women and raising Orthodox children. Although some would disparage this as "missionary-dating," the validity of this type of Orthodox witness—the strong family life, the observation of the liturgical cycle within the home, the Old World pieties like home altars festooned with vigil lights and icons—played its part in the renaissance of Orthodox spirituality and the birth of the American Orthodox Church.

Unfortunately, none of the ethnic jurisdictions provided any guidance in this matter. It was more often than not a go-it-alone type of practice that could just as easily lead to heartache as it could to spiritual growth.   To the extent that the various jurisdictions addressed the idea of interfaith marriages at all, it was usually in a tactless manner. Only when the divorce rate (for *all* marriages) started sky-rocketing would they begin to confront the issue.

The Calendar Question

Perhaps the most vexing question facing the Orthodox faithful in North America was the issue of the calendar. Patriarch Meletius IV of Constantinople convened a council in May of 1923 in which not every church was invited or in attendance (specifically, the Churches of Serbia, Greece, Cyprus, Alexandria, Antioch, Jerusalem, Bulgaria and Russia). Given the recent tumult of the Armistice, the fall of the Romanov dynasty and the expulsion of the Greek armies from Turkey by Kemal Ataturk, such poor attendance was not unusual. Still, it should have given pause to Meletius in undertaking so bold a reform.

From its inception, the Church followed the old Julian calendar. Because of its inaccuracies, the Julian calendar no longer corresponded with the earth's position *vis-à-vis* the sun. Specifically, March 21st on the Julian calendar did not correctly identify the vernal equinox. This discrepancy had been noticed centuries before by Pope Gregory XIII, who commissioned a panel (which included the Polish astronomer Copernicus) to revise the Julian calendar. Because of the open hostility between the Eastern churches and the West at this time, this correction was resolutely ignored. The end result was that by the 20th century, the Julian calendar was 13 days behind the Gregorian calendar.

Although the purpose of Meletius's synod was to make the Gregorian calendar the official calendar of the Orthodox Church *in toto*, the fact that a great number of the national churches were unable to attend this synod forced Meletius to suggest a compromise. Basically, the fixed feasts and fasts (e.g., the Nativity, Epiphany, the Holy Apostles' fast, the Transfiguration and the Assumption) were to follow the Gregorian ("new") calendar, whereas the variable feasts and fasts (e.g., Great Lent, Pascha, the Ascension and Pentecost) were to follow the Julian ("old") calendar. Eventually, many of the national churches accepted this compromise, although the Churches of Russia, Serbia, Jerusalem and the Athonite communities did not. In the United States, the Greek archdiocese accepted this proposal, and in due time, the Antiochians would as well. The Metropolia, upon receiving its independence from Moscow, eventually adopted the new calendar.

The "Non-Canonical" Jurisdictions

It is the calendar question that is, in fact, the defining characteristic of the more traditionalist Orthodox jurisdictions in North America. As to their overall numbers, the 22 "non-canonical" jurisdictions are easily dwarfed by the 10 SCOBA-sanctioned jurisdictions.[8] The largest is ROCOR, with 44 parishes and 13 monasteries in North America. Next comes the Russian Orthodox Autonomous Church in America, which has five parishes and three monasteries, and then the True Orthodox Church of Greece, with six monasteries and a miniscule number of parishes. Despite the beauty of their services, their adherence to principle and the piety exhibited by their flocks, these jurisdictions are dwindling. Even within ROCOR, a division is growing between those priests who are more open about the need for reconciliation with Moscow and those who hold an uncompromising approach. The former tend to be allied with Archbishop Laurus, whereas the latter tend to congregate around Bishop Gabriel. Recently, with the election of Archbishop Laurus as Metropolitan of ROCOR (2001), chances of reconciliation with Moscow appear more likely than they have at any other time.

\Though the nature of the calendar is certainly a bone of contention, other issues dominated their relations with the SCOBA jurisdictions. For many, this included liturgical laxity and a de-emphasis on monasticism. The non-canonical jurisdictions also objected to the increased role of the laity in the American exarchates and their willingness to ignore the episcopate. The "old" calendar versus the "new" divided American Orthodoxy into those who saw themselves as the true guardians of the Old World faith standing against those who wanted to make everything new.

This division of course is rather simplistic. Many of the more strict-observance Orthodox detect a return to traditionalism within the SCOBA jurisdictions. Monasticism, fasting and confession are on the rise in many parishes. Likewise, many within SCOBA discern a fidelity to piety and asceticism that were in abeyance during the latter part of the 20th century. In the words of Bishop Kallistos Ware, for example, the fidelity of ROCOR to "[t]he ascetic, monastic and liturgical traditions of Orthodox Russia...are something of which western Orthodoxy stands greatly in need."[9] Even vociferous critics of ROCOR such as Alexander Bogolepov concede the piety and faithfulness of ROCOR worshipers to Orthodoxy, finding fault only with "the canonicity of its organization."[10]

The Controversy over the Celebration of Pascha

The date of Pascha was itself emblematic of the disunity that the Orthodox Church in America faced. Rather than try to reconcile the issue of the proper observance of the Lord's Resurrection, Orthodox jurisdictions were still fighting the Gregorian/Julian calendar controversy.

The battles over the calendar masked the issue of unity. While Orthodoxy continued to fight within itself, it lost its third and fourth generations to the secularization of American culture or the evangelical denominations. Increasingly, many Orthodox activists felt that American pluralism must be confronted with a monolithic, united American Orthodox Church. The intramural battles over the calendar ignored the fact that the West uses only the Gregorian Calendar. Even with the Protestant Reformation, none of the Reformed churches that broke away from Rome adopted the Julian calendar, recognizing the Gregorian calendar as being more accurate. All of the West, therefore, celebrated Easter on the same date.

Orthodox immigrants quickly discovered that the date for Pascha and Western Easter normally do not fall on the same Sunday. For most Orthodox living in America, the real calendar question was the question of the date for Easter, not which astronomical calendar was used. That the Orthodox Church in America debated instead which was the correct Orthodox calendar indicated how far the Orthodox in America had to go in order to become an American Orthodox Church.

Further Threats to Unity: The Liturgical Crisis

The Divine Liturgy, with its timeless nature, has endured essentially unchanged despite the many crises that have buffeted the Church throughout its history. This is not to say that the various liturgies have not undergone adaptation over the centuries (the Liturgy of St. John Chrysostom, for example, is shorter than that of St. Basil the Great), or that minor changes have not been added to the petitions (e.g., "…travelers by land, sea *and air*.").[11] Likewise, various liturgies existed throughout the united Christendom of the first millennium in different regions of the Roman world. Examples included the Mozarabic (Spain), Gallican (Gaul) and the Sarum Rites (Britain) in addition to the Antiochian and Alexandrian liturgies of the Byzantine East. Be that as it may, even within these various rites, a remarkable consistency predominated,[12] and clerics were loathe to either add or subtract formulas based on individual whims or the dictates of fashion.

The Orthodox Church guarded her worship. Why she did so was expressed by the Latin credo *lex orandi, lex credendi* ("how we pray is how we believe"). This was famously stated in the second century by Bishop Irenaeus of Lyons: "Our opinion is in accordance with the Eucharist and the Eucharist in turn establishes our opinion."[13] These statements provided the standard response to would-be reformers who sought to introduce novel formulas and practices; this in turn kept heresy from distorting the faith. The liturgies of the Church had a practical effect: by their timelessness and rigidity, they kept the Church whole.

The most glaring example of the opposite phenomenon of course was the addition of the Latin word *filioque* to the Creed in the Roman Catholic Church. This distorted the concept of the Trinity and led in time (and by circuitous route) to the introduction of other heresies such as the papal monarchy and the mandatory celibacy of priests, to say nothing of the Great Schism of 1054 itself.[14] Indeed, the conservative impulse against the *filioque* was very strong in the West, where it was expressly condemned for at least 400 years by the papacy until 1014, when it was officially inserted into the Creed by the Roman pontiff. As more than one commentator has pointed out, the unilateral acceptance of this formula actually gave a date from which historians can point to a "clear and unmistakable doctrinal difference between [Greek East and Latin West]."[15]

As for modern Orthodox worship, nowhere has the seduction by the West been more pronounced than in the introduction of musical instruments (primarily the organ) in the worship services of the Church. The introduction of the organ began as a well-intentioned attempt to standardize hymnody and to assist priests, who were often left to the mercy of ill-trained chanters. Unfortunately, the organ created a musical approach more concerned with imitating Western musical styles than promulgating the use of the traditional Eastern *oktoechos*, or eight-tone odes, which the entire liturgical cycle conforms to. Many choirs took to wearing brightly colored robes (yet another deviation from Orthodox ecclesiology), which gave a priestly cast to those who were otherwise barred from ordination. In addition, mixed choirs were also viewed as a means to stanch the generational losses that were pervasive in American Orthodoxy. It was thought by many that the best way to train young people in the hymnody of the Church was via piano or organ. (This of course is standard practice among Protestant groups, and full-blown musical combos are now an integral part of evangelical worship.)

Given the conservative nature of the Church, the first hymnodies tended to mimic rather well the original monophonic chant that had been used since time immemorial in one fashion or another. In the Greek jurisdiction, George Anastassiou produced the first standardized hymnody that made use of Western notation, thereby allowing everyone to sing the responses and hymns without having to rely on the complicated Byzantine notes that only the most highly trained chanters could follow. In fairness to him, his liturgy followed rather closely the traditional Byzantine chant. Unfortunately, his insistence on the use of the organ, and his rather bizarre statements regarding its supposed use in the Byzantine church,[16] would lead others to take bold steps and go off on musical tangents that were more operatic in nature and employed many different melodies.

Some of these composers (such as Theodore Bogdanos, Tikey Zes and Frank Desby) would produce some remarkably beautiful arrangements, and in time, Anastassiou's simpler arrangement would fall by the wayside and be derided as unsophisticated in comparison. In fairness, many of the newer arrangements would employ Slavonic and Byzantine elements, though only as a starting-point for the increasingly complex compositions that followed. This phenomenon was not unknown in Greece, for that matter; the world-renowned composer Mikis Theodorakis, for example, produced a more traditional liturgy that was widely acclaimed, whereas Dimitri Papastolou produced a hauntingly beautiful *Orthodox Symphonic Liturgy* with the support and imprimatur of Archbishop Iakovos.[17]

Despite the beauty of many of these works, their increasing complexity made it cumbersome for many in the congregation to chant the responses. Moreover, the polyphonic and often conflicting melodies ensured that choirs remained the preserve of all but the most musically inclined individuals (at least initially). In some of the larger parishes, the choir director and organist even received a stipend. Choirs, which according to Orthodox ecclesiology were always considered to be adjuncts to worship to help the congregation do its part, often became virtuosos instead. Choirs became performers and no longer co-participants with the congregation and the priest.

The complexity of the newer compositions were very often beyond the capabilities of all but the most dedicated choirs; this made it all but impossible for the congregation to follow. The liturgical admonition that all should sing "with one voice and one heart" became a dead letter in many parishes.[18] Especially in the Greek archdiocese, congregations were reduced to being mere observers in worship. The more traditional practices of OCA, and an increasing number of Antiochian parishes as well as Old Calendar parishes, by avoiding the introduction of the organ, kept the professionalism of their choirs in check with strong congregational participation.

As in so many other instances, the absence of a united American Orthodox Church ensured that there would be no direction in this regard. If organs could be admitted, why not string quartets? Why not symphonies?[19] Or a rock liturgy? However, the ultimate indictment against ethnic jurisdictions remained the fact that, as of yet, there was no standard English translation of the services. Efforts to improve poor translations led to the introduction of further heretical elements, including politically correct speech in many of the different liturgical formulas.[20]

Iconography suffered much the same fate as Orthodox hymnography. Many churches have Renaissance-quality icons, which, though beautiful, are likewise extra-canonical (at best) and are thus theologically unsettling.[21] Iconography is as much a liturgical element of the Church as the hymns, and they reinforce the timelessness of both the church building itself and the doctrinal purity of the faith. As to the architecture found in all too many parishes (and all jurisdictions), the less said, the better. The architectural maxim "doctors bury their mistakes, architects have to live with theirs,"[22] was tossed out the window countless times, but nowhere more notoriously than when the famed American architect Frank Lloyd Wright was allowed to design an Orthodox church in Milwaukee, a creation which some have derisively termed the "mother ship."

Conversion and the Orthodox Renaissance

Nowhere is the lack of leadership more evident than in the issue of the conversion phenomenon that picked up steam in the 1980's. For the first time in American history, non-cradle Orthodox started coming into the Church in startling numbers. Previous to this time conversions were mainly through marriage; now, however, grown men and women who had never heard of Orthodoxy, much less ever known a Russian, Serb or any of the other immigrant Orthodox, began a journey to Orthodoxy that often began in the evangelical or charismatic movement. Thousands of disgruntled Protestants of all stripes and Catholics who desired a more structured prayer life emanating from a historic faith began studying Orthodoxy seriously. Indeed, many parishes in the United States today, particularly in the Midwest, South and West, have parish councils and clergy drawn from the ranks of converts.

In the 1980's, the Evangelical Orthodox Church petitioned the Greek Orthodox Archdiocese of North and South America for entrance and when rebuffed, turned to the Antiochian archdiocese instead. The dam burst and a flood of American non-ethnic converts found the Orthodox faith. Soon, Old Calendar as well as New Calendar Orthodox parishes began experiencing something entirely new: adult chrismation and even baptisms of entire families. Evangelists and speakers addressed congregations in the manner of Protestant circuit riders, exhorting the cradle Orthodox to be true to their Christian roots.

In 1976, the ratio of baptisms to chrismations was roughly 11:1, by 2000, this ratio had shrunk to 7:1.[23] Part of this was due of course to increased interfaith marriages; however, anecdotal evidence of grown men and women entering the Church either through chrismation or even baptism were widespread. In the Antiochian jurisdiction, evangelism and conversion became the norm, and many parishes re-instituted the Litany of the Catechumens immediately following the *Synaxis* (the Liturgy of the Word). The Antiochian archdiocese created the Department of Missions and Evangelism with Fr. Peter Gillquist (former head of the Evangelical Orthodox Church) as its director. The OCA likewise took the lead in establishing mission churches that are often "multi-ethnic" or even non-ethnic, particularly in the South and West.[24] The Greek jurisdiction lagged in responding to this phenomenon. Still, even within Greek parishes, converts entered, in some cases in significant numbers. Indeed, the growth that was largely fueled by the conversion phenomenon resulted in the addition of 150 parishes (in all jurisdictions) between 1975 and 1995.[25]

Not all of this was viewed in a positive light. Many of the immigrant parishes simply did not know how to deal with this influx. Some priests felt that the converts were "too conservative" and that, if they were not watched, they could "stir up trouble." Often, they would point to the Ben Lomond affair as a prime example of what could go wrong if too many converts entered the faith. On the other hand, converts to Orthodoxy were among the biggest givers in a typical parish and have been praised from the pulpit for their example. Indeed, many priests and bishops privately admit that if it were not for these new members, many parishes would no longer be viable.

Regardless of the Ben Lomond affair, the Antiochian jurisdiction led the way in creating a template for receiving converts into the faith, including allowing the use of the Western Rite, mandating the use of English in the services of the Church and giving converts positions of authority within the archdiocese. One of the more interesting convert-priests was Fr. A. James Bernstein, one of the founders of the "Jews for Jesus" movement that had come to prominence in America in the early seventies. He is at present a priest in the Antiochian jurisdiction. Indeed, many of the priests in the Antiochian and OCA came from different faith backgrounds, and five of the bishops of the OCA likewise came from different denominations. Even within the Greek jurisdiction, convert-priests are becoming more common. According to sources in the Metropolis of Denver (GOA), about one-third of all clergymen in that diocese are either converts or of non-Greek origin.

From the fresh breath of evangelism, Orthodoxy regained its vitality. Converts began publishing magazines and journals such as *Again, The Orthodox Word, The Handmaiden, The Christian Activist* and *The Road to Emmaus.* Publishing houses likewise grew out of the conversion movement, including Conciliar Press and Regina Orthodox Press, imprints which are able to publish books that the official organs of the SCOBA jurisdictions choose to shy away from for whatever reason. Likewise, English hymnody was improving markedly, and several high-quality CDs and audiocassettes were being produced and marketed. Examples of groups who produced these recordings include First Fruits, Kerygma and the St. Vladimir's Seminary Octet. Father John Finley, a former Southern Baptist and now an Antiochian priest, wrote music for the Trisagion service that was both beautiful and easily sung. It quickly became widely popular and a mainstay of Orthodox hymnography.

Orthodox vitality also became evident in the arts. Significant classical composers of the late 20th century converted to Orthodoxy; among them were John Tavener (whose funeral dirge for Princess

Diana's funeral was heavily influence by Byzantine themes) and the famed Estonian composer Arvo Part. To make part of this understandable, an essay written for *Image: A Journal of the Arts and Religion,* a periodical with an intellectual evangelical perspective, discussed Tavener's conversion to the Orthodox Faith thusly:

> In 1977, however, [John] Tavener turned his back on the Western tradition and entered the Russian Orthodox Church. He has said, "It sounds very extreme, but I think sacred art has gone downhill since the Middle Ages. I feel I've come into contact with what icon painting is, with the primordial kind of Orthodoxy that the West has never had; the fact that the Byzantine tone system is practically unchanged, the fact that Greece never had a Renaissance...However impressed I am by Michelangelo, the simple Greek peasant icon means much, much more to me. Or to give a musical example, I'm deeply moved by the very simple harmonic music they sing at the Russian Orthodox cathedral."[26]

Some of the luminaries of the convert movement whose writings have provided the intellectual firepower behind the Orthodox "renaissance" include the likes of Kimberly Patton, Philip Sherrard, Fredericka Mathewes-Green, Jim Buchfuehrer, Clark Carlton, Jaroslav Pelikan, Seth Farber, Frank Schaeffer and Timothy (Bishop Kallistos) Ware. Their books and articles have made them familiar faces not only to cradle Orthodox, but to the wider American audience as well. (Mathewes-Green, for example, is a regular contributor to *National Public Radio,* and has appeared on C-SPAN) Likewise, exhibits of Orthodox iconography in several museums throughout the 1980's-1990's were very well attended by the general public and heightened an appreciation for the impact that Orthodoxy has made on Eastern Europe and the Balkans.

The Greek Orthodox hierarchy, concentrated as it was on the East Coast, found it difficult to turn away from the old country and face fully toward Americans wanting to convert. Nowhere was this more evident than during the tenure of Archbishop Spyridon (1997-99), who, though American-born, exhibited a Europeanist attitude once in power. During his pastorate, a blind eye was turned by the Greek archdiocese towards the growing interest in Orthodoxy among non-Greeks. Evangelical churches that wished to join were rebuffed and, as usual, turned to the Antiochian archdiocese or the OCA.

The spearhead for this occurred in 1985, when the Patriarch of Antioch, Ignatius IV, traveled to the United States. He and Metropolitan Philip, head of the Antiochian Archdiocese of North America, took the lead in embracing the conversion of America by meeting with representatives of the Campus Crusaders who wanted to convert.[27] He declared, "Orthodoxy is the best kept secret in America" and then created a Department of Missions and Evangelism to make sure the secret got out. In 1987, Metropolitan Philip Saliba welcomed 3,000 former Campus Crusaders into the Church with the simple words, "Welcome home!" He ordained many of their pastors as priests. Protestant pastors began knocking on the doors of Antiochian churches; many converted and brought their congregations with them.[28] More than one visitor to an Orthodox Church found themselves confronted by a bewildered member who asked in amazement, "Why are you here? What do we have that you could possibly want?" The answer to those questions fueled the Orthodox Renaissance. America had discovered the Orthodox faith. There would be no turning back.

CHAPTER 11

LIGONIER AND THE CHALLENGE TO THE OLD WORLD

The Prelude to Ligonier: Patriarchal Concerns

Patriarch Athenagoras (r. 1948-1972), though a strong individual in his own right, was at his peak upon his election to the patriarchal throne. The years following were characterized by a slow, steady decline brought about by the active hostility of the Turkish government and the enforced isolation that he endured. In 1955, violent, anti-Greek riots broke out in Istanbul, a catastrophe from which the Greek community never recovered. The ecumenical patriarchate went into a steep and, apparently, irreversible decline.

There were some high points during Athenagoras's tenure. An example would include the time when he met with Pope Paul VI in Jerusalem in 1966, an action that proved that he was a "bold visionary," certainly one willing to confront those elements within the Church for which no *rapprochement* with Catholicism was possible.[1] Likewise, his spearheading of the first Pan-Orthodox Conference on the island of Rhodes in 1961 clearly showed that he was serious about inter-Orthodox unity. His own vision in this regard was that the Rhodes Conference would be the first step leading to a "Great and Holy Synod," or what some would call "the Eighth Ecumenical Council."

Despite these significant accomplishments, his successor, Dimitrios (r. 1972-91), by all accounts a "man of peace and prayer,"[2] could do nothing but watch with increasing dismay as this decline continued. The patriarchal complex itself mirrored this decay. Although Dimitrios became the first ecumenical patriarch to visit the United States in 1990, his ignorance of English meant that his words and actions were largely ignored by the increasingly American Greek archdiocese. Even so, while visiting the Cathedral of St. Nicholas in Washington D.C., he categorically declared that the ethnic divisions found in American Orthodoxy were "truly a scandal."[3] The fact that he spoke these words in an OCA church meant that the earlier breach between the OCA and Patriarchate Athenagoras had tacitly been healed.

With the election of Bartholomew Archandonis, the Metropolitan of Philadelphia, to the patriarchal throne in 1991, there was no reason to suspect that Orthodox unity in America would not proceed. By all accounts, Bartholomew possessed qualities that could make him another Athenagoras. Unlike Athenagoras, who had to fight divisive battles during his pastorate in the United States, Metropolitan Bartholomew was immune from this type of infighting, given the fact that he was the titular head of a moribund see. This allowed him to pursue an ambitious academic career, including post-doctoral work at the Pontifical Academy of Rome. Because of his erudition and wide travels, he cultivated excellent relations with the Vatican and the World Council of Churches.

Ironically, he hailed from the same island (Imvros) as Iakovos, and both men shared many of the same leadership qualities. Unfortunately, these similarities put them on a collision course from which only one of them would remain standing. Regardless of the underlying tension, all appeared calm on the surface.

During the 32nd Biennial Clergy-Laity Conference of the Greek Orthodox archdiocese held in Chicago, Metropolitan Spyridon Papageorge of Italy, viewed by many as an eventual successor to the aging Iakovos, gave a well-received speech that left no doubt as to where he and Patriarch Bartholomew stood on the matter of unity. In his address to the clergy and laity of the Greek archdiocese, Spyridon plainly stated that both he and Bartholomew wanted an end to the "ethnic ghettoes" that divided Orthodoxy in America. His words denouncing ethnic insularity at the expense of "our spiritual identity" were clearly a broadside aimed at many of the Greek-Americans who still looked to the Greek archdiocese primarily as a bastion of culture. Thus, in the view of many American bishops, it was obvious that the time had come to cut the "Gordian knot of nationalism," to use Spyridon's own words.[4]

The Ligonier Statement

Taking their cue from Metropolitan Spyridon, 29 American bishops, representing all of the canonical Orthodox jurisdictions, took it upon themselves to end their self-imposed ethnic isolation. They met five months later at Ligonier, Pennsylvania, from November 30 to December 2, 1994, under the auspices of the Antiochian archdiocese at the Antiochian Village.

The event itself was harmonious, and Iakovos graciously receded into the background as Ligonier was the under the jurisdiction of Metropolitan Philip, who was thus the host and official prime mover behind the conference. It was Philip who actually addressed the convocation of bishops, and it was Bishop Dmitri Royster of Dallas (OCA) who gave the official response. By all accounts, amity and unity of purpose abounded. The assembled bishops came to an agreement and issued a statement declaring their intention of forming a united American Orthodox Church.

The "Ligonier Statement" itself was uncontroversial and contained no negative mention of the ancient patriarchates or disparagement of the immigrant nature of the Orthodox Church. To the contrary, both the role of the Old World patriarchates and the immigrant origins of the jurisdictions were written about in a positive light.[5] With acute attention to canonical detail, the bishops who met at Ligonier followed Orthodox protocols. There was no attempt to create an *ad hoc* religious denomination. The Ligonier Statement was a serious document that chose to address in a sober and thoughtful manner the canonical deficiencies that hindered the ethnic jurisdictions in their evangelistic mission and their relationships with each other.

Unfortunately, the Ligonier Statement was viewed by some of the patriarchates as a "power grab" by Iakovos, who heretofore had been accused *sotto voce* of cultivating a "cult of personality." Many feared that he was on the verge of having himself proclaimed as "Patriarch of America." Some of the Old World patriarchates were scared of losing their American dioceses simply for economic reasons.

One of the signatories, Metropolitan Christopher of the Serbian exarchate, openly admitted that the ultimate goal of the Ligonier conference was not only unification, but also autocephaly.[6] The fact that this interview (as well as Christopher's comments) was conducted on videotape and was distributed to parishes all over North America showed there was no hidden agenda at Ligonier. Regardless, Ligonier disturbed not only the Old World patriarchates, but some priests and laymen in America as well. More than a few were perfectly happy with the *status quo.*

Regardless of such concerns, it was clear that the conferees were more concerned about the canonical irregularities that plagued American Orthodoxy than they were about their own place in the pecking order. Many of the bishops headed dioceses within the various jurisdictions that, after decades of struggle, had acquired vast properties and maintained impressive institutions such as orphanages, seminaries, youth camps, parochial schools, philanthropies and so on. Each of the most senior hierarchs had something to lose with unification. If they had been merely interested in aggrandizing their own power further, they would have left matters as they were. Iakovos, Philip and Theodosius, who between them controlled the lion's share of parishes in North America, were all old men. Iakovos himself was in failing health. If it were he who was to be elected the first Metropolitan of the American Orthodox Church, it would have been done with the recognition that his reign would not be a long one. Either one of these three men was therefore looked upon as a transitional figure, and not an empire builder.

What began as a sincere plea for an end to disunity eventually accomplished exactly the opposite. Why did it fail? Clearly, the view that this was a power grab by Iakovos played some part. It is believed that one of the signatories of the Ligonier Statement, Bishop Vsevolod of the Ukrainian archdiocese, told Bartholomew that Iakovos was getting ready to have himself declared "Patriarch of America." Although the goal of unity had been openly declared as desirable in Spyridon's earlier address to the Greek archdiocese, the inflammatory reportage of the Ligonier Conference by this particular conferee may have caused Bartholomew to question the motives of the signatories. It is just as possible that other forces, which had no desire to see a united Orthodox witness in the United States, were at work behind the scenes.

Patriarch Ignatius IV of Antioch, for example, first supported American unity and eventual autocephaly and spoke bold words to that effect in Chicago of 2000 during the annual Antiochian convocation.[7] However, when Metropolitan Philip took Ignatius up on his offer, the latter started to make excuses, accusing the American church of being "immature" and "not yet ready" for autonomy.[8] (The war of words continued for several years until June of 2002, when the Holy Synod of Antioch finally relented and granted "full autonomy" to the Antiochian archdiocese.[9]) Although Ignatius seemed to be the point man in the battle against autonomy in the immediate post-Ligonier imbroglio, it was Bartholomew who would receive most of the blame in time.

The Removal of Iakovos

Since Bartholomew's accession to the patriarchal throne, the see of Constantinople under went a renaissance of sorts. Churches had been rebuilt, and relations with the secular government of

Turkey improved markedly. The patriarchal compound in the Phanar district had been revitalized thanks to the efforts of former President Jimmy Carter and the benevolence of Theodore Angelopoulos, an Athenian steel magnate. Bartholomew himself was well-known as a major theologian and ecclesiastical figure in international circles, and after becoming Patriarch of Constantinople, an indefatigable sojourner not unlike Pope John Paul II. In addition, he kept up the theological school at Halki, refurbishing it for the day when, it was hoped, the Turkish government would allow it to reopen. (The Turkish government had closed it in 1972). Although the Christian population of Istanbul remained negligible—perhaps less than 3,000—it was hoped by some within the Phanar that, with eventual Turkish entry into the European Union, Christian immigration into Turkey would stanch the continuing hemorrhage.[10]

Whether Bartholomew feared the loss of financial support from America in the event that an American Orthodox Church become a reality, or whether he feared the loss of American political clout in facing the Turks, or whether it was nothing more than a power struggle between two strong men, in 1997 Bartholemew sent a delegation from the Holy Synod of Constantinople to force Iakovos' resignation. After a 39-year career as the dean of American Orthodoxy, the longest tenure in American Orthodox history, Iakovos was forced to step down. For many, Orthodoxy in America had begun with his tenure, as it was Iakovos who brought the Church to the American consciousness. Despite missteps along the way, to the fullest extent possible, Iakovos bridged ethnic divisions and forged an Orthodox consensus. He almost succeeded in creating the American Orthodox Church.

The End of an Era: Spyridon Replaces Iakovos

To replace the giant void left in North America, Bartholemew sent his protÈgÈ, Spyridon Papageorge, who in 1994 addressed the

Chicago clergy-laity conference and spoke bold words of unity. As Metropolitan of Italy, Spyridon, like Bartholomew, was well-educated, urbane and conversant in several languages. The fact that he was American-born and thus cognizant of American mores and customs seemed to be a feather in his cap. He had been groomed for this job.

In his inaugural speech at the archdiocesan cathedral in New York (1997), Spyridon, again to thunderous applause and in the presence of bishops from every other ethnic jurisdiction, once more affirmed the need to move beyond ethnic ghettos.[11] Even though Iakovos was going to be replaced, it seemed to everyone that his legacy would continue; and given Spyridon's relative youth, it appeared that unity was just around the corner. Moreover, the end of ethnic factionalism had the imprimatur of Bartholomew himself, or so it seemed.

To effect the transition from Iakovos to Spyridon, and possibly to weaken opposition to himself, Bartholomew unilaterally divided up the former Archdiocese of North and South America into four separate metropolitan districts: Canada, the United States, Central America, and the Caribbean and South America. Although from a cultural and demographic standpoint this made eminent sense, the legality of it remained an open question.[12] Since the former archdiocesan structure was headquartered in New York state, some looked to the possibility of bringing suit against the Phanar in civil court, charging that such an action violated the charter of the archdiocese, which empowers only the biennial clergy-laity conferences to effect such a change. More ominously, the nine diocesan seats that had been created in 1977 under the earlier charter had now been downgraded to mere auxiliaries in a move reminiscent of what Athenagoras had done 60 years earlier to the dioceses of Chicago, Boston and San Francisco. Although the bishops of these cities remained in residence within them, they were stripped of their titles and deprived of any canonical authority. Like Athenagoras,

Spyridon had aggrandized power within his own person (although, it must be said, this was done under the orders of the Phanar).

Spyridon, however, was still viewed as a unifier rather than a spoiler, and no lawsuit was brought. Although Spyridon's new title ("Archbishop of America") was clumsy and possibly non-canonical (as was the earlier title "Archbishop of North and South America," since one can only be a bishop of a city, e.g., "Archbishop of Athens and All Greece"), the majority of parishioners within the Greek jurisdiction accepted matters as they stood. Still, rumblings were being heard, not only among many of the laity, but from the recently downgraded bishops as well.

Spyridon: The Beginning of the End

Unfortunately for Spyridon, events quickly spun out of control. The catalyst for opposition to him occurred during a party that took place on February 27, 1997, (that particular day is also called *Tsiknopempti*, or "Roast-Beef Thursday") on the campus of Holy Cross in Brookline, Massachusetts. According to eyewitnesses, an archimandrite from Greece who was pursuing post-graduate studies made a homosexual pass at a Palestinian undergraduate at the party. This party was by all accounts a raucous affair in which alcohol flowed freely. The undergraduate reacted violently to the overture and punched the priest in the face, giving him a black eye. A disciplinary committee made up of four senior priests from the faculty looked at the facts and concluded that, based on the best available evidence, the archimandrite had indeed provoked the incident and should be censured.[13]

Had things proceeded under the cloak of secrecy, the chances of this incident becoming known would have been minimal. However, Spyridon came to the aid of the priest in question and unilaterally fired the four tenured priests from the staff of Holy Cross, a high-handed, and possibly illegal, action that sent shock waves across parishes all over the nation. In the words of one priest, Spyridon blundered because "you don't come into town wanting to make changes with both guns blazing."[14] The priests in question, the Rev. Drs. George Dragas, Alkiviades Calivas, Theodore Stylianopoulos and Emmanuel Clapsis, had instructed nearly every Orthodox priest in North America who had graduated from Holy Cross within the last 30 years and were very well regarded by the vast majority of them. Clearly, Spyridon had overestimated his power, if not his authority.

Things then went from bad to worse. The fact that the priests in question were married men and the censured priest a homosexual led to scurrilous accusations about Spyridon and the coterie around him. The latent opposition to Spyridon was now joined by a growing number of the married clergy. In short order, the bishops of the Greek archdiocese formed another flank of opposition to him. In order to silence this flank, Bartholomew promoted five of the most senior bishops to the rank of metropolitan and gave them authority of extinct dioceses in Asia Minor, essentially an empty gesture since they still were auxiliary bishops without the right to ordain men on their own authority. For a while, it appeared that this move worked. To quiet the situation at Holy Cross, Spyridon recruited Bishop Isaiah of Denver (before he was elevated to the rank of metropolitan) as president until a newer one could be found. His tenure lasted one year.

The Orthodox Christian Laity (OCL), a group that had agitated for reform and unity since its founding in 1987, was joined by the self-styled Greek Orthodox American Leaders (GOAL). Together, they spearheaded the opposition to Spyridon. These groups set up a website that targeted dissent against Spyridon, the new charter, and by extension Patriarch Bartholomew. This website, *Voithia* ("help" in Greek), carried the subtitle "For the Good of the Church."[15] *Voithia* served as a clearinghouse for dissent and presented views counter to the official organ of the Greek jurisdiction, *The Orthodox Observer*, which was slavish in its devotion to the official line. In short order, GOAL started to overshadow the OCL, possibly because the latter group had gone off on other tangents, such as questioning the idea of a celibate episcopate and the all-male priesthood, among other things.

In an effort to spread the word, GOAL somehow acquired the archdiocesan mailing list and sent a mass mailing to every steward of the archdiocese, an action that certainly skirted the law if not actually broke it. Spyridon chose to sue GOAL in civil court, but the newly elevated metropolitans (Methodius of Boston, Iakovos of Chicago, Maximus of Pittsburgh, Isaiah of Denver and Anthony of San Francisco) chose not to join him in the suit, citing Paul's exhortation to Christians (1 Corinthians 6:1) against using secular authority to enforce church discipline. Spyridon was therefore undercut by the most senior bishops of the Greek archdiocese.

The momentum against Spyridon continued to grow. The newly elevated metropolitans chafed at the fact that, despite the grandiosity of their titles, they were essentially straw men. In fact, their actual titles in Greek bordered on the ridiculous. For example, Metropolitan Anthony of the Dardenelles held the title *"Proedros* of San Francisco;" *proedros* literally means "president." According to one source, one of the metropolitans complained that "if I went around calling myself 'President of Y', people would think I'm nuts."

In order to avoid this absurdity, their titles were rendered in English to "Presiding *Hierarch* of Y". This was essentially a distinction without a difference, as the only change in status that this afforded them was that, from now on, during the Great Litany, priests and deacons only had to commemorate their diocesan bishop (as "Archbishop John of Y") who was now a member of the "Holy Eparchial Synod." The new metropolitans in turn commemorated only the ecumenical patriarch. A somewhat clumsy situation was created whereby the new metropolitans were themselves archbishops and thus technically equal to Spyridon. By not mentioning the name of the archbishop in New York, the essential unity of the archdiocese was therefore called into question. In effect, a divide-and-conquer stratagem had been employed.

Despite the metropolitans' displeasure and their publication of an open letter to the ecumenical patriarch that GOAL mass-mailed to every home in the archdiocese, they were openly told in one meeting at the Phanar in January of 1997 that there was nothing they could do.[16] Supporters of Spyridon, in response to the tactics employed by GOAL, set up a rival organization, Greek Orthodox American Stewards (GOAS), that countered the claims of GOAL with their own charges. Some of the charges leveled by Spyridon's partisans against the GOAL/*Voithia*/OCL nexus included the accusation that the opponents of Spyridon wanted to "de-Hellenize" the Church and do away with Greek festivals. (As to the latter charge, one parish council president wrote on the *Voithia* website: "Great! Where do I sign up?") Other charges overstepped the bounds of propriety and accused prominent laymen of attempting to bribe the patriarch.[17] By leveling this accusation, they in effect called into question Bartholomew's own integrity in suggesting that he was susceptible to such gross gestures.

The Removal of Spyridon

Spyridon's pastorate was not without its successes. For one thing, he managed to effect reconciliation between one of the Old-Calendar Greek dioceses headed by Bishop Paisius of Tyana (headquartered in Astoria, New York) in April of 1998. Together with Paisius's deputy, Bishop Vikentios of Apameia, this diocese, with its one monastery and 12 parishes and missions, was brought back into the canonical fold, although it was allowed to retain its liturgical schedule.[18] It was during this time as well that the archdiocese entered the age of the Internet and developed its web page and even broadcast services live. During Spyridon's tenure, Patriarch Bartholomew conducted two pastoral visits to the United States. The first one, in 1997, was quite successful on its own merits and heightened American awareness of Orthodoxy. It also enabled the Greek archdiocese to temporarily unite and sweep their differences under the rug. By the time the second one occurred a year later, the mood was far more subdued and it was nowhere near as well publicized.

However, the blunders committed by Spyridon and his partisans outweighed these few successes. Some of these blunders included financial misfeasance in the procurement of a home on Long Island for the archbishop valued at $1.1 million. Because of procedural irregularities, the 10% down payment was lost. Accusations that he wanted to bring the Philiptochos's treasury under his direct control led to estrangement with the leaders of this charity. The OCMC (Orthodox Christian Mission Center), which is also under the auspices of the Greek Orthodox archdiocese, likewise resisted efforts by him to restrict its independence.

Other missteps included demoting Fr. Robert Stephanopoulos, the dean of the archdiocesan cathedral and perhaps the most senior priest in the Greek jurisdiction, and replacing him with an archimandrite loyal to Spyridon. (Father Stephanopoulos is also the father of George Stephanopoulos, a political operative in the Clinton administration.) This action further eroded what little support he still enjoyed.

Indications of the deterioration were on display at the Clergy-Laity Congress of 1998 (held in Orlando, Florida), when angry words were exchanged publicly between Spyridon and the leadership of the Philoptochos. Early the next year, officials in the Diocese of Denver requested that the parish of the Annunciation in Houston, Texas, the largest in the Diocese of Denver (and the fourth largest in the archdiocese), withhold its annual assessment to New York. According to one parish council member, diocesan officials requested that the money be placed in an escrow account until it could be released at a time deemed "more appropriate."[19]   Daily updates on the *Voithia* website described a crisis atmosphere, and it quickly became obvious that, sooner or later, the issue would come to a head.

The "last straw" happened in June of 1999, when several other parishes withheld their annual assessment from the archdiocese; this resulted in a crisis of confidence that could not be repaired as long as Spyridon was at the helm. A critical mass had been reached, and Bartholomew realized that Spyridon's tenure had become untenable. In due course, Patriarch Bartholomew "accepted" Spyridon's resignation and reassigned him to the non-existent Metropolis of Chaldea, an empty gesture that was mitigated somewhat with a generous retirement package. To his credit, Spyridon wrote a conciliatory letter absolving anybody from blame and asking for forgiveness for any actions he may have taken that upset the integrity of the archdiocese. He entered a self-imposed exile in Portugal.

Aftermath: Whither American Orthodoxy?

To replace Spyridon, Bartholomew installed Metropolitan Demetrios Trakatellis, a pre-eminent theologian, scholar, published author and educator at Harvard University. In the words of many who knew him, he was a "scholar's scholar" or a "living saint." With this action, Bartholomew diffused the tense situation that had engulfed the Greek-American archdiocese during the tumultuous years of Spyridon's pastorate. Demetrios, who had to receive permission for a transfer from the Church of Greece, was a conciliator and viewed by many (because of his age) as a transitional figure. It was felt that his tenure would salve the wounds that festered and allow the Greek jurisdiction time to draw its own conclusions about the future of American Orthodoxy.

Although Demetrios was above reproach and any rational criticism, the clarion call of unity and autonomy could not be silenced forever. Many of the Greek bishops, particularly the metropolitans, felt that some effort had to be made to increase American control over the archdiocese. Negotiations with the patriarchate continued, but both sides talked past each other. The Phanar, in a stunning gesture of bad faith, rejected out-of-hand many of the American metropolitans' proposals. This, however, was not well-publicized, so amity continued for the time being.

The situation did not last, however: in early 2002, Patriarch Bartholomew issued a new charter for the archdiocese that many believed aggrandized even more power to the Phanar.[20] Although Demetrios had been spared the vituperation inflicted upon Spyridon, certain elements viewed his episcopate as a scheme to foil American unity and independence by other means.[21] Elements of GOAL and its website, *Voithia*, both of which voluntarily disbanded upon the removal of Spyridon (as they had promised to do), reassembled and redoubled their efforts and concentrated their firepower in the newly revitalized Orthodox Christian Laity. They attempted to raise one million dollars in an effort to "alert" every Greek Orthodox parish in the United States about the new "patriarchal" charter.

Several of the larger parishes petitioned the archdiocese for copies of the new charter. At first they were met with silence. However, under the growing pressure of the OCL and its concentrated effort, the archdiocese relented and sent copies to every parish council member in the United States for their "input."

This was a hollow gesture. Despite asking for lay input, the archdiocese instructed the parish priests to inform the laity that this was a "good will gesture only for informational purposes," since the Church is a "hierarchical church" and as such the laity must accept the charter regardless. This backfired on the Phanar, as every parish that viewed the new charter rejected it out of hand.

The Orthodox of America had grown restless. Other jurisdictions felt the winds of change as well. In the OCA, for example, the Holy Synod announced that Metropolitan Theodosius would retire in June 2002 due to health concerns (he had suffered a minor stroke the year before).[22] More dramatically, the Patriarchate of Antioch granted "full autonomy" to the Antiochian archdiocese.[23] Both bodies, it was believed, had timed the announcements of these actions in preparation for the Clergy-Laity Congress of the Greek archdiocese, which was to be held in the summer of 2002 in Los Angeles. Indeed, leaders from both bodies had privately informed the Greek hierarchy that they would welcome a Greek bishop as metropolitan of the American Orthodox Church and, if need be, place themselves under the *omorphorion* of the Patriarch of Constantinople as part of an autonomous (but united) American church. Metropolitan Philip of the Antiochian archdiocese spoke words to this effect in the Greek ethnic press.[24] Other clergymen and lay leaders from the other jurisdictions gave the same endorsements as well.[25]

While the autocephalous status of the OCA made this a cumbersome task to accomplish canonically speaking, the willingness of the OCA to accept Greek and even Phanariote hegemony underscored a strong desire to end the decades of strife and division. The question remained as to whether the Greek-American delegates would have the courage to "cut the Gordian knot of nationalism once and for all." Would they discuss these issues openly in Los Angeles, or would they shrink from the prospect of a united, independent American Orthodox Church? The Orthodox of North America looked to the Greek Archdiocese. Would they too cast their vote for a united American Orthodox Church?

Unity Derailed

Unfortunately, the Los Angeles Clergy-Laity Congress was anything but amicable. Delegates were told ahead of time that unity and autonomy were not to be discussed. Under intense pressure from several delegates, however, Archbishop Demetrios staged a strategic retreat and made last-minute changes to the agenda. He would allow the first two plenary sessions of the congress to be devoted to discussion of the charter. Each line would be read and commented upon by the delegates. Motions would be entertained and amendments would be offered and submitted to the Phanar.

What transpired was an often acrimonious debate. Many delegates were alarmed by the grandiosity of the events, such as the entrance of the Knights of St. Andrew[26] into the Cathedral of St. Sophia to a trumpet fanfare. (The metropolitans themselves were ushered in by a symphonic fanfare replete with spotlights during the opening session Monday morning.)

Many of the subcommittee meetings were poorly attended and little was accomplished.[27] Indeed, the entire congress was one of the most poorly attended in recent history.[28]

In the final analysis, the congress itself was viewed by many as an utter failure. Assurances were made by the hierarchy that the recommendations by the combined clergy and laity *vis a vis* the charter would be submitted and considered by the patriarchate. Few took them at their word. Many of the delegates, including clergy, left before the closing of the session. More than a few remarked that they would never again attend future congresses.

The question posed by the other jurisdictions to the Greek-Americans had, for all intents and purposes, been answered. Unity was put on the back-burner and autonomy was out of the question. As for the charter itself, the overwhelming majority of the changes suggested by the delegates were ignored by the ecumenical patriarchate.

CHAPTER 12

TOWARDS AN AMERICAN ORTHODOX CHURCH

Collegiality, Autonomy and the Territorial Principle

In considering the history of the Orthodox Church, it is useful to understand certain key elements that make the Orthodox faith distinctive from the churches of the West. For one thing, the self-understanding of the Orthodox Church is that it is not headed by any one man serving as a vicar of Christ, but by Christ Himself. In this sense, it preserves the apostolic tenor that pervaded the Church as found in the Acts of the Apostles, whereupon St. James, the first Bishop of Jerusalem, sat as president of the apostolic council and was the spokesman for the *ekklesia* as a whole, and not for himself alone (Acts 15).

This conciliarity pervaded the Church throughout its early history. When the episcopate became more formalized, protocols were developed and certain bishops of major metropolitan areas were afforded more prestige; but in the final analysis, all bishops were viewed as equals. It was for this reason that, when complicated theological matters needed to be decided, Church councils were convened with standing invitations sent out to as many bishops as possible rather than having one or two of the more prominent bishops decide the issues privately.

Since bishops enjoyed theoretical equality, it stood to reason that the Church, though unified in doctrine, was necessarily constituted of individual dioceses whose sole authority was their respective bishops. In the office of the bishop, therefore, the juridical, legislative and executive functions were concentrated in the same man. It was for this reason that councils were of extreme importance within the Church. Without councils, doctrine could develop independently along regional lines, thereby nullifying any unity in faith. Doctrine had to be recognized unanimously for it to be valid. This even extended to more mundane matters such as the observance of the festal cycles and the requirements for marriage. Only future councils could modify the decisions (canons) of past councils. In order to understand what is meant by the "canonical irregularity" of the Church in the United States today, one must first examine the decisions of the Church councils.

A Communion of Churches

At its fundamental level, the Church is a bishop and the parishes he personally oversees. In geographical regions, local bishops meet together in local synods to discuss common issues faced in their region. When they meet in synods, one bishop is the presiding officer of the synod, but he has no authority *over* the other bishops. Since bishops are equal, the Orthodox Church is ultimately a "communion of...sister churches, united in faith, sacramental life and canonical order, but in other respects, fully self-governing...having the capacity to manage its own affairs and select their own bishops...without recourse to another church."[1]

The bishops within a nation oversee the Church in the nation. Thus there are the Greek, the Russian, and the Serbian Orthodox churches, for example. While there is a patriarch or other titled chief presiding officer within each national church, this officer is no more than a bishop equal to all other bishops. The collegial nature of the Orthodox Church stands in stark contrast to the monarchial nature of the Catholic Church, where the Bishop of Rome is above the other bishops within the church. (Indeed, the closest analog in the West to the Orthodox Church is the Anglican Communion.)

The various national Orthodox churches are "fully self-governing" (i.e., "autocephalous"). Ecumenical councils established many of them at a time when the Patriarchate of Rome was still part of the united, pre-schism Christian Church.[2] As bishop of the imperial city, the Bishop of Rome enjoyed a "primacy of honor" as "first among equals" (*primus inter pares*), but his canonical authority did not extend beyond the bounds of his diocese, large though it was. As president of the episcopate, he did enjoy certain prerogatives that the other patriarchs did not, but they were of a more juridical, rather than legislative or executive, nature. For example, a bishop condemned by a local synod of heresy or some other irregularity could appeal to the pope for a retrial; if the latter thought there was any merit to his appeal, he would allow a synod of bishops from at least three contiguous dioceses to reconsider the verdict. Even the pope could not overturn the second verdict.[3] Since the Great Schism of 1054, when the Bishop of Rome separated the West from Orthodoxy, the primacy of honor passed to the bishop of the new imperial city, the Archbishop of Constantinople, later known as the ecumenical (i.e., "imperial") patriarch.

During the period of the ecumenical councils (from the fourth through the eighth centuries) independent, local churches were proclaimed by majority vote. For example, canon 2 of the second ecumenical council (Constantinople) determined that five of the eastern dioceses (Alexandria, Antioch, Asia Minor, Pontus and Thrace) were to be autocephalous.[4] The third ecumenical council (held in Ephesus), declared the Church of Cyprus to be independent of the Church of Antioch.[5] Later, Asia Minor, Pontus and Thrace were subsumed into the Patriarchate of Constantinople. During the fourth council, held in Chalcedon, the Bishop of Constantinople was accorded patriarchal status and placed second in relation to the Bishop of Rome, superseding the Patriarch of Alexandria.[6] The creation of patriarchates and autocephalous churches thus is well attested by conciliar precedent, and its historicity cannot be denied by any patriarchate.

What are the requirements for a self-governing church? First of all, a self-governing church possesses "two distinguishing marks": (1) The right to resolve all internal problems on its own authority, independent of all other churches and (2) the right to appoint its own bishops, among them their presiding head of the church.[7] As to who can elect bishops, the canons are quite respectful of local customs (the laity, for example, may or may not be involved in the actual election; however, they must assent to the candidate at least during his ordination). Despite the latitude allowed in the actual election of bishops, canon 4 of the first ecumenical council (Nicaea) mandated that at least three bishops appoint (and at least two must consecrate) another bishop. At the very minimum, then, no region can have fewer than three bishops if it is to be autocephalous.

In order to become autocephalous, a region must first be part of an already-existing church. The reason for this is that the Orthodox Church in its totality is part of the same organic whole. There can be no "independent" dioceses or jurisdictions that arise spontaneously of their own accord. In the example cited above, Cyprus was first part of Antioch, one of the most ancient of the patriarchates. Likewise, Albania, Bulgaria, Serbia, Russia and Greece were originally part of Constantinople, and Poland, Czechoslovakia, Japan and Finland were originally part of Russia and so on.

Once the first requirement that there be at least three *ruling* bishops (not auxiliaries) in a region or territory was met, a second, equally important requirement had to be met for independence to be recognized: only dioceses that were *outside* the boundaries of the mother church could have a claim to autocephaly. In other words, the boundaries of the new church must conform to the "civil" (i.e., secular) pattern.[8] This condition was met when the Russian Metropolia, a functioning diocese of the Russian Orthodox Church, was cut off from the Russian empire by the sale of Alaska to the United States in 1867. The American branch of this church was now part of a new polity and, following the commandments of St. Paul, owed allegiance to the nation in which it now resided (c f Romans 13:1-3, Titus 3:1). In fact, the Holy Synod of Russia granted permission to the clergy of its American diocese in 1906 to commemorate the President of the United States by name during its services rather than Czar Nicholas II.[9]

The territorial principle is of ancient standing in the Church. The apostolic canons that date from the synod of Antioch in 341 and the synod of Laodicia in 343[10] mandated territorial integrity: "The bishops of every nation (*ethnos*) must acknowledge him who is first among them (Apostolic Canon 34)." Of course, some insist that *ethnos* denotes an ethnic group;[11] however, canon 9 of the Council of Antioch in 341 defined *ethnos* as being a province, not a group united by racial or linguistic ties.[12] Saint Tikhon's idea of ethnic auxiliary dioceses—though laudable in intent—therefore were canonically problematic.

The boundaries of national churches were established by territoriality and not ethnicity. Various ethnic groups inside a single political territory could not establish their own ethnic churches.[13] Ethnicity was "significant only so far as it coincided with the territorial principle, but did not override it."[14] Apostolic canon 34 was reiterated in the late 19th century when certain Bulgarians living in areas claimed by Greece requested a Bulgarian bishop rather than their Greek hierarch. This heresy, called "phyletism" (tribalism) was condemned outright by the council of Constantinople (though in this instance, the intent may not have been laudable). Regardless of intention, the effect of this condemnation is straightforward: tribalism can have no place within the Church.

Autocephaly and How It is Proclaimed

Following the foundation of the apostolic churches (Ephesus, Antioch, Rome, etc.), Orthodox ecclesiology provided two methods for the formation of an autocephalous (or "local" or "national") church. They are: (1) its declaration as such by an ecumenical council and (2) the granting of independence by a pre-existing "mother church." [15] In both cases, however, it should be noted that a local church *could only arise from a pre-existing church*. This is because, in Orthodox eyes, the Church is an organic whole, founded by Jesus Himself in Jerusalem *ca* AD 30. From the original mother church of Jerusalem, therefore, the Apostles radiated first to Antioch, then to Alexandria, Rome and so on, establishing churches in each of these cities.

For many centuries, however, Constantinople has argued that the preferred method for granting autocephaly is by declaration of an ecumenical council or by permission of the Patriarchate of Constantinople itself. As such, the autocephaly of the Church of Cyprus, for example, or the elevation of Jerusalem and Constantinople to patriarchal status is non-controversial since ecumenical councils decreed these actions. In reality, these councils merely ratified claims of autocephaly that were declared by these churches or already granted to them by their mother churches. Nor was there anything sacred about the number of autocephalous churches or about the primatial order. Indeed, the Bishop of Rome was recognized as the first among equals simply because Rome was the premier city of the classical world. The Bishop of Alexandria likewise was viewed second only to the Pope simply because Alexandria was the second-most important city in the Roman Empire. When Constantinople replaced Rome and Alexandria as the political and cultural capital of the Empire, the council of Chalcedon ruled that its bishop was now second only to Rome (canon 28). The primatial order, therefore, is an *administrative* decision and not a *theological* one.

Councils do not arise in vacuums but are called to solve problems; the first council was called to settle the Arian controversy and the date of Pascha, for example. The fourth council, which elevated the Bishop of Constantinople to patriarchal status likewise addressed the issue of his status in relation to the Popes of Rome and Alexandria. Therefore, the ratification of autonomy presupposes an already-existing claim of independence that the council must address. This means that the second method is in reality the first means by which a church becomes independent, whereas the first method, the ratification of its autocephaly by an ecumenical council, is posterior to it.

With the Great Schism of 1054, the era of the councils passed. In the absence of a new council, the ecumenical patriarch used canon 28 of the fourth ecumenical council as its authorization for being the sole source for declaring autocephaly. In a letter to Alexis II, Patriarch of Moscow and All Russia, dated April 11, 2002, Ecumenical Patriarch Bartholomew cited canon 28 as to his authorization for declaring the Estonian church to be autocephalous from Moscow in addition to his interpretation of the American crisis. Alexis, in his reply, disputed Bartholomew's interpretation of the canon and reminded Bartholomew of the history of the Church regarding the principle of territoriality established by the apostolic canons. Alexis cited the "the historical facts showing that until the 1920's, the Patriarchate of Constantinople had no actual power over the entire Orthodox diaspora in the world, nor did it claim this power."[16] Bartholomew was concerned about America and its "division of the Orthodox, in defiance of the sacred canons, especially among those living in Western countries, into ethnic and racial groups and churches led by bishops elected on ethnic and racial grounds, who were often not the only ones in each city and sometimes not in good but hostile relations to one another. It is a disgrace for entire Orthodoxy and a reason for unfavorable responses working against it."[17] The issue between Bartholomew and Alexis was not the crisis in America. On that they were agreed. The issue was who was to blame and whose task it was to resolve the situation.

Because Bartholomew believed a church becomes independent only with Constantinople's approval, he blamed the American mess on the Church of Russia for having granted independence to the Metropolia. Alexis on the other hand believed that mother churches should grant independence to those national churches to which they have given birth. He defended granting autocephaly in 1970 and blamed Constantinople for the present mess: "It is sad that the holy Church of Constantinople did not support the 1970 Act and did not help in ensuring the unity desired so much. This remains to this day a cause of disorder and dissatisfaction with their status felt by many Orthodox people in America."[18]

The innovative arguments of the ecumenical patriarchate notwithstanding, the method practiced throughout the history of the Church was for a mother church to grant autonomy to a metropolitan district that had been cut off from it because political boundaries had changed (and which has at least three active dioceses headed by bishops). The recent correspondence between Bartholomew and Alexis identifies the differences between a monarchial and a collegial approach, the differences between Constantinople and the rest of the Orthodox world.

How Can Unity be Affected?

Before unity can be demanded, every American Orthodox must understand one salient fact: as long as we are dependencies of Old World patriarchates, our own Christian witness will be mitigated. The tumultuous history of the Orthodox Church in America is filled with several instances of interference from the Old World that hobbled the Orthodox witness in North America. Very often, these incidents occurred at the behest of anti-Christian secular or Islamic governments. Several of the most venerable and ancient patriarchates are not independent of forces hostile to Christianity and are hostages to external political realities and agendas. The following are examples of this situation: (1) Archbishop Tikhon of New York asked for a Greek bishop to help minister to Greek immigrants, the Turkish sultan refused the Patriarch of Constantinople permission outright; (2) Metropolitan Sergius, *locum tenens* of the Moscow patriarchate, attempted to force loyalty oaths to the Soviet government on all American priests of the Metropolia; (3) the Soviet government forced the Patriarchate of Moscow to place all American bishops of the Metropolia under interdict, forbidding them from celebrating the services of the Church on three different occasions; and (4) the Living Church used the American judiciary to force the Metropolia to turn over its cathedral in New York City.

All of the above examples happened in the pre-World War II era. They did not stop during the Cold War. Modern examples include: (1) the Church Abroad was able to interfere in the affairs of the Metropolia, again by means of the American judiciary, which ruled that it could not declare autonomy without going through the "normal" channels because it was "merged" with the Church Abroad and (2) Patriarch Alexis I of Moscow (Metropolitan Sergius's successor) issued a decree that said Russian-Americans were forced by "theological" necessity to be loyal to the Soviet state.

Even with the fall of the Soviet state, interference by secular and anti-Christian overlords is still rather common: (1) the unity that Metropolitan Spyridon of Italy proclaimed was necessary in 1994 was stopped dead in its tracks, most probably by the Turkish government, which welcomed the resultant anarchy that engulfed the Greek-American community and (2) during a pan-Orthodox meeting of all the heads of the autocephalous Churches held in Israel and the Palestinian Authority in January of 2000, Patriarch Ignatius IV of Antioch was forbidden to attend by his overlord, President Hafez el-Assad of Syria.

It is one thing to demand unity, it is quite another to implement it. The first question concerning unity—is unity necessary?—has been answered in the preceding pages. By now it should be obvious: not only is it necessary, but anything less than unity is non-canonical. Multiple jurisdictions that are currently in place are a canonical nightmare. Ten jurisdictions deem themselves canonical while deeming the other 22 non-canonical. Why, for example, is "The True Orthodox Church" non-canonical but the Greek Orthodox Archdiocese of America canonical? All of the ethnic exarchates are, strictly speaking, in schism from the Archdiocese of the Aleutians and North America, which was established in 1799.

The second step on the road to unity already has been taken with the establishment of SCOBA and the convocation of various inter-Orthodox symposia of clergy and lay theologians. The third step also has been taken, which is to say that clergy representing the various jurisdictions have concelebrated hundreds of times. The fourth step is no less important: the people, the *laos*, must demand unity. With the establishment of various laity-led organizations such as the Federation of Orthodox Churches, Orthodox Christian Laity, Orthodox People Together and such, we are certainly well on our way of achieving this goal. All laymen in all jurisdictions must declare, "Enough of this division!" and they must hold their clergy accountable.

The final question then is: how is the United States to be administered as one Church? Of course, problems of real estate and incorporation must be tended to so that no legal irregularities are committed. For this reason, a legal committee of attorneys and theologians under the chairmanship of an auxiliary bishop who has no diocesan position must be appointed. Each new diocese must be viewed (for legal purposes only) as a new corporation. The purpose of this committee would be to make sure that no city has more than one bishop and that all diocesan properties, parishes and institutions are merged into the new corporation. Canonical order should be followed as much as possible. The presiding hierarch should be the Archbishop of Washington, DC and his title should be Metropolitan of the United States. Likewise, each diocesan seat should be in the capital city of a state. Each bishop should be equal to his peers but, for purposes of unity, the metropolitan may make the first appointment of priests and deacons.

As for how many dioceses the new Church should have, for the 40 or so canonically ordained bishops who comprise the 10 jurisdictions of SCOBA, each one could be given a new diocese headquartered in one of the 40 largest cities of the United States. They should each convene a biennial clergy-laity conference in their respective dioceses and likewise meet in the alternate years in an All-American Council to be chaired by the primate of the Church. These 40 or so diocesan bishops would of course comprise the Holy Synod of the United States, and it would be their duty to elect the new primate upon vacancy of that office. As for the election of diocesan bishops, they should be chosen from a list of candidates nominated by the clergy and laity of the diocese in question. This list should then be forwarded to the Holy Synod of the United States for election.

Because of the vast size of the continental United States, it may be appropriate to consider dividing the country into metropolitan regions or archdioceses such as the Far West (to include Alaska and Hawaii), the Mountain West, the Midwest, the Southwest, the South, the East Coast (New York, New Jersey and Connecticut), the Ohio Valley, New England and the Mid-Atlantic (Washington, DC; Maryland; Delaware and Virginia). The Archbishop of the premier city in each region (e.g., Los Angeles, Denver, Dallas, Chicago, Atlanta, New York City, Pittsburgh, Boston and Washington, DC) could be designated as "metropolitan" of that specific region, but, given the canonical parameters that mandate the official equality of each bishop, this would be an honorific title rather than an administrative one.

Every archdiocese and/or metropolitan region should be encouraged not only to build and maintain parishes but have at least one men's monastery, one women's monastery, a parochial school and an orphanage. If the idea of a metropolitan district is accepted, then each one of these regional subdivisions should have a seminary for the training of priests and deacons and a yearly consistory for the training of chanters, choir directors and parish council members.

The role of the laity is not to be downplayed either. In keeping with the directives of the All-Russian Sobor of 1917 as well as countless American councils, it is vital that the laity be given as much a role to play as possible. Indeed, the push for unity is largely the result of the laity as the hierarchy has been too easily controlled by overseas patriarchates in the past. It is for this reason that laymen and laywomen seriously consider the formation of lay fraternities such as *Zoe* in Greece or the Trophy-Bearers in Russia, which are comprised of dedicated laymen involved in secular professions and trades but who have an abiding love for the Church and fierce dedication to it. An excellent example at present in the United States is the Philoptochos Society, a sorority of dedicated laywomen who are concerned with the alleviation of poverty. Likewise, brotherhoods could be organized that supports traditionalism in iconography, hymnography or Orthodox standards of architecture. Endowments could be set up which could provide seed money to parishes that are struggling to implement reforms along these lines.

Brotherhoods have been the hallmark of American civic life from its very inception. De Tocqueville himself commented on the pervasiveness of societies dedicated to temperance, abolition and the like during his travels in the United States in the 1830's. Today, of course, there are more of these societies, and many have been helpful in promoting various Orthodox jurisdictions in the past, even though they were not of an ecclesiastical nature themselves (e.g., AHEPA). Perhaps church-dedicated groups such as Orthodox People Together, Orthodox Christian Laity, Syndesmos, etc., could reassess their missions and reconstitute themselves into lay brotherhoods (or sisterhoods). These new groups could be all male or all female or open to both of the sexes.

The need for such dedicated organizations is great simply because the clergy are constrained from taking leadership roles on certain issues, and some of them may not possess the requisite skill. Laymen who are independent of the administrative hierarchy have much to offer in bolstering the prophetic ministry of the Church, and it is very often from activist groups that reform can occur (as was the case with the removal of Archbishop Spyridon). Men drawn from their ranks can be trained in theology and homiletics so that the ancient office of lay preacher (*kyrix*) is reactivated. (In many lands of the Old World, it was the preacher who delivered the sermon following the Gospel reading.) These men could travel from parish to parish, serving in the Sanctuary and in delivering the homily, and provide continuity between parishes that would strengthen inter-Orthodox ties.

The Rite of Catechumens should be re-instituted, and churches should be refurbished with Narthexes and adult baptisteries that can accommodate them. Soup kitchens and homeless shelters should be erected in every major city with or without government help. In order to implement evangelism and accommodate adult baptism, an honest assessment of the office of deaconess must be undertaken as well. The task is daunting, but for those who know their history, none of this is novel to Orthodoxy.

Nor should we forget the central rite of what makes us Orthodox Christians: the Divine Liturgy itself. The language issue must be resolved immediately. A liturgical commission of all jurisdictions must meet to standardize the use of English. Simply put, the language must be elegant but understandable, the music should be as far from performance-based as possible and iconography should likewise be faithful to Orthodox norms. The time is right to re-educate the people that they are the Royal Priesthood and not hostages to elitists who view them as observers rather than participants.

Of course, many of the Old World patriarchates fear the loss of their American exarchates, believing that they would suffer. It does not follow that this would be the case. God has been exceedingly kind to us in America with our vast resources. Despite our traditional ethnic insularity, we have established viable missions through the OCMC and the IOCC, which together raise millions of dollars yearly for the alleviation of suffering and the evangelism of the Gospel to thousands in the third world. It is thus impossible to believe that a united American Church would ignore the mother churches from which we sprang. Indeed, by the consolidation of dioceses, ministries and institutions, the cost-savings could be significant and surpluses therefore could be spent more wisely. The avenues open to the people of the Church, as well as to world Orthodoxy in general, would be greatly expanded if the various ethnic jurisdictions would unite as the American Orthodox Church.

Where Do We Go from Here?

The time for unity is long past. What Metropolitan Spyridon discussed in 1994, what alarmed Patriarch Dimitrios of Constantinople during his visit here in 1990, is what we have been living with since the 1920's—a non-canonical situation that will eventually undermine the faith. Because of this disunity, there is no Orthodox identity in the United States; instead, we are balkanized in ways that ensure that we will not be taken seriously in the foreseeable future.

Consider the recent events of September 11, 2001, the worst terrorist attack in history. Three days after the attacks, at the National Cathedral in Washington, DC (on the feast day of the Holy Cross, no less!), religious leaders representing Catholicism, Protestantism, Judaism and even Islam were present; yet not one Orthodox bishop was invited to give a prayer. What witness could we have provided the American people and Christendom in general-

—indeed, all of Western civilization—had all canonically-ordained Orthodox bishops celebrated a doxology of the Holy Cross? The witness, of course, would have been that we in the East have carried the Cross countless times in the past, against the hordes of Attila, Mohammed, Tamerlane and Lenin, often paying the ultimate price. Our witness at this ecumenical prayer service would have told our countrymen, "Take comfort. The hour is bleak. But it is not the end."

Who among the great historians doubts that, if the Byzantines had not held the line against Islam for as long as they did, Western civilization would not have progressed? If the Serbs had not sacrificed their nation at the Field of Kosovo in 1389, would the Catholics under King John Sobieski have been able to repel the Turks at the Gates of Vienna?[19]

Those who are secularly minded think that life would not have been essentially different under a resurgent Islam. They rightly point out that Christianity is allowed to exist under Muslim regimes and, to a point, they are correct. But let us think about the nature of the Church in the Islamic world: is it by any stretch of the imagination free or robust? Christians in the Near East, whether they are Orthodox, Catholic, Nestorian, Anglican, Evangelical or Coptic, practice their faith in a hostile environment that differs from the Soviet oppression only by degree, not kind. Our most ancient patriarchates—Antioch, Alexandria, Constantinople and Jerusalem— are in real danger of extinction. What makes the average Western Christian think that their own denominations would have been more viable had Charles Martel not turned back the Moors at Poitiers in AD 832, a victory granted to him only because the Byzantines had destroyed the navy of the caliphate 100 years earlier?

How are we to minister to the West in our present state? The challenges facing civilization from new-age occultism, materialism and Islamo-fascism are going to be even more horrific than what we have experienced even now. The ancient patriarchates are moribund and the Russian and Slavic churches are hobbled economically, only now rising from the rubble of communism. Either the American exarchates unite as the canons of the Church mandate, or we will have no choice but to cede the battlefield to the heterodox Charismatic and Evangelical churches that, for all their faults, are unabashed in their devotion to the Gospel (despite their misinterpretation of it).

This book is not about doing away with food-festivals or ethnic parishes; it is about maintaining the purity of the faith. This can only be done if we are one American Orthodox Church. To believe otherwise is the height of foolishness. For us to evangelize America we need to be true to our Orthodox tradition, revitalize our liturgical life, partake of the sacraments with sincerity and boldly proclaim the Gospel, not in touchy-feely, politically correct language but in the way Orthodoxy has traditionally proclaimed the eternal truths of Christianity. A fragmented church would not have survived 300 years of Roman persecution. A fragmented church would not have survived 500 years of Islamic persecution. A fragmented church would not have survived 70 years of horrific Soviet persecution. A fragmented church will not be able to survive individualistic and secularized modern America. It is for good cause that our Lord prayed for the unity of the Church. He knew we could not survive without it.

That they all may be as one, as thou, Father, art in me, and I in thee, that they also may be one in us: that the world may believe that thou has sent me. (John 18:21)

THE AMERICAN ORTHODOX CHURCH

The Mission of the Church to America and the Non-Orthodox

In discussing the history of the various jurisdictions of American Orthodoxy, it almost seems as if the Church were an afterthought in the history of the American experience. The vast migrations that usurped the Kodiak mission, overwhelming its ability to create an authentic native American Orthodoxy, can be viewed as unfortunate in light of the more normative Orthodox experience. Certainly, the eclipse of the Church in Alaska and its continuing impoverishment remains a scandal.

Nevertheless, the Orthodox Church is what it is. The waves of immigrants that planted parishes, often in defiance of canonical norms, must be viewed as providential in the final analysis. In spite of the uneven nature of sacramental observance, the highly uncanonical nature of multiple jurisdictions, the ethnic squabbling and uneven liturgical practices, Orthodoxy in America is not without its successes.

All too often, we forget that the Church is a theanthropic institution, which is to say that it is divine as well as human. Despite its many apparent failings, the Church has as its head Jesus Christ, who is the same yesterday, today and forever.[1] For every misstep made by Orthodox Christians, there have been successes. Some of these include charities such as the International Orthodox Christian Charities, which dispenses essential needs and services to impoverished people regardless of creed the world over. The Philoptochos, which dispenses charity to needy people in the United States, is the largest ladies benevolent association in America.

The Orthodox Christian Missions Center is active in countries all over the third world. They have built churches in Ghana, Kenya,

Cameroon and Indonesia, to list only a few. Through their Support a Mission Priest Project (SAMP), they are able to underwrite the salaries of indigenous clergy. Likewise, they sponsor American medical missionaries to help provide basic medical care to our Orthodox brethren in the third world. In Central America, they send Americans to help build housing; in Alaska, dilapidated churches are being rebuilt.

One of the largest orphanages in the United States, Trinity Services (formerly Guadalupe Homes), is run by the Greek Orthodox Archdiocese of America. It is headquartered in California and provides housing, basic educational and medical services for thousands of homeless, destitute or otherwise orphaned children of every race and ethnicity. Trinity, OCMC, IOCC, and other such institutions are indications that American Orthodoxy is breaking out of its ethnic ghettos and shedding it tribalism in favor of realizing its mission to the broader, non-Orthodox world. This can only be for the good of all involved.

Spiritual Renewal

Since the fall of the Berlin Wall, American parishes have been sending church supplies to recently reopened churches in Romania, Yugoslavia, Ukraine and even Russia. Orthodox monasticism, which had been almost non-existent in America, is now vibrant and growing. Monasteries for both men and women are no longer unusual. By some estimates, there are well over 200 such institutions all over the United States.[2] Although a majority of these are old calendarist and not associated with the SCOBA-led jurisdictions, they provide a vital spiritual link to Orthodox laymen of all jurisdictions.

Part and parcel of this spiritual renewal is the interest in the Jesus Prayer, asceticism and more frequent sacramental participation. Renewed interest in Byzantine and Slavonic chant, traditionalist iconography and attendance at Vespers and Matins is also on the increase. Fasting during Great Lent is no longer viewed with automatic derision by some of the more assimilated members of the Church. Many choose to stand throughout the services of the Church, despite the presence of pews.

The presence of Orthodox Christians and clergymen in the pro-life movement is also on the increase. Though nowhere near as vocal as the Catholic and Evangelical churches, the Orthodox Church has maintained a consistent teaching on this subject, as it has on other issues (such as homosexual unions, polyamory, etc.) that are tearing apart the fabric of American society. Many disenchanted Christians from other denominations are flocking to Orthodoxy simply because of the spiritual wounding they have experienced from their own churches' accommodation to the *zeitgeist*. Orthodoxy, in spite of its own self-inflicted wounds, provides to all who wish to partake of it a consistent, scriptural worldview that does not succumb to the whims of the moment.

To be sure, part of this interest in a more authentic observance of Orthodoxy can result in zealotry, bigotry and even fanaticism. Anti-Semitism, never completely eradicated from the Christian tradition, can rear its ugly head among some of the more extreme elements of Orthodoxy. Often, these elements make common cause with the environmentalists, anti-globalists and other paranoid elements within the secular world. Sometimes, however, the willingness of many secularists to tar the Orthodox Church with the anti-Semitic paintbrush is unfair, since the indigenous Christians of the Holy Land themselves have suffered greatly because of the policies of Israel. Unfortunately, the Church, particularly its (dwindling) Arab component invites such accusations due to its schizophrenic view of Islam. (The often sympathetic views of many of the Old World patriarchs towards Islam in general and Mohammed in particular are theologically distressing to the say the least.[3])

Where Do We Go from Here?

The idea that Orthodoxy in America is at a crossroads is certainly not new. It must be said, however, that with the tumult following Ligonier, it has acquired an urgency that is very reminiscent of the cleavage of the Metropolia from Moscow in 1918. Unlike the period from 1918 to 1960, however, the American church cannot simply muddle along any longer.

The reason for this is obvious: the immigration that kept the ethnic exarchates functioning is now over and done with. Orthodoxy in America cannot continue to survive as it is presently constituted. Although it has done much to shed its xenophobia, the fact remains that the continuing existence of ethnic jurisdictions will always hinder its vision as a "native" church.

Under these conditions, the creation of social services such as Trinity, IOCC, etc., is almost an afterthought. Although they certainly indicate a willingness to provide a Christian witness to the non-Orthodox, their long-term survival depends on an official, American Orthodox presence. Likewise, evangelism cannot proceed until the Orthodox in America come to the realization that, despite its Evangelical/Enlightenment roots, America is no longer a Christian nation. The pluralism that is celebrated among our secular elites is but a transition stage from one orthodoxy (a Protestant one) to another (Islam? Materialism? Neo-paganism?).

Orthodoxy must become American, evangelical and united. Else, it will fail, and likely, America with it.

NOTES

PROLOGUE

[1] Alexander Bogolepov, *Towards an American Orthodox Church: The Establishment of an Autocephalous Orthodox Church,* (Crestwood, New York: SVS Press, Rev. ed., 2001), p.89.

[2] Much of the information for this chapter comes from a lecture series (*The Orthodox Church in Alaska*) given by Fr. Michael Oleksa and produced by the Eagle River Institute of Orthodox Christian Studies, which was delivered over the period of August 1-5, 1997, at St. John Orthodox Christian Cathedral, Eagle River, Alaska.

[3] Timothy (Bishop Kallistos) Ware, *The Orthodox Church* (London, England: Penguin, 1993), p. 173.

CHAPTER 1

[1] Timothy Ware, *The Orthodox Church* (London: Penguin, 1993 ed.), p. 173.

[2] Mark Stokoe, O*rthodox Christians in North America: 1794-1994* (Orthodox Christian Publications, 1995), p.6.

[3] Ibid.

[4] Ibid, pp. 7-8.

[5] Ivan Golikov, an earlier partner of Shelikov's, had been attacked in 1781 by an Aleut war party that sank his ship and murdered most of his crew.

[6] Britannica 2000

[7] Stokoe, Op. cit., p. 8

[8] Ibid.

[9] To this day, Ivan Khuskutov's name is synonymous with "bogey-man" among Aleuts. He later became commandant of Ft. Ross, where his house is maintained as a historical site today.

[10] "St. Herman of Alaska: Ascetic and Wonderworker," www.ptialaska.net/~stherman/stherman/htm.

[11] Ibid.

[12] Oleksa, Op. cit.

[13] St. Herman's feast day is commemorated on December 13.

[14] "St. Juvenaly, Protomartyr of America," www.ptialaska.net/~stherman/stjuven.htm.

[15] St. Juvenaly's feast day is commemorated on September 24.

[16] The highest office, that of Patriarch of Moscow, had been forced into abeyance by Peter the Great in the 17th century. Therefore the highest office then extant was that of Metropolitan of Moscow.

[17] The story of Innocent of Irkutsk had a profound influence on the young John Popov, and he took the name Innocent when he received monastic tonsure later in life. Upon graduation from the seminary, he took as his surname Veniaminov, after Bishop Benjamin, the rector, a man whom John looked upon as a father.

[18] Ware, Op. cit., p. 181.

[19] Oleksa, Op. cit. Contrary to popular belief, the Jesuits had nothing to do with Peter's martyrdom. "Jesuit" was simply a common Russian idiom for any Roman Catholic priest at that time.

[20] Stokoe, Op. cit., p. 15.

[21] Aleksei II, "St. Innocent," www.cygnus.uwa.edu.au/~jgrapsas/pages/innocent/htm.

[22] St. Innocent's feast day is celebrated on March 31.

[23] The Russian-American Trading Company had established Ft. Ross in 1812. The name Ross is actually derived from the word "Russia."

[24] Oleksa, Op. cit.

[25] St. Peter the Aleut's feast day is celebrated on September 24.

[26] Oleksa, Op. cit.

[27] Stokoe, Op. cit., p. 15.

[28] St. Jacob's feast day is celebrated on July 26.

[29] According to Oleksa, the Russian population never amounted to more than 700 men, women and children at any one time during the Alaskan colonial period.

[30] Acts 2:8.

[31] Matthew 28:18-20.

[32] Stokoe, Op. cit., pp.15-16.

[33] Ibid.

[34] Oleksa,Op. cit.

[35] Stokoe, Op. cit., p. 20.

[36] Ibid, p. 22.

CHAPTER 2

[1] Timothy Ware, *The Orthodox Church*, p. 75.

[2] Ibid.

[3] For an excellent summary of the expansion of Orthodox Christianity northward, see *The Orthodox Church*, pp. 73-86.

[4] Kenneth Scott Latourrette, *A History of Christianity* (New York: Harper & Row, Publishers, 1953), p. 287.

[5] See Matthew Perry, *The Middle East: Fourteen Islamic Centuries* (Englewood Cliffs, New Jersey: Prentice Hall, 2nd ed., 1992); Bat Ye'or (trans. Miriam Kochan and David Littman), *The Decline of Eastern Christianity under Islam: From Jihad to Dhimmitude, Seventh-Twentieth Century* (Rutherford, New Jersey: Fairleigh Dickinson Univ. Press/Associated University Presses, 1996); and Sir Steven Runciman, *The Great Church in Captivity* (Cambridge, England: Cambridge Univ. Press, 1968).

[6] See Luke 12:42-48.

[7] See Fr. Alexander Schmemann's "Holy Things Are for the Holy," printed as the Appendix in *Great Lent* (Crestwood, New York: SVS Press, 1996, pp. 107-133), for a discussion of the spiritual decay that has transpired within Orthodoxy since its subjugation by Islam.

[8] Philip K. Hitti, *History of the Arabs* (New York: St. Martin's Press, 10th ed., 1970), pp. 734-735.

[9] Immigration statistics are often unclear in regards to the Turkish Empire. Syrians, Palestinians and even Levantine Jews were often designated simply as "Turkish" immigrants.

[10] Stokoe, Op. cit., p. 31.

[11] Many proud liberals of the 19th and early 20th centuries were driven by the need to acculturate non-Protestant immigrants into the folkways and religiosity of Anglo-Saxon Americans. Exemplars included Horace Mann who created the American system of public education as a reaction against the growing Catholic parochial system. One of Mann's avowed purposes was divesting non-Protestant children of their "superstitious" religious practices in favor of more correct Protestant piety. Even revolutionaries like Benjamin Franklin were horrified by the prospect of Germans "overwhelming" the native English stock in his beloved Pennsylvania.

[12] Theodore Saloutos, *The Greeks of the United States* (Cambridge: Harvard Univ. Press, 1964), p. 69.

[13] E.D. Karampetsos, "Mining the Past: Helen Papanikolas and the Greeks of Utah," (*Odyssey,* Jan/Feb 2002), p. 54.

[14] Stokoe, Op. cit., p. 31.

[15] Ibid, p. 30.

[16] Stokoe, p. 22.

[17] Ibid, p. 32.

[18] Ibid, p. 19.

[19] Ibid, p. 33.

[20] Ibid, p. 32.
[21] Ibid, p. 21.

[22] Ibid, pp. 45-53.
[23] Ibid, pp. 45-53.
[24] Saloutos, Op. cit., p. 121.
[25] Stokoe, Op. cit., p. 32.
[26] Ibid, p. 48.
[27] Ibid, p. 40.
[28] Ibid, p. 25.
[29] Ibid, p. 33. Ostensibly, the Church had sound theological reasons as well for ignoring the diaspora Greeks' requests as a major encyclical against phyletism (tribalism) had just been issued in 1870.
[30] Ibid, p. 22.
[31] "…and from the Son." These words had been added to the Nicene Creed in Spain in the sixth century in an effort to fight the Arianism of the Visigoths. It was not normalized in the West as a whole until the 10th century, the effect of which was to precipitate the schism between East and West.

The issue of the canonicity of the Uniates has always been a problem for both Roman Catholicism and Eastern Orthodoxy, not only in North America but in Europe as well. Despite the recent papal encyclical *Orientale Lumen*, which effectively reversed *Ea Semper*, for example, the quasi-autonomous nature of the Eastern Rite churches has never set well with the Roman curia, which is overwhelmingly Latin in domination. Be that as it may, recent Orthodox persecutions of Uniates in Eastern Europe since the fall of the Soviet bloc are unconscionable. Bishop Kallistos Ware rightly condemns such actions (Ware, *The Orthodox Church*, pp. 164-65) as a stain on our faith.

[32] Stokoe, Op. cit., p. 26.
[33] Ibid, p. 26.
[34] Ibid, p. 26.
[35] Ibid, p. 27.
[36] Ibid, p. 29.
[37] Ibid, p. 29.
[38] Ibid, p. 29.
[39] Ibid, p. 30.
[40] Ibid, p. 29.
[41] His feast day is commemorated on May 7.
[42] Ibid, pp. 47-48.

[43] See for example Helen Papanikolas's books on this subject, *The Greeks of Carbon County* and *Toil and Rage.*

[44] Aristeidis Papadakis, *The Christian East and the Rise of the Papacy* (Crestwood, New York: SVS Press, 1994), p. 120.

[45] Stokoe, Op. cit., p. 50.

[46] Ibid, p. 50.

[47] Ibid, p. 50.

[48] Saloutos, Op. cit. This bill was never passed.

[49] Stokoe, Op. cit., p. 48.

[50] Ibid, p. 48.

[51] Ibid, p. 51.

[52] Ibid, p. 51.

[53] The remittances made by Greek men alone amounted to over 100 million dollars. Indeed, Greece became so dependent upon these monies that it suffered a hemorrhage of manpower, which cause great social dislocations (Stokoe, Op. cit., p. 31).

[54] Saloutos, Op. cit., pp. 74-75.

CHAPTER 3

[1] Stokoe, p. 41.

[2] Ibid, p. 39. It must also be remembered that the federal government encouraged Protestant missionaries to go to Alaska and convert the "heathen" from Orthodoxy, which most American intellectuals at the time disdained. The government granted subsidies to the various sects and divided up the Alaskan landscape among them (cf Fr. Michael Oleksa, *The Orthodox Church in Alaska*).

[3] Bishop Gregory Afonsky, *A History of the Orthodox Church in America: 1917-1934* (Kodiak, Alaska: St. Herman's Seminary Press, 1994), p. 12. Although Afonsky's numbers include Greeks, Greek (as well as non-Greek) trustee parishes are not included as they were not under the jurisdiction of the Russian archdiocese.

[4] Ibid, p. 10

[5] Isabel Florence Hapgood, *Service book of the Holy Orthodox-Catholic Apostolic Church* (Englewood, New Jersey: Antiochian Orthodox Christian Archdiocese, 7th ed., reprinted 1996).

[6] Ibid, "Preface to the Second Edition."

[7] Afonsky, pp. 39-40

[8] Ibid, p. 42

[9] Saloutos, Op. cit., p. 127.

[10] Ibid, pp. 32-33.

[11] Ibid, p. 33.

[12] Ibid, p. 37.

[13] Ibid, p. 37.

[14] "The Life and Conduct of Our-Father-among-the-Saints Raphael, Bishop of Brooklyn," www.prophora.org/palmpsrings/Raphael.htm.

[15] Ibid, p. 46. See also "The Life of St. Raphael" in *Our Father Among the Saints Raphael Bishop of Brooklyn* (Englewood, New Jersey: Antakya Press, 2000), pp. 1-6.

[16] "The Life of Raphael," Op. cit.

[17] Stokoe, Op. cit., p. 48.

[18] "Bishop Nikolai Velimirovich: Serbia's New Chrysostom," www.roca.org/oa/158/158f.htm.

[19] Stokoe, Op. cit., p. 38.

[20] Metropolitan Bartholemew Arhandonis, "The Participation of the Laity in the Synods of the Greek-Byzantine Church," available on www.voithia.com/content/qmpBartholo.htm.

[21] There had in fact been two preparatory conferences in 1905 and 1906 by clergymen alone in anticipation of the All-American Sobor (Stokoe, Op. cit., p. 38).

[22] Saloutos, Op. cit., p. 122.

[23] This was especially true of Bulgarians and Greeks, who were routinely misidentified with each other (Ibid, p. 98).

[24] Ibid, p. 108.

[25] Ibid, p. 107.

[26] Ibid, p. 129.

[27] Ibid, p. 133.

[28] Ibid, p. 130.

[29] Ibid, p. 133.

[30] Constance J. Tarasar and John H. Ericksson, eds., *Orthodox America 1794-1976: Development of the Orthodox Church in America,* (The Orthodox Church in America, Dept. of History and Archives: Syosset, New Jersey, 1975), pp. 212-13

[31] Saloutos, Op. cit., p. 124.

[32] Stokoe, Op. cit., pp. 51-53.

[33] Ibid, p. 53.

[34] Ibid, p. 33.

[35] Ibid, pp. 47-48.

CHAPTER 4

[1] Stokoe, *Orthodox Christians in North America: 1794-1994* (Orthodox Christian Publications Center: 1995), p. 60.

[2] Ware, *The Orthodox Church: New Edition* (London, England: Penguin Books, 1993 ed.), p. 150.

[3] Stokoe, Op. cit., p. 58.

[4] Ibid, p. 58.

[5] Bellavin, Patriarch Tikhon, (*Epistle of Oct. 26, 1918.*) See also Ware, *The Orthodox Church*, "Whoever does not condemn [the czar's murder] will be guilty of his blood." p. 150.

[6] Stokoe, Op. cit., pp. 56-58.

[7] Ware, Op. cit., p. 176.

[8] A. Bogolepov, *Towards an American Orthodox Church: The Establishment of an Autocephalous Orthodox Church* (Crestwood, NY: SVS Press, 1980 ed.), p. 57.

[9] V. Rev. M. Polsky, *The Canonical Position of the Supreme Church Authority in the USSR and Abroad,* (Jordanville, NY: 1940), pp. 113-14, p. 126.

[10] Bogolepov, Op. cit., pp. 59-60.

[11] Ibid, p. 58.

[12] As it continues to do so even at the present.

[13] These of course were not the only jurisdictions that were formed during these tumultuous times. By the 1930's, there were four competing Antiochian jurisdictions.

[14] 34th Apostolic Canon: "The bishops of every nation must acknowledge him who is first among them."

[15] Bogolepov, Op. cit., p. 57.

[16] Ibid, p. 91.

[17] Ibid, p. 91.

CHAPTER 5

[1] Bogolepov, Op. cit., p. 58.

[2] Ibid, p. 71.

[3] Bishop Gregory Afonsky, *A History of the Orthodox Church in America: 1917-1934* (Kodiak: St. Herman of Alaska Seminary Press, 1994), pp. 41-42.

[4] Saloutos, Op. cit., p. 136.

[5] *Memorandum on Opinion,* Superior Court of Los Angeles: *The Church of the Transfiguration et al* vs. *Rev A Lisin et al, 1948.*

[6] Bogolepov, Op. cit., pp. 57-88.   See especially canons 4 and 5 of the first ecumenical council and canon 9 of the council of Antioch.

[7] Ukase no. 398, May 5, 1922.

[8] Boris Talentov, "The Moscow Patriarchate and Sergianism," [published in *Russia's Catacomb Saints,* Ivan Andreev (Platina, CA: St. Herman of Alaska Brotherhood, 1982) pp. 463-86].

[9] Bogolepov, Op. cit., pp. 13-14, 19-20.

[10] Ibid, p. 65, quoting canon 4 (Nicaea, A.D. 325): "A bishop can only be ordained after he has been designated a bishopric."

[11] Ibid, p. 72, quoting canon 17 (Chalcedon, A.D. 451): "Let the order of the ecclesiastical parishes follow the political and municipal pattern." See also canon 38 (Quinisext council in Trullo, A.D. 691): "…let the order of things ecclesiastical follow the civil and public models."

[12] Ibid, p. 69.

[13] Ibid, pp. 72-73. Admittedly, the acceptance of the Church Abroad's statutes as binding on America was the result of several different deliberations occurring over different periods of time and in various sobors. The actual "acceptance" of these statutes as a whole was in reality an open question.

[14] Ibid, pp. 73-74.

[15] Ibid, pp. 74-75.

[16] Ibid, pp. 75-77.

[17] Ibid, p. 75.

[18] Ibid, p. 77.

[19] Ibid, pp. 91-93.

[20] Ibid, p. 92.

[21] Ibid, p. 92.

CHAPTER 6

[1] Ironically, throughout the Middle Ages, Constantinople was always commonly referred to as "the city." In Greek, "to the city," is *eis tein poli,* which became to the Turkish ear *is-tan-bul.*

[2] Bat Ye'or, *The Decline of Eastern Christianity under Islam: From Jihad to Dhimmitude,* p. 27.

[3] Ibid, p. 89.

[4] Mark Stokoe, *The History of the Orthodox Church in North America: 1794-1994* (OCPC: 1995) p. 32.

[5] Ralph Harper, *Journey from Paradise: Mt. Athos and the Interior Life* (Quebec, Canada: Editions du Beffoi, 1987) p. 67.

[6] Theodore Saloutos, *The Greeks of the United States* (Cambridge, Mass: Harvard Univ. Press, 1964) p. 281.

[7] Ibid, p. 283.

[8] Ibid, p. 284.

[9] Ibid, p. 284.

[10] Ibid, p. 284.

[11] Ibid, p. 284.

[12] Ibid, p. 285.

[13] Ibid, p. 285.

[14] Ibid, p. 287.

[15] Ibid, p. 288.

[16] Ibid, p. 290.

[17] Ibid, p. 292.

[18] Ibid, p. 292.

[19] Ibid, p. 292.

[20] Ibid, p. 292.

[21] Ibid, p. 291.

[22] Ibid, p. 126.

[23] Ibid, p. 286.

[24] Ibid, p. 317.

[25] Ibid, p. 295.

[26] Ibid, p. 295.

[27] Ibid, p. 295.

[28] Ibid, p. 295.

[29] Ibid, p. 296.

[30] Ibid, p. 297.

[31] Ibid, pp. 300-301.

[32] Ibid, p. 301.

[33] Ibid, p. 300.

[34] Ibid, p. 301.

[35] Ibid, p. 302.

[36] Ibid, p. 302.

[37] Ibid, p. 301.

[38] Ibid, p. 294.

[39] Ibid, p. 307.

[40] George Anastassiou, *Armonki Leitourgia Ymnodia* (1944, 7th ed.) p. 235. The author's comments regarding the use of organs in Orthodox hymnody during the Byzantine era are entirely laughable and his research completely spurious. For one thing, there is no such thing as a "Jewish Church," for another, until the 20th

century, organs were never used in synagogue worship, and then, only in the most liberal wings of Reform Judaism.

[41] In my own home parish of Holy Trinity (Tulsa, Oklahoma), several parishioners stormed out of the church when, in 1935, the priest commemorated King George II of Greece, who had just been restored to the Greek throne. When one man (a royalist) asked another why he was leaving, the latter one replied loudly in Greek for all to hear: "He is not my king!" (Personally related to me by the late Don G. Metevelis.)

[42] Saloutos, Op. cit., p. 371.

[43] Archbishop Dmitri, the present Bishop of Dallas and the South (OCA), was received into the faith in Dallas, Texas, along with his sister, the late Dimitra Royster, by then-Archbishop Athenagoras in 1940, when they were both teenagers.

CHAPTER 7

[1] www.antiochian.org/Archdiocese/History/archdiocese.history.htm
[2] Ibid.
[3] Afonsky, Op. cit., p. 46.
[4] www.antiochian.org
[5] Ibid.
[6] Stokoe, Op. cit., p. 79.
[7] Ibid, p. 79.
[8] www.antiochian.org
[9] Ibid.
[10] Fr. Joseph Allen, *Widowed Priest: A Crisis in Ministry,* (Minneapolis, Minn: Light and Life Publishing, 1994).
[11] Personal reports given to the author by two priests in the Antiochian archdiocese who wish to remain anonymous.
[12] Rev. D. Abramtsov, "A Short History of Western Orthodoxy," (www.westernorthodoxy.com).
[13] Saloutos, Op. cit., p. 135.
[14] Ibid, p. 135.
[15] Abramtsov, Op. cit.
[16] For a complete inquiry into the Evangelical Orthodox Church, please read Fr. Peter E. Gillquist's own account: *Becoming Orthodox: A Journey to the Ancient Christian Faith* (Ben Lomond, Calif: Conciliar Press, revised edition, 1992).
[17] Stokoe, Op. cit., p. 109.
[18] www.antiochian.org/News/ben_lomond.htm .
[19] Ibid.

[20] www.sspeterandpaulonline.com

[21] Ibid.

[22] The Orthodox Church in America, though it has its roots in the Russian Orthodox Church, is no longer considered to be an "ethnic" Orthodox Church.

CHAPTER 8

[1] After the second episcopate of Metropolitan Platon, the American archdiocese of the Russian Orthodox Church became unofficially known as the "Metropolia" and it retained this name until it received autocephaly from the Moscow patriarchate in 1970. After this date, it became known officially as the "Orthodox Church in America."

[2] This unfortunate type of ethnic chauvinism was imposed as well on the Bulgarian Orthodox Church when it was first evangelized in the ninth century. When the Bulgar khans threatened to submit to papal authority unless their customs were respected, the Byzantine hierarchy relented. Fortunately, other such examples of a Greek-only liturgy being imposed on a non-Greek population are exceedingly rare. According to Ariesteides Papadakis, the liturgical language of the Nubian church (roughly modern Sudan) was also Greek and remained so until the 12th century. As to why the natives chose Greek as opposed to Coptic remains a mystery (Papadakis, *The Christian East and the Rise of the Papacy*, Crestwood, NY: SVS Press, 1994, p. 128).

[3] Stokoe, Op. cit., p. 48.

[4] Ibid, p. 48.

[5] Ibid, p. 48.

[6] Ibid, p. 48.

[7] Ibid, p. 49.

[8] Ibid, p. 49.

[9] Ibid, p. 49.

[10] Ibid, p. 50.

[11] Ibid, p. 50.

[12] Archbishop Theodosius Lazor, the Primate of the OCA, served in this capacity until his retirement in 2002.

[13] *Ea Semper*. This papal bull was quite strident in its pro-Latin bias. The position of the Roman Catholic Church today is almost the exact opposite, as elucidated in *Orientale Lumen* (1995), which commends the Orthodox churches for their "…combined respect and consideration for individual cultures with a passion for the universality of the Church, which they tirelessly [strive] to achieve." ("Gospel, Churches and Culture," *Orientale Lumen.7*).

[14] Stokoe, Op. cit., p. 69.

[15] *Yearbook of the Greek Orthodox Archdiocese of America: 2002*, Op. cit., p. 154.

[16] Stokoe, Op. cit., p. 69.

[17] Ibid, p. 29.

[18] Ibid, p. 51.

[19] Bishop Gregory Afonsky, *A History of the Orthodox Church in America: 1917-1934*, p. 45.

[20] www.hirrs.hartsem.edu

[21] Ibid.

[22] Stokoe, Op. cit., p. 50.

[23] Ibid, p. 79.

[24] Ibid, pp. 79-80.

[25] Ibid, p. 80.

[26] Ibid, p. 80.

[27] Ibid, p. 80.

[28] Ibid, p. 80.

[29] Ibid, p. 81.

[30] Ibid, p. 81.

[31] Ibid, p. 81.

[32] Ibid, pp. 81-82.

[33] Alexander Bogolepov, *Towards an American Orthodox Church*, p. 55. Trifa had to take monastic vows and be re-ordained as deacon, priest and then finally as bishop.

[34] Ibid, p. 55.

[35] Ibid, p. 56.

[36] Stokoe, Op. cit., p. 82.

[37] Ibid, p. 81.

[38] Ibid, p. 82.

[39] Ibid, p. 82.

[40] Ibid, p. 82.

[41] www.hirr.hartsem.edu

[42] Ibid.

[43] www.hirr.hartsem.edu

[44] Stokoe, Op. cit., p. 48.

[45] Fr. D. Rogich and V. Kesich, *Serbian Patericon: Saints of the Serbian Orthodox Church, Vol. I,* (Forestville: St. Paisius Abbey Press, 1994). Sourced on www.roca.org/oa/158/158f.htm.

[46] *Yearbook 2002, Greek Orthodox Archdiocese of America*, p. 160.

---

[47] www.hirr.hartsem.edu.

[48] www.uocc.ca/index.html.

[49] A skete is a monastic brotherhood on a small scale. Generally speaking, its monastic rule is not as rigid as those of larger monasteries.

CHAPTER 9

[1] Saloutos, Op. cit., p. 374.

[2] Ibid, p. 374.

[3] Ibid, p. 374.

[4] Ibid, p. 375.

[5] Ibid, p. 375.

[6] SCOBA, to its credit, (even at this early stage) has never shied away from the ultimate goal of an autonomous American Orthodox Church.

[7] Bogolepov, A., *Towards an American Orthodox Church,* (SVS Press: Crestwood, 1980 ed.) p. 107.

[8] Ibid, p. 107.

[9] Ibid, p. 107.

[10] Ibid, pp. 107-8.

[11] Ibid, p. 108.

[12] Particularly in respect to the United States' support of the State of Israel. Ironically, Arab Christians are often accused by radical Islamists of being a "fifth column," much to their detriment. Since the foundation of the Jewish state, the Christian component of the Near East has shrunk considerably, particularly in Israel itself. In reality, the decimation of the Arab Christian population began before the partition of the British Mandate of Palestine. Regardless, if present demographic trends continue, Arab Christians of all denominations within Israel itself as well as the Occupied Territories will disappear within the next 20 years.

[13] *Letter of July 16/29, 1927,* (W. Emhardt, *Religion in Soviet Russia,* 1929), pp. 146-50.

[14] Bogolepov, Op. cit., pp. 99-100.

[15] Ibid, p. 99.

[16] Ibid, p. 100.

[17] Ibid, p. 105.

[18] Ibid, p. 105.

[19] Ibid, p. 123.

[20] Ibid, p. 99.

[21] Ibid, p. 96-7.

[22] Ibid, p. 110.

[23] Ibid, p. 90.

[24] Ibid, p. 111.

[25] Ibid, p. 94.

[26] Ibid, p. 103.

[27] Ibid, p. 104.

[28] Ibid, xii. J.H. Erickson, "Forward" [Bogolepov, *Toward an American Orthodox Church*, (SVS Press: Crestwood, 1980 ed)].

[29] Erickson, Ibid, p. xii.

[30] Ibid, p. xiii.

[31] Ibid, p. xiv.

[32] Ibid, p. xiv.

[33] Stokoe, Op. cit., p. 94. Athenagoras's pique was in part due to the fact that he had met years earlier with a delegation from the Metropolia who wished to joined the ecumenical patriarchate. Rather than anger the Patriarch of Moscow, Athenagoras told them "you are Russians, go back to your mother church. No one can solve your problem except the Russian Church."

[34] Once, an elderly priest of my acquaintance decided to give the priestly blessing *"eirene eimen"* ("peace be unto you") in English. Unfortunately he said "peace on you" and was greeted with snickers from the congregation. Needless to say, any more attempts at English were put on hold by the priest in question.

[35] Related to the author by Don G. Metevelis. The incident in question took place during the early 1950's in my home parish.

[36] See, for example, Fr. Patrick Henry Reardon's essay, "The Newest Liturgical Monstrosity," [Frank Schaeffer, *Letters to Father Aristotle* (Regina Orthodox Press: Salisbury, MA, 1995), p. 181].

[37] *Iakovos, A Legacy* (1996, videotape produced by GOTelcom).

[38] Personal observation by the author in meetings held with him over a period of several years.

[39] Woodrow Wilson, cited by Linda Bowles in her syndicated column, *The Daily Oklahoman,* Dec. 24, 2001, p. 6A.

CHAPTER 10

[1] In fact, the Ku Klux Klan reached its apogee in the 1920's. It was during this time that President Warren G. Harding was initiated into the Klan at a special service held in the White House itself. This is doubly ironic as it was widely rumored that he was of African descent himself and had even spoken in favor of civil rights for African Americans during his presidency.

[2] See, for example, Archbishop Damascene of Athens's encyclical as to the incompatibility of an Orthodox Christian being a member of esoteric lodges.

[3] According to many reliable sources, the apogee of affiliation within Masonry was the immediate post-World War II period, where it was estimated that one of every five men in the United States were members of Masonic lodges.

[4] Fr. Seraphim Rose, *Orthodoxy and the Religion of the Future* (Platina, Calif: St. Herman of Alaska Press, 1990),p. 147.

[5] Ibid, p. 218.

[6] Stokoe, *Orthodox Christians in North America: 1794-1994*, (OCPC: 1995), p. 92.

[7] *Yearbook of the Greek Orthodox Archdiocese: 2002*, p. 90. In 1976, the "inter-Orthodox" marriage rate was 54%, but by 2000, this had shrunk to 38%. This figure however is not reflective of the actual number of interfaith marriages, as many of those labeled "inter-Orthodox" are in reality weddings between an Orthodox spouse and a non-Christian who was baptized in the Orthodox Church in order to remove the canonical impediment that would have ordinarily prevented the wedding from transpiring in the first place.

[8] Stokoe, Op. cit., pp. 1-3. See also the monograph "How Many Eastern Orthodox are there in the USA?", which can be accessed at www.ocl.org/Hartford%20Institute.htm.

[9] Bishop Kallistos Ware, *The Orthodox Church,* (London, England: Penguin, 1993 ed.), p. 77.

[10] Alexander Bogolepov, *Towards an American Orthodox Church: The Establishment of an Autocephalous Orthodox Church* (Crestwood, New York: SVS Press, 2001 ed.),p. 88.

[11] To their credit, neither St. Basil the Great nor St. John Chrysostom would have added their names to their respective liturgies. Indeed, it is hotly debated today how much they contributed to the formation of these rites.

[12] Regardless of these regional variants, the liturgy itself contained the same basic rubric since Apostolic times: the Liturgy of the Catechumens (*synaxis*), whose climax was the Gospel reading/homily, and the Liturgy of the Faithful (Eucharist), whose climax was Holy Communion.

[13] St. Ireneus of Lyons, *Against Heresies,* iv. 18, 5.

[14] Admittedly, identifying the Great Schism from this date is rather arbitrary as nobody at that time, East or West, viewed the actions of Cardinal Humbert de Candida Silva or the counter-reaction of Patriarch Michael Cerularius as being final or irrevocable [Aristeides Papadakis,*The Christian East and the Rise of the Papacy* (Crestwood, New York: SVS Press, 1994), p. 14]. For example, there was a "mute schism" some years earlier that was caused when the Patriarch of

Constantinople failed to mention the Pope in the Dyptichs (ibid, p. 14), but this was the result of faulty lines of communication plus the fact that the situation was rather chaotic as there had been three claimants to the see of Rome at one time. Likewise, the Great Schism did not become effective until the ravages of the Fourth Crusade permanently poisoned the atmosphere between East and West. Only in retrospect and for the purposes of clarity was this particular date chosen.

[15] Papadakis, Ibid, p. 14.

[16] Anastassiou, G., *Harmoniki Leitourgia Hymnodia,* (1944, 7th ed.), p. 325.

[17] Experimentation in symphonic adaptations had in fact first appeared in Russia in the 19th century with compositions by both Rachmaninoff and Tchaikovsky, though they tended to adhere closely to the original Slavonic.

[18] See for example St. Jerome's observation in his *Epistle to the Galatians*: "Often when the congregation of a church responded with an 'amen' or 'Lord have mercy,' you could hear a rumbling like that of thunder."

[19] The canonical strictures against all musical accompaniment in the worship services of the Church are unambiguous. St. Clement of Alexandria, for example, states: "Only one instrument do we use, the word of peace with which we honor God, no longer the old psaltery, trumpet, drum and flute." St. John Chrysostom states: "David formerly sang in Psalms, also we sing today with him; he had a lyre with lifeless strings, the church has a lyre with living strings. Our tongues are the stings of the lyre…" St. Simon (founder of Simonopetra on Mt. Athos) states: "At the church services chant with solemnity and devoutness, and not with disorderly vociferations."

[20] Within the Greek Orthodox archdiocese, for example, many different forms of the Nicene Creed are used.

[21] One priest told me that many of his colleagues consider the hyper-realistic icons in the Cathedral of St. Sophia (Los Angeles) to be so disconcerting that it appears that the Theotokos is wearing lipstick. One widely circulated rumor in fact states that Spyros Skouras, the benefactor of that church (and former president of Twentieth Century Fox), had Loretta Young serve as the model for the Platytera!

[22] As quoted in "Building an Architecture of True Orthodox Vision: Past, Present and Future," (Christ J. Kamages, *The Christian Activist: A Journal of Orthodox Opinion,* Vol. 10, Winter/Spring, 1977), p. 43.

[23] *Yearbook of the Greek Orthodox Archdiocese: 2002,* p. 90.

[24] Stokoe, Op. cit., pp. 108-9.

[25] Ibid, p. 109.

[26] John M. Hodges, "Windows into Heaven: The Music of John Tavener," *Image: A Journal of the Arts and Religion,* (Summer: 1995, No. 10), p. 88.

[27] Fr. Peter Gillquist, *Becoming Orthodox: A Journey to the Ancient Christian Faith* (Ben Lomond, Calif: Conciliar Press, rev. ed., 1992), p. 147.

[28] The stories of some of those making their journey to the Orthodox faith is told in *Coming Home: Why Protestant Clergy are Becoming Orthodox,* (Peter Gillquist, ed., Ben Lomond, Calif: Conciliar Press, 1992).

CHAPTER 11

[1] Bishop Kallistos Ware, *The Orthodox Church: New Edition,* (Penguin Group, LTD: London, 1993 ed.), p. 129.

[2] Ibid, p. 129.

[3] Ibid, pp. 174-75.

[4] Metropolitan Spyridon Papageorge, "Keynote Address," 32nd Biennial Clergy-Laity Congress, Chicago, Illinois, July 7, 1994.

[5] "We respectfully petition His All-Holiness the Ecumenical Patriarch to convene a world conference of mission representatives to help coordinate Orthodox mission strategies and efforts around the world."

[6] Metropolitan Christopher, *A New Era Begins* (videotape of the Ligonier Conference of Bishops, Nov. 29-Dec. 2, 1994, produced by Orthodox People Together).

[7] The comments of Patriarch Ignatius IV of Antioch can be accessed at www.voithia.org.

[8] Theodore Kalmoukos, "Antiochian Archdiocese Prepares for Autonomy," *National Herald* July 21-22, 2001 ed.

[9] In remarks delivered to the Orthodox Christian Laity in Los Angeles, July 1, 2002, Charles Ajalat (former director of International Orthodox Christian Charities) declared that, contrary to earlier statements issued in preparation of the Los Angeles congress by Metropolitan Anthony of San Francisco (GOA), Patriarch Ignatius IV had indeed declared the American exarchate to be "fully autonomous." Anthony's earlier broadside appeared to be part of a well-orchestrated effort to muddle the facts, hoping that, in so doing, the delegates to the Los Angeles Clergy-Laity Congress would be confused as to the actual facts of the matter.

[10] The revitalization of the Phanar and the Archdiocese of Constantinople under the auspices of Patriarch Bartholomew is based on the author's own research as gathered during a pilgrimage that he (Michalopulos) made to Istanbul in 2000. As to the possibility of increasing Christian immigration to Turkey, this appears dubious at present.

[11] Metropolitan Sypridon Papageorgiou, "Inaugural Address," *Enthronement Ceremony,* Sept. 21, 1996 (on videotape produced by GOTelcom).

[12] "Charter Revisions: Are they legal?" A rather lively discussion ensued on the internet regarding these changes. Ultimately, they were not challenged. (May be accessed at www.voithia.com.)

[13] "Laographos," *The Greek Press,* July 13, 1997.

[14] Personal conversation with a priest at the 1998 Clergy-Laity Conference (Orlando, Fla).

[15] www.voithia.com

[16] According to one source, Bartholomew pointed his finger at Spyridon and told the metropolitans: "You see that man there? He's going to be your archbishop until the day he dies!" Interestingly, some of the metropolitans' criticisms *vis a vis* Spyridon's administrative style were expressed using the Slavonic word *sobornost* ("conciliarity") and his supposed tactlessness in this regard.

[17] "Laographos," *The Greek Press.* See also www.voithia.org.

[18] *Yearbook of the Greek Orthodox Archdiocese of America: 2002,* p. 151.

[19] Personal conversation with a member of the executive committee of the parish council that year.

[20] Holy Synod of the Ecumenical Patriarchate, "Joint Draft of the Proposed Charter of the Greek Orthodox Archdiocese of America."

[21] Personal correspondence with members of the OCL and diocesan officials.

[22] OCA "Letter on the Retirement of the Metropolitan."

[23] Kalmoukos, Op. cit.

[24] Kalmoukos, Op. cit.

[25] Personal conversations with priests and parish council members of the OCA.

[26] The Knights of St. Andrew, also known as the "Archons," are prominent laymen who are recognized by the archdiocese after years of service to the Church. They are named on the Sunday of Orthodoxy in the archdiocesan cathedral.

[27] The author was a delegate to two of these committee sessions. At the one that was called to implement the archdiocesan budget for the coming year (and chaired by Metropolitan Iakovos of Chicago), the Diocese of Chicago was in open revolt, questioning the method of financing the archdiocese. The crux of the matter was the desire to reverse the present procedure in which all monies go directly to New York and then a portion goes back to the dioceses. The motion failed.

[28] Out of the total of 2,200 delegates that were allowed to attend (four from each parish), approximately 700 were registered, barely a quorum.

CHAPTER 12

[1] John H. Ericson, ("Foreword," [Bogolepov: *Toward an American Orthodox Church,* 1980 ed.]), p. ix.

[2] Ibid. p. xix.

[3] Bishop Kallistos Ware, *The Orthodox Church* (London: Penguin, 1993 ed.), p. 27.

[4] Bogolepov, Op. cit., p. 7.

[5] Canon 8, AD 431 (cited by Bogolepov, pp. 7-8).

[6] Canon 28 (cited by Bogolepov, p. 14).

[7] Bogolepov, Op. cit., p. 8.

[8] Canon 38, Council in Trullo (AD 691): "…let the order of things ecclesiastical follow the civil and public models."

[9] Bishop Gregory Afonsky, *A History of the Orthodox Church in America: 1917-1934* (Kodiak, Alaska: St. Herman's Seminary Press, 1994), p. 10.

[10] Nikon D. Patrinacos, *A Dictionary of Greek Orthodoxy* (Minneapolis, Minnesota: Light & Life Pub., 1994), p. 10.

[11] During the height of the Spyridon crisis, *The Orthodox Observer,* for example, printed essays attributed to faculty at Holy Cross that stated that the ethnic jurisdictions were "desirable" and "consistent" with many of the canons.

[12] Bogolepov, Op. cit., p. 12.

[13] Indeed, this was a relatively recent phenomenon beginning in the Old World with the establishment of the Church Abroad. The American experiment with the Lebanese auxiliary diocese was largely ignored and quite probably unknown to the majority of Old World Orthodox.

[14] Ibid. p. 12.

[15] Erickson, Op. cit., pp. i-xxiii. See especially the section "Autocephaly and How it is to be Proclaimed," pp. xvi-xix.

[16] Letter from Alexis II to Bartholomew, translated into English from Russian. Copy sent by fax from Greek Orthodox Patriarchate of Damascus (Antioch). Fax: 963-11-5424404, dated January 8, 2003.

[17] Patriarch Bartholemuew cited canon 28 in his letter no. 129 of Aprill 11, 2002, to Patriarch Alexis II of Moscow and All Russia.

[18] Alexis II, Op. cit.

[19] Alan Jacobs, "Shame the Devil," *Books and Culture: A Christian Review* (Vol. 8, No. 2, Mar/Apr 2002), p. 38. This is no idle question: according to Jacobs, Rebecca West's editor, when reviewing her *magnum opus, Black Lamb and Grey Falcon,* she wondered during the blitz of London if history would have turned out differently had the Serbs been victorious over the Turks at Kosovo in 1389.

EPILOGUE

[1] Hebrews 13:8.

---

[2] If sketes are included, the number, together with Canada, rises to some 400. Caution must be exercised, however, as more than a few of these are not only old calendarist, but wholly independent from even the major old calendar jurisdictions. There is simply no way of determining the state of inter-communion that exists among some of these institutions.

[3] The late Patriarch Parthenius III of Alexandria (r. 1987-2001), for example, stated that Mohammed possessed the vocation of prophet to some extent. Likewise, Patriarch Bartholomew of Constantinople has on more than one occasion stated that Islam was a "religion of peace;" this, in the immediate aftermath of the September 11, 2001, attack on the United States. He has traveled extensively to Iran and the Arabian peninsula stating his views openly, often being broadcast on Al-Jazeera, the Arabic-language all-news channel. Even Bishop Kallistos Ware's historical description of Mohammed (towit: "When the Prophet died in 632..." [*The Orthodox Church*, p. 29]), accepts the Islamic attributions without comment, thereby normalizing his self-styled vocation.

Bibliography

Afonsky, Bishop Gregory, A History of the Orthodox Church in America: 1917-1934, (Kodiak: St Herman's 1994)

Archdiocese of America, Greek Orthodox, Yearbook 2002

Azkoul, Rev Dr Michael, The Toll-House Myth: The Neo-Gnosticism of Fr Seraphim Rose, (Dewdney: Synaxis Press)

Bogolepov, Alexander, Toward an American Orthodox Church: The Establishment of an Autocephalous Orthodox Church, (Crestwood:SVS Press, 1963, 1991 rev ed.)

Coniaris, Fr Anthony, Introducing the Orthodox Church: Its Faith and Life, (Minneapolis: Light and Life, 1982)

Durant, Will, The Reformation: A History of European Civilization from Wyclif to Calvin: 1300-1564, (New York: Simon and Schuster, 1957)

Durant, Will and Ariel, The Age of Reason Begins: A History of European Civilization in the Period of Shakespeare, Bacon, Montaigne, Rembrandt, Galileo and Descartes: 1558-1648,(New York: Simon and Schuster, 1961)

Evans, M Stanton, The Theme is Freedom: Religion, Politics and the American Tradition, (Washington: Regnery Gateway, 1994)

Farber, Seth, Eternal Day: The Christian Alternative to Secularism and Modern Psychology, (Salisbury: Regina Orthodox Press, 1988)

Frazier, Terry L, A Second Look at the Second Coming: Sorting Through the Speculations, (Ben Lomond: Conciliar Press, 2000)

Gillquist, Fr Peter E, Making America Orthodox, (Brookline: Holy Cross Orthodox Press, 1984)

Lincoln, W Bruce, The Romanovs: Autocrats of All the Russias, (New York: Dial press, 1981)

Massie, Robert K, Peter the Great: His Life and World, (New York: Ballentine, 1980)

Oleska, Fr Michael, Orthodox Alaska, (Crestwood: SVS Press, 1992)

Papadakis, Aristeides (in collaboration with John Meyendorff), The Christian East and the Rise of the Papacy, (Crestwood: SVS Press, 1994)

Pelikan, Jaroslav, Jesus Through the Centuries: His Place in the History of Culture, (New Haven: Yale Univ Press, 1985)

Rose, Fr Seraphim, Orthodoxy and the Religion of the Future, (Platina: St Herman of Alaska Brotherhood, 1990)

Saloutos, Theodore, A History of the Greeks in the United States, (Cambridge: Harvard Univ Press, 1964)

Schaeffer, Frank, Dancing Alone: The Quest for Orthodox Faith in the Age of False Religions, (Brookline: Holy Cross Press, 1994)

Schaeffer, Frank, Letters to Father Aristotle: A Journey through Contemporary American Orthodoxy, (Salisbury: Regina Orthodox Press, 1995)

Stokoe, Mark, Orthodox Christians in North America: 1794-1994, (Orthodox Christian Publication Center: 1995)

Tarasar , Constance J, et al, Orthodox America 1974-1976: Development of the Orthodox Church in America, (Syosset: OCA, Dept of History and Archives, 1975)

Trevor-Roper, Hugh, The Rise of Christian Europe, (London: Thames and Hudson, 1965)

Ware, Bishop Kallistos, The Orthodox Church: New Edition, (London: Penguin Books LTD, 1993 ed.)

Ware, Bishop Kallistos, The Orthodox Way, (Crestwood, SVS Press, 2001, Revised Edition)

Whelton, Michael, Two Paths: Papal Monarchy-Collegial Tradition,(Sailsbury: Regina Orthodox Press, 1998)

Woodhouse, C M, Modern Greece: A Short History, (London: Faber and Faber, 1968)

Articles/ Essays

Aleskii II, Patriarch, "St Innocent",
www.cygnus.uwa.edu.au/~igrapsas/pages/innocent.htm

Archandonis, Metropolitan Bartholemew, "The Participation of the Laity in the Synods of the Greek-Byzantine Church, (Kanon III, 1977), pp 33-38

Christopulos, Mike, "Book Review: The Struggle Against Ecumenism", The Sword, Sept 1998. (May be accessed online at www.cybercome.net/~htm/Sword.htm)

Christ, Fr Bill, "Instruments in Church Music," The Light (Tulsa: Dec 2001).

Chronopoulos, Metropolitan Isaiah of Denver, "The Dangers of Multiple Orthodox Jurisdictions in the United States, " (1991, may be accessed at : www.ocl.org)

Conomos, Dimitri, "Orthodox Byzantine Music," (Univ of British Columbia: Greek Orthodox Archdiocese of America, 1990-96)

Hodges, John Mason, "Windows into Heaven: The Music of John Tavener", Image: A Journal of the Arts and Religion, (Summer 1995, No 10)

Jacobs, Alan, "Shame the Devil", Books and Culture: A Christian Review, (Mar/Apr 2002)

Jenkins, Philip, "A Global Pentecost", Books and Culture: A Christian Review, (Mar/Apr 2002)

Kamages, Christ J, "Building an Architecture of True Orthodox Vision: Past, Present and Future," The Christian Activist: A Journal Of Orthodox Opinion, (Winter/Spring 1997).

Reynolds, Gabriel Said, "Muhammed Through Christian Eyes", Books and Culture: A Christian Review, (Jan/Feb 2002)

Rogich, Fr Daniel, et al, "Bishop Nikolai Velimirovich: Serbia's New Chrysostom", Orthodox America (may be accessed online at www.roca.org/oa/158/158f.htm.)

Sames, John, ed. "Byzantine Music History," (2001. As yet unpublished but an excellent resource material of Byzantine hymnography and Patristic sources).

Saroka, Fr Vladimir, "Orthodox Music Today: Integrating Our Traditions," The Word Magazine, (Nov 1994), p 6-9.

Triaditsa, Bishop Photius of, "The 70th Anniversery of the Pan-Orthodox Congress in Constantinople: A Major Step on the Path Towards Apostasy", Orthodox Life, Nos 1 & 2, 1994. (May be accessed online at www.orthodoxinfo.com/ecumenism/photii.htm)